ESCAPE FROM RED CHINA

By Robert Loh

ESCAPE

as told to Humphrey Evans

FROM RED CHINA

Coward-McCann, Inc. New York

FOREWORD

WHEN I agreed to write this book with Robert Loh, he insisted that I should depict him in such a way that the readers would despise him. He said that in Communist China, no one with honor, integrity and honesty could retain these virtues and survive; because he did survive, he must lack these virtues and therefore be despicable. If the readers simply learn that only an utter scoundrel can live in the New China—Loh believes strongly—they will have gone far toward understanding Chinese Communism.

Loh learned to understand Chinese Communism the hard way —he lived it. He lived in constant danger, and mere survival required him to be utterly ruthless. Nevertheless, he clawed his way from near the bottom of the social scale to a position of considerable importance.

The story of Loh's life in the New China is not pretty, but it gives us a vivid detailed picture of the society which is evolving

5

under Marxist-Leninist Maoism. For this reason alone, we can be grateful that Loh fought to survive. Few of us can imagine living in a society which repudiates the basic human values, but I believe that most otherwise decent people would behave much as Loh did. I doubt if any Western reader will consider that Loh's behavior was reprehensible. He himself never lost awareness of the human values, and his struggle was for the chance to live again as a decent human being. Moreover, in his effort to endure, Loh never betrayed or endangered others.

This book, in fact, could not be written until after certain central figures in the story were dead. Other characters could be protected adequately by giving them changed names, by disguising their physical appearances, and by giving them different jobs or titles. For others who would not suffer reprisals because of the publication of Loh's story, we nevertheless changed names; this was partly to save them possible embarrassment, but also in the effort to simplify Chinese names for Western readers.

Westerners find the Chinese names confusing because of their unfamiliar sounds, but the names themselves are remarkably simple; most of them consist of a one-syllable family name followed by a two-syllable given name. To help readers identify the characters easily, we generally have called men by only their one-word family names and women by their two-word, hyphenated given names.

The name problem was simple, however, compared to the problem of presenting the characters themselves accurately. Loh speaks English well enough, but to explain to me so that I could put into English precisely what the characters said, did and felt was infinitely complicated; often I had to write and rewrite the same scenes innumerable times in order to achieve an effect that was neither over- nor understated.

Both Loh and I believed that this effort to be accurate was ex-

6

tremely important. Anyone who has lived in the New China hates the regime, and his temptation is to pour out his bitterness in violent terms. The one really startling aspect of Communist China, however, is the fact that a small group of men has been able to achieve complete control over 650 million unwilling people. To make this achievement understandable, the Communists' reasons for attempting it, the techniques they developed for the purpose, and the discipline they acquired in the process must be described rationally and truthfully. In short, this book is not intended to lament what has happened in China; it is intended to picture how and why it happened.

Loh's story is especially suitable for this purpose, because his experiences brought him into direct contact with many different aspects of Communist China. Along with this—and just as important—is the fact that Loh is one of the few escapees who did not leave close family members behind on the China mainland. Actually he is the only Chinese refugee I have found who can describe his experiences fully without fear that reprisals will be taken against relatives.

I am sure that the reader will agree with me that his experiences were extraordinary indeed.

—HUMPHREY EVANS

ESCAPE FROM RED CHINA

CHAPTER 1

Still must the wounded heart seek peace;
Interminable are my wanderings.

—CHU YUAN

I CAN RECALL the moment when living in Communist China became intolerable for me. It was at 11:05 P.M. on July 7, 1954. The night had been stifling in Shanghai, and rain had fallen earlier. When I came out of the Democratic League Building into Bubbling Well Road, the wet streets seemed to make the air too thick to breathe.

I was exhausted. I had just been to the third meeting in six days of my Communist-sponsored political discussion group. After a long day in my office at the flour mills, the physical effort of attending these meetings was bad enough, but the strain was worse. The smallest error—a mistaken response, a wrong gesture, a slip of the tongue—could mean catastrophe. People who live with fear eventually lose their awareness of it, but the tension remains and has serious effects. What bothered me most was constant fatigue. I desperately needed more rest in order to stay sufficiently alert for the continual struggle to survive.

In this, however, I was no different from the others in the crowd I joined that night in Bubbling Well Road. As always, I was surprised to find so many people still up at this hour. In the old days, of course, the streets had been crowded at every hour. Neon signs would have been garishly bright, and the people would have been dressed in many different styles and colors. They would have milled about, some moving quickly and others slowly. And above the traffic sounds, their voices would have been heard, chattering, calling, cursing, shouting, laughing.

But now no one spoke. The only sound was the shuffling of thousands of feet. Everyone moved at the same tired pace. Everyone had the same worried look and wore similar drab clothes. The only light came from the street lamps that made dim yellow pools at regular intervals along the wet pavement. Occasionally a motorcar swished by, arrogantly important.

Like me, the others still up had been to the grimly serious political meetings and were intent only on getting to bed.

I had gone the few paces to the corner of Gordon Road, however, when I suddenly came alive. Moving toward me out of the shadows was a face I knew better than any other. It belonged to Li-li. I had not seen her for two years, but she was seldom out of my thoughts. Even in a shapeless uniform, she was beautiful. From Li-li I had learned how close it was possible to be to another human being; I think that neither of us was ever really complete without the other.

And now we found ourselves unexpectedly face to face. The place, the time and the crowd were forgotten. We were aware only of each other. The moment lasted an age in which was concentrated all the anguish and bliss that knowing Li-li had meant.

But then the moment was gone. Li-li vanished into the crowd.

I felt sharp pain as I realized she had made no sign of recognizing me. I knew that she had felt my presence, but not one muscle had betrayed it; her pace had not faltered, her facial expression had not changed, and no light had come into her eyes.

I was struck then by another realization that was even worse. During that moment of awareness with her, I too had completely hidden my feelings. Not even the most sharp-eyed observer would have suspected that Li-li and I had ever met.

What made this seem so shocking was not that under the Communist regime our romance had been thwarted. Lovers can be kept apart by many circumstances in any society. Moreover, I knew that the Communists were indifferent to our feelings; they were concerned only with how we acted. Li-li and I that night reacted instinctively. Each of us feared that recognition might expose the other to danger. The instinctive reaction made me realize that the Communists, simply by applying constantly the stimulus of fear, had acquired such complete control over us that our actions could be made to deny our most natural and decent inclinations.

At home that night, I tossed and turned for hours on hot damp sheets. Having faced the fact that the Communists completely controlled my behavior, I considered fully for the first time just how I was being made to behave. At this point, I perceived how much I had been deluding myself about the Communists' intentions, for when I saw myself clearly as they had remolded me, I was filled with loathing and horror. I felt that if I were ever again to become a self-respecting human being, I would have to be free.

By all logical reasoning, however, my chances of getting away from Communist control were nil. An unsuccessful attempt would mean the end of me. Nevertheless, just before dawn rain fell again and for a moment a cool breeze refreshed my room. I made up my mind. Thereafter, every thought I had, every action I took, every word I spoke would be toward one objective: to devise and implement a successful plan to escape.

If the story of my escape is to be understood, however, I must tell it from the beginning.

CHAPTER 2

In spring I slept unconscious of the dawn;
I heard the carefree chatter of the birds...
— LI PO

WHEN I made up my mind to escape, I knew that I would have an obstacle from within myself. If I were successful, I would be leaving forever the one place on earth where I belonged. Such a step is painful for anyone, but I think that my background gave me a special attachment to Shanghai.

My parents typified Shanghai's peculiar combination of the ancient and modern. My father, for example, was a deeply religious Buddhist, but he was also fond of American jazz; he once even won a cup in a Charleston contest. Again, although he was a serious classical scholar and had come from a long line of famous scholars, he made his living as an investment broker.

The extreme contrasts of the city were also exemplified in my parents. No two people could have been more unlike. My father's family had had social standing but little money. My mother had been the beautiful spoiled daughter of *nouveau riche*. My father preferred simplicity, but my mother tended to ostentation. One time, I remember, a friend told her that Madame Chiang Kai-shek had a pair of hose that cost $18; my mother immediately stated that *she* had a pair costing $24. She wanted the best clothes, the largest mansion, the most lavish parties and the biggest cars. My father always rode the streetcar to work, he ate only vegetarian food and his study was starkly furnished.

Like Shanghai itself, however, my parents' differences were harmoniously blended. My father, for instance, indulged my mother in her whims, and cooperated fully in the social life she loved. Meanwhile, she saw to it that he had time each day, alone and undisturbed, for study and meditation. Moreover, we spent part of each summer at a Buddhist monastery retreat, and my mother always acted as though she enjoyed it. Despite their differences, they united in lavishing attention and affection on their children.

I was born in November 1924, the second of three sons. Later we had a baby sister who was the family favorite. We lived in a Western-style mansion with a huge enclosed garden. We were raised in the Chinese style, however, with a large group of relatives and servants who were like family members, and we had little contact with outsiders.

My first real contact with outsiders came from four White Russian bodyguards hired by my father. The guards were big simple men who enjoyed our children's games as much as we did. We regarded them affectionately, but in those days White Russians in Shanghai performed the most menial and degrading labor; in Chinese, the word "Russian" came to mean anything that was the shoddiest of its kind. From an early age, I thought that the worst possible fate was to become, like the Shanghai Russians, a despised refugee in a foreign land.

The other Shanghai foreigners were indirectly responsible for our needing the guards. The city was dominated by British and French, but the government was corrupt. Officials often cooperated with gangsters with whom kidnapping was a common form of extortion. My mother was too lively for the restrictions of being adequately guarded, and was kidnapped twice. Fortunately, the gangsters rarely harmed their captives, nor did they demand exorbitant ransom. The payments were made with police connivance. We children suffered terrible shock when our mother was taken. I hated gangsterism, and blamed it on the foreigners.

My worst childhood shock, however, came in 1936 when I was almost twelve. Our baby sister died. The effect on my parents was disastrous. In his grief, my father lost interest in his business; he made some wrong investments and lost almost all his money. This additional catastrophe was too much for my mother, and within a few months she also died. Her relatives tended to blame my father—at least, he believed they did, and certainly thereafter they treated him coolly. My father and his sons were drawn closely together. He gave us even more attention and affection. Moreover, although he was only thirty-two, he never remarried. He threw himself into his work. He wanted to obtain for us the material comforts that, I think, he felt he owed to our mother.

The effect of all this was to make me dissatisfied with our class. We had to give up our mansion and all extravagance, but we were not so poor that we endured real hardship. Nevertheless, our relatives humiliated us and our friends abandoned us. We felt alone in a hostile world. I came to scorn the values of the rich. This scorn, together with my bitterness toward the foreigners, turned my sympathies toward the Chinese masses whom I felt were victimized by both groups.

I myself felt victimized during that same year when my older brother and I were sent as boarders to the Shanghai University High School. The institution was run by Southern Baptist missionaries, but was considered one of the two best schools in Shanghai. We could afford only enough to cover the basic expenses and thus were unable to keep up with the social life of the other students.

My school life was made worse by the fact that my classmates were older. Previously we had studied with tutors at home, and I had progressed beyond my age group. Having been completely sheltered, my brother and I knew nothing about getting along with our contemporaries, and we were painfully shy. Our older, richer and more worldly classmates took every advantage of us; we were made the butt of their ridicule and jokes.

A year later, in 1937, however, the Japanese occupied Shanghai. This was another blow to my national pride, and it increased my bitterness against foreigners. The Japanese sealed off the International Settlement and the French Concession and posted sentries at the Garden Bridge between the two parts of the city. Every Chinese who crossed the bridge was forced to make a ninety-degree bow to the sentries. If a sentry felt that a bow was not made with sufficient humility, the Chinese was slapped across the face and made to go on bowing until the sentry was mollified. The Japanese seemed to take special delight in subjecting the most dignified elderly persons to this humiliation. To us, the sight of an old man or woman being beaten by a rough young Japanese soldier was almost unbearable. Most Chinese therefore avoided the bridge, and we in the foreign section were largely isolated.

The Japanese permitted foreign schools to operate only within

18

the foreign section. In this area, Shanghai University had only one of its buildings, the Commercial School. Thus this one building now had to be used by the entire institution. High school classes were held there in the mornings, the colleges used it in the afternoons, and the commercial school had it in the evenings. My brother and I now could live at home, and we had to endure our classmates only a few hours a day.

These circumstances pleased us, but the quality of our education was threatened. Overcrowding, economic chaos, and the deliberate encouragement given to official corruption by the Japanese caused a deterioration in morality and discipline that affected the schools. Professors received so little pay, because of the inflation, that they had to take two or more jobs to make a living, and pupils therefore received inadequate attention. Teachers also tutored their students privately, and this became a form of bribery; students could demand passing grades, whether they studied or not, by paying tutoring fees. Anyone with a little money now could enroll and purchase credits toward a degree. Thus, for example, young party girls sometimes entered the university, partly to find clientele among the rich playboys and partly to claim the higher social status of "college students." Because we could not afford tutoring bribes, I could make passing grades only by studying so hard that my competence could not be denied.

Moreover, my father, with his love of learning, encouraged us in every way possible. Because of the disordered times, he dreamed of a new strong China in which my brother would be a great scientist and I would become a famous statesman. I therefore began to think seriously about the country's problems, and I turned to the study of political science. By the time I entered the university, I was in the group of serious students. Among my classmates, those with the sophistication to go to night clubs, drink and have affairs with women were admired and envied, but the few of us who really studied were given genuine respect.

The respect I earned was increased by the fact that the famous Dr. Stewart Yui, head of the Political Science Department, took personal interest in me. He invited me to his house with the advanced students so that I could hear expert discussions on the subject. He made me read political science books not included in the course. Above all, he encouraged me to formulate and express my own ideas. I came to admire him as much as I did my father; more important, through his help I experienced an awakening of self-confidence.

My self-confidence was boosted further by the fact that my father's fortunes were slowly improving. His success, oddly enough, came largely from the confused conditions. By now, World War II had started. After Pearl Harbor, all Westerners were interned and Western business interests were taken over by the Japanese. Business conditions were chaotic. Inflation was uncontrollable, and black-marketing was everywhere. The vaguest rumor caused the stock market to fluctuate wildly. Most businessmen speculated to keep ahead of inflation, and investment brokers therefore were busy. My father refused to handle the more dubious speculative deals. Thus his profits were low but his business was more stable. As his reputation for honesty grew, the number of his clients increased, and finally he commanded a good share of the investment trade.

My father himself continued to live, as always, with spartan frugality, but he shared his new prosperity lavishly with his employees and his sons. My allowance grew until I found that I was receiving as much money as the sons of the richest industrialists. I began entertaining my few friends in the best restaurants, and soon I attracted the attention of the playboy set.

One day, I was flattered to be invited by a popular member of this group to tea in the Peacock Hall of the Park Hotel. When I arrived, I found that he was sitting with a girl. He introduced me casually to Li-li, and from the moment I saw her I could not take my eyes away from her. My new friend kept up a stream of small talk. Li-li listened attentively, nodding from time to time and occasionally smiling or murmuring a reply. I do not think I said a single word to her. If she was upset by my silent staring, she did not show it. Just before we left, she turned to me, and I felt her glance as a physical shock. "Your friend tells me," she said, "that you are one of the most brilliant students at the university."

I stammered something that must have denied the compliment, because she said, "You must not belittle yourself with too much modesty."

Thereafter, I thought of Li-li constantly, and I wanted desperately to see her. I sought out my new friend, but he did not bring Li-li with him again. Finally, I found the courage to mention her. "That girl—Li-li," I said. "I thought she was charming. Maybe she has a friend or someone so that we four could go out..."

A look of surprise came into my friend's face. "Are you crazy?" he said. "You can see that cutie whenever you want. She's a taxi dancer."

My first reaction was anger. I could not believe him. Li-li had been modest, dignified and intelligent; anyone in the Park Hotel would have taken her for a girl of good family. Nevertheless, my friend insisted that if I wanted to meet her, I would have to go with him to the Sing Hwa Ballroom in the French Concession.

Two days later, therefore, he led me up a beautiful staircase and I found myself in a small, dimly lit dance hall. The walls were mirrored, and I could see about fifty tables, perhaps half of which were occupied. The men seemed normal middle-class

ESCAPE FROM RED CHINA

types, but I felt I was in a sinister place, and I was shaking with nervousness as we were shown to a table.

My friend called a man who I thought was a waiter but who turned out to be a kind of go-between. In cheaper dance halls, customers bought tickets which they gave to the girls for dances. In this medium-class place, however, the go-between arranged for the partners, and the payment was unfixed and was more discreetly handled. Thus my friend told the go-between that we would be pleased to have Li-li join us.

A moment later, I saw her walking toward us, and I forgot everything else. When she recognized us, she looked pleased. She greeted us gravely and sat down. My friend chatted with her easily, and I envied his savoir-faire. Nevertheless, he was good enough to tell Li-li that I had wanted to see her.

"I'm glad," she said, smiling at me. "Do you wish to dance?"

I answered that I did not know how, and she offered to teach me. On the floor, I found that holding her around the waist was so disturbing that I could not concentrate on what to do with my feet. Suddenly I stopped. "I just can't believe you work in a place like this," I said.

She looked up at me reproachfully. "Nevertheless, Mr. Loh, I am only a taxi dancer." She said it with neither shame nor self-pity.

I took her arm and led her back to the table. My friend was dancing with another girl. Alone with Li-li, I was less tongue-tied. I wanted to know everything about her.

Li-li's father, I learned, was too poor to arrange a good marriage for her, but she had managed to graduate from high school. She thus would have been able to get a respectable position such as a secretary, but because of the inflation few salaried jobs paid a living wage. A taxi dancer's earnings, however, could be impressive. Li-li did not like the work, but she was glad to be able to help her family.

Most Shanghai taxi dancers were of low class, and the majority, if not prostitutes, could be bought easily enough. A few of the more attractive and intelligent, however, refused to sell themselves at any price, and carefully established a reputation for respectability. These taxi dancers became popular and probably earned more than the "party girls." Their social status may not have been high, but they were respected by their clients. Such a girl could hope eventually to become at least the second wife of a rich man. Li-li belonged to this group. She had become a taxi dancer only a few months before, but already she was much in demand. I did not like what she was doing, but by the end of that first afternoon my admiration for her was greater than ever.

I told her that I wanted to see her again the next day, but she shook her head. "You do not belong here," she said. And then, to my delight, she suggested that we go on a picnic the following Sunday.

I lived the next few days in a fever of anticipation. On Sunday, I found that Li-li's family lived in two meagerly furnished rooms over her father's firewood shop. While I waited for Li-li to finish dressing, her father told me of all his bad luck. His business was poor, he complained, and he could not hope to earn a living chauffeuring, which was his real profession. To my consternation, I learned that he had once been the driver for a relative of mine.

When Li-li appeared, however, the day brightened again. Because of fuel shortage, pleasure cars were prohibited, and I had to take her on the back of my bicycle. She rode holding me around the shoulders, and I wished the journey would last forever. We went to the Lung Hwa temple in the suburbs. I found that I was no longer shy with her, and we laughed and talked with complete naturalness. We had our picnic in the temple garden and afterward went in to kneel to the Buddhas. Li-li whispered to me that she wanted our fortunes told. I took the container that stood at the foot of the idol, and spilled the bamboo splinters out on the floor. We each picked one and went to an old priest. He studied the numbers on our splinters and then solemnly gave us correspondingly numbered slips of paper. My fortune told of a happy and successful future, but Li-li's could not have been worse. A shadow fell across the otherwise perfect day. Back in the garden, Li-li squeezed my hand. "Don't be sad," she said. "That was the right fortune for me. If my fate was not meant to be miserable, I would be in a college instead of a cabaret." Then she added, "I am happy that you will have such good fortune."

I was deeply touched. Without thinking, I found that I had caught her shoulders and was pressing my mouth against hers. Her lips were warm and submissive. Finally she drew back, but I still held her tightly as though I could protect her from all the misfortune in the world.

In the months that followed, I saw Li-li at least once or twice a week. Nevertheless, I did not make love to her. I felt that if I made her my mistress, I might be ruining the reputation she needed in order to become something better than a taxi dancer. I think that she appreciated my restraint, and in any case we were happy only when we were together. We always had much to talk about, and we communicated our innermost thoughts and feelings without embarrassment.

One day, in my last semester at the university, my brother told me that our father was upset about my being involved with a "low woman." I protested dramatically that Li-li was respectable, and that I was doing nothing wrong. "If you say so, I'll believe you, but don't expect anyone else to," my brother said.

I found he was right a week later when Dr. Yui also talked to me about Li-li. He accused me of becoming a playboy and said he was disappointed in me. I tried to make Dr. Yui understand what kind of a girl Li-li really was, but I failed. I mollified him somewhat by reminding him that I stood at the head of my class and that therefore my studies had not suffered.

Li-li sensed my distress about this situation and drew me out. As always, she reacted with calm sensibility. By this time, there nad been much talk of my going to the United States for postgraduate study in political science. I had put off making the decision only because I dreaded the idea of not seeing Li-li for as long as a year or two. She now advised me that by announcing my intention to go, I would satisfy both my father and Dr. Yui.

Li-li was right. Dr. Yui was obviously relieved, and my father remarked that he was glad I would be breaking off my "blatant affair with a common woman."

Breaking off with Li-li, even temporarily, required all my will power. I made her promise to wait for my return when I intended to marry her. At the pier, I stood by the ship's rail and waved to the people who had come to see me off. In one group was Dr. Yui and some of my university friends. In another stood my father and a number of our relatives. And alone near by was Li-li. I knew that she was full of the virtues that my father and Dr. Yui themselves accepted and had taught me to appreciate. If they rejected her, therefore, the fault was not in either Li-li, my father or Dr. Yui, but in our disrupted society which perverted our basic values. As the ship pulled away, I wept bitterly.

During the voyage, I wrote to Li-li every day, but gradually the excitement of new experiences dispelled my melancholy. Some of the other Chinese passengers were Nationalist officials going to America on government business, but the majority were students. A fourth of the students were children of Nationalist officials or, like me, from rich families. The rest were poor but

25

industrious; through competitive examinations they had earned permission to buy dollars at the former legal rate—a tiny fraction of the inflated rate—and thus were actually being subsidized by the Nationalist Government. We called these students "noodle-eaters," not out of disrespect—indeed many of them were brilliant—but because they were so dedicated they gave little thought to such worldly matters as food.

Three of the "noodle-eaters" were also going to the University of Wisconsin, and the four of us therefore became a group. During the stopover in Hawaii, we saw the sights in our first foreign city and we were impressed that Honolulu was exactly as the Hollywood films depicted it.

We therefore expected the mainland also to be like the films. San Francisco looked like any big city, but we were too afraid of gangsters to explore much of it. The train trip, however, promised a safe glimpse of America from a coach window, and we anticipated it eagerly.

We were amazed that the country was so sparsely settled. The mountains were dramatic, but the plains were monotonous and the infrequent villages identically drab. In Cheyenne, Wyoming, the train stopped for two hours and, with the porter's encouragement, we made a short foray beyond the station.

Most of our fear came from being strangers in a confusing country. We thought we knew English, for example, but we understood little of what we heard; the Americans spoke so quickly in a bewildering number of dialects. Another reason for our fear concerned money. My companions were each carrying traveler's checks for about $1,000 and I had more than $5,000. We did not associate traveler's checks with safety; they were merely a means by which foreign travelers could carry dollars. We thought that dollars in such large amounts were sure to tempt robbers.

After a short walk from the station, we entered a restaurant. At least we thought it was a restaurant; now I know it was a "bar and grill." The place was dark and smelled of disinfectant and stale beer. We found a table and ordered hamburgers and tea from a huge woman with a booming voice. When she left, we had a chance to look around the place. With growing horror, we saw that it was only too familiar. Every cowboy film had shown the same bar and the same stag's head. The loungers at the bar spoke with the same drawl and wore much the same costumes.

We all had the same idea at the same time. Always, in the films showing this sort of place, a fight started and shooting went on until the air was blue with gunsmoke. Our table was placed so that we might well be caught in a withering crossfire. My companions wanted to leave immediately. I had the same impulse, but I resisted such an undignified retreat. Thus we waited tensely— I was clutching the pad of traveler's checks in my pocket—until we were served. We took one bite of the food, paid the check and then left.

If our fear seems absurd, remember that in Shanghai lawlessness was very real—my mother had been kidnapped twice because of it. Moreover, we associated it with the Westerners, and for years Hollywood films had been pounding away at the idea that violence and brutality were accepted, and even respected, aspects of American life.

Safe aboard the train again, the porter asked us why we had returned so soon. I explained that we had seen all we wanted to see. The porter agreed. "You see one, you see them all," he said.

I asked if Madison would be like this.

"Oh, no," he replied. "It's *cold* in Madison."

I realized he thought I was referring to weather. Thus he implied that except for weather, all American towns were like

Cheyenne. I must confess that I was depressed for the rest of the trip.

Imagine my delight, therefore, to find that Madison was like nothing we had seen in the films. It was a dignified town with tree-shaded streets and four beautiful lakes; its atmosphere was dominated by the academic life of the university. I quickly lost my fears, and settled down to a pleasant life of casual study and social activity.

I boarded with a couple named Agnes who, I was astonished to learn, were in their seventies. People of this age in China were apt to be so infirm as to need constant attention. Mr. Agnes, however, although retired on a pension after 50 years with a railroad company, participated energetically in civic affairs. Mrs. Agnes, besides running a house, keeping a boarder, and entertaining friends, did expert dressmaking. Neither of them did what they did because they needed money, but because they enjoyed it. I was much impressed.

I was able to impress the Agneses with stories of China. Mrs. Agnes especially liked to hear about the respectful treatment given to elderly persons. Her own sons had families of their own and lived in nearby towns, but visited their parents only on rare holidays. To me this seemed disgraceful neglect. Before long, the Agneses treated me like a son. Because of this happy relationship, I was able to learn American customs quickly.

Some American customs disturbed me. In the classrooms, for example, the students showed little respect for the professors; often they argued with and even contradicted the teachers. Moreover, this almost arrogantly independent attitude of students was actually encouraged.

The attitude of students toward the opposite sex also disturbed me. In the Memorial Union Building, the sofas and chairs were usually filled with couples locked in passionate embrace. In those

28

days, it was called "smooching," and I was told that as a pastime it was only distantly related to sex. What little "smooching" Li-li and I had done, however, was quite explosively otherwise, and I could not imagine myself doing it in public.

Eventually I did learn to appreciate the American way of life. Oddly enough, my teacher was a fellow countryman. My father thought that I should see as much as possible of the United States, and for this purpose he sent me a generous sum to buy a motor-car. This was late 1947, and cars were still difficult to obtain. I was advised that the person most likely to help me was a young Chinese in Milwaukee with the improbable name of "Charlie" Chan. I realized that he must come from the famous Chan family of industrialists; my father knew them, and I therefore telephoned "Charlie." He said he could "fix me up," and he gave me a Milwaukee address to which I was to go the next day.

The address was a house belonging to a short and rather fat American who greeted me with a warm handshake. "Any pal of Charlie's is a pal of mine," he said.

Charlie came in then. He was tall and gangling; he had a narrow forehead, thick eyebrows and a lopsided grin. After shaking my hand, he put an arm around our host's shoulder. He made what I thought was an unkind remark about the size of our host's stomach. Our host, however, only laughed, and both men traded friendly insults. Finally, the American said, "Charlie, you'll kill me. You'll send me to the poorhouse."

Charlie replied, "Cut out that stuff, Joe. If I had your money, I'd get the classiest jalopy this side of Hollywood."

I understood nothing of this exchange, but I was lost in admiration for a fellow countryman with such a perfect command of American idioms. Moreover, a few minutes later I was sitting behind the wheel of my new car, a large Buick Roadmaster with innumerable special gadgets.

29

Charlie had me drive him to the Allis-Chalmers establishment, where he worked. He said he wanted me to meet "some of the boys." He took me into the office of a middle-aged man. "Bob," Charlie said to me, "this is Hal. He's my boss. But one of these days he may be working for me in Shanghai. How about it, Hal?"

"I'd like that, Mr. Chan," Hal replied, and I could see that he was charmed by Charlie as everyone else seemed to be.

During the next hour, I could see also that Charlie was perpetrating an innocent hoax on the firm's employees. He was sharing with me a piece of delightful irony which he knew only I would fully appreciate.

In Shanghai, Charlie's father was a man of formidable wealth whose textile and flour mills were spread all over China. The father had seven sons. Four were by his wife, and three were from a concubine. The four legitimate sons were given every advantage, but the concubine's sons received second-rate treatment; they could never hope to control any part of the Chan holdings. Charlie, youngest of the concubine's sons, had come to America to learn about the machinery which Allis-Chalmers supplied in huge quantity to the Chan mills. For this reason the people at Allis-Chalmers treated him with much friendliness. In effect, Charlie became what he had no chance of being in China: the scion of the famous Chan family. He was touched by the kindness of the Allis-Chalmers people, and I think he had made about half of them hope to go to China to live like Oriental potentates in his employ.

Before I left that day, Charlie invited me to go on a "binge" with him in Chicago the next weekend. I did not know what a "binge" was, but when I told my friends in Madison that I was going on one, they seemed impressed. Charlie drove me to Chicago in his magnificent Lincoln. At the hotel, everyone seemed delighted at Charlie's arrival; he strode through the place passing

30

out large tips, and we were whisked up to a luxurious suite. After changing, we set off on a tour of the night clubs. They were similar to the few I had seen in Shanghai, but the floor shows usually were too sophisticated for me to understand.

Late in the evening, we were at a place featuring a distinctive American art which even I could understand: strip tease. Charlie, obviously, was a connoisseur. He stamped his feet, whistled shrilly through his teeth and called encouragement to the girls whose performance he especially appreciated. I would have been embarrassed by his lack of dignity except that his enthusiasm won genuine admiration from the other guests.

After six girls had performed, Charlie asked me which one I had liked the best. I mentioned the only one whose name I happened to remember: Dixie. She was a lively brunette with a well-rounded figure. "Good choice," Charlie said. "I'll fix it up for you."

I did not know what he meant, but later Dixie and another of the performers joined us at our table. Apparently both girls considered Charlie an old friend. When we left the night club, they accompanied us. Back at the hotel, Charlie and his companion began what at the university was called smooching and then disappeared into his bedroom.

Dixie stood up, yawned and stretched. "I've had a rough day," she said. "Come on, honey, let's go beddie-bye."

Her words made no sense to me, but she took my hand and led me into my bedroom. She sat on the edge of the bed, kicked off her shoes and began to unfasten her stockings. Only now did I understand what Charlie's "I'll fix it up for you" meant. I was panic-stricken. I wanted to run but I had nowhere to go.

Dixie looked up and saw my consternation but misinterpreted it. "You had a bit too much to drink, didn't you?" she said sym-

31

pathetically. She pulled me down beside her. "Let Dixie help you," she said, and began deftly to undress me.

In the months that followed, Charlie took me on "binges" all over the United States. Almost every weekend we took a trip to some new place, and during longer holidays we went to the more distant corners of the country.

And everywhere we went, Charlie was always perfectly at home. If the place was small, his ploy was to stop some man on the street. "Friend," he would say, "my name is Chan. Everyone calls me Charlie. You have a great little town here. Where can a guy get himself a drink and a girl?"

I know that if I had tried that, I would get myself a punch in the head, but with Charlie it always worked. Within a few minutes, the stranger would be an old friend, and we would be off on a new adventure.

In cities, getting to know people quickly was more difficult, but Charlie's system was foolproof. He would rent the most impressive limousine available and give the chauffeur a large tip. Thereupon, the chauffeur's duty was to see that we were provided with the best that the city offered in the way of entertainment. By the middle of 1948, I had what was, in effect, a road map to loose living in America.

I did not really approve of loose living, and I was relieved when it came to an abrupt end. Charlie received a cable saying that his brother had been killed in an accident. The brother also had been one of the concubine's sons. For the first time, I saw something penetrate Charlie's devil-may-care attitude. Within only a few days he was on his way back to China. I knew that his main concern now was for his other brother from the concubine mother. Charlie felt that this brother, coping alone with the indifference of the Chan family, would need his help.

Not long after, another occurrence helped to jolt me out of my

32

immaturity. My father, from whom I had received regular weekly letters, suddenly stopped writing. Just when I was becoming frantic with worry, I received a letter from him in Taiwan. He said that he was closing out his interests in Shanghai but now had decided against Taiwan and planned to settle in Hong Kong. This news surprised me, but I was not alarmed, because my father treated the matter so casually.

Later, however, I had a letter from my brother giving me the true story. Because the bulk of my father's investments had been in real estate, he had lost heavily by leaving Shanghai. In effect, he was starting his business again from the bottom. Our previous experience with such a catastrophe was one of the most vivid memories I had. My brother's news therefore was a shock. I felt guilty about the money I had wasted on "binges" with Charlie, and disgusted with the playboy life. I changed my ways drastically.

Fortunately I had not neglected my studies. Moreover, my increasing knowledge of political science took on special significance with the rise of Communist power in China. Events at home were moving quickly. We Chinese students at the university felt a growing excitement at the prospect of dramatic changes, and we began to meet constantly to discuss the latest political developments.

To understand how we felt about these developments it is necessary to appreciate that Chinese history is a record of cultural achievement longer than any other, and that our pride in our civilization is correspondingly great. Our forefathers had difficulty in comprehending the true significance of the impact of the seemingly barbarian West. They tended to credit the Westerners only with possessing more powerful weapons. The Japanese were the first Asians to perceive that Western strength was not merely in a few fortuitous technological tricks, but in a society organized

33

so that technology was stimulated to limitless development. The Japanese reorganized their society along Western lines and within scarcely a generation became so strong that they could subjugate most of the great China mainland. The shock effect this had on the Chinese people cannot be overemphasized. We no longer doubted that if our country was to survive in the modern world, we would have to rebuild it in the Western image.

Dr. Sun Yat-sen's original image of a new China had incorporated Western ideas, but his revolution had failed. Expediency had forced him to compromise fatally with self-interest groups. After Sun's death, his political party, the *Kuomintang* or "Nationalist Party," became dominated by corrupt and inefficient officials who could not command the support of the Chinese or the respect of foreigners. The country was humiliatingly weak and disunited. We of the younger generation, therefore, were fired with the determination to build a new social order.

At first, few of us took the Communists seriously. We had little respect for Marxist theories which prescribed a rigid and wholly alien social pattern. On the other hand, judging from the rapidity with which the Communists were conquering the China mainland, they seemed impressively strong. Also impressive was Mao Tse-tung's article, "On the New Democracy"; he wrote that in China, under Communist Party leadership, a new democratic society would be established first and that socialism would be introduced gradually after the "New Democratic Revolution" had been completed.

Thus, most of the Chinese students in America were confused about the Communists but critical of the Nationalists. The long-established Chinese Students Association, to which we all automatically belonged, was controlled by a pro-Nationalist clique and became increasingly unrepresentative of actual Chinese student opinion. In the middle of 1948, another association for Chinese students was formed, "The Society for the Spread of Science." I was asked to join it, but I refused because I had studied no science. Nevertheless, I did attend a few meetings. The discussions were solely on politics, and no scientific subjects were raised. Moreover, the members were sharply critical of the Nationalists.

I did not know it, but this was my first contact with a Communist front organization. I also did not know at the time that the Communists had planted two underground agents among the 150 Chinese students at Wisconsin University. One of these was named Yung Won-yuan. He identified himself with the group of 100 or so "noodle-eaters." Like them, he was serious and studious and lived frugally. Later, under the Communist regime, he became the dean and secretary-general of the Shanghai College of Finance and Economics. I knew him only casually in the U. S., but I met him many times after I returned to Shanghai. I learned only then of his underground work in Madison.

The other agent was Frank Chou. He was suave, good-looking and popular, especially with girls. He worked with the so-called playboy group of Chinese students and I knew him well. He was not my type, but he seemed to pay special attention to me. I thought his interest in me concerned mainly my car; occasionally he would talk me into chauffeuring him while he sat in the back smooching with an American girl. In any case, he was acquainted with me well enough to know that I had no Nationalist sympathies.

This one fact may well have saved my life. Under the Communists, Frank Chou was to become one of the top officials in the People's Bank. Later, without a favorable report from a man of such rank, I would not have been able to clear myself of suspicion as to whether I had engaged in any anti-Communist activities while I was in the U. S.

At the time, however, none of the students suspected that these two were Communist agents. Neither of them ever discussed Communism. They were outspokenly anti-Nationalist, but because by now the Communists were the only alternative to the Nationalists, this was as effective as pro-Communist agitation. Also, neither agent ever took a leadership position either in the front organization or in any activity which benefited Communist goals. Instead, they were adept at persuading others to take the desired action while they remained discreetly in the background. They invariably chose people who were completely innocent of any Communist connections.

My own political feelings at the time were intense but negative. Academically, I disapproved of Communism, but I actively disliked the Nationalists. The flaw in the logic of contrasting people and an idea was an asset to the Communists, as we now know well, but in 1948 the same flaw was prevalent in much of American liberal thinking.

The thinking expressed in the more intelligent section of the press in the United States was largely in favor of the Chinese Communists. The American conservatives, on the other hand, seemed so obsessed with Communists that they saw Marxist socialism in every effort toward social reform. Because such reform was irresistible and inevitable, the Communists needed only to be identified with it in order to be carried almost automatically into power. The few people who voiced the opinion that the Communists posed the greatest single threat to the necessary social progress seemed to be rejected by both the liberals and the conservatives.

In 1948, however, the Chinese Communists still had not revealed their real intentions. They were said to be scrupulously correct and disciplined; they promised progress, order and justice—everything that the people wanted desperately and that the

Nationalists had failed to provide. By now, their victory in China was assured. Our only choice was to back a reactionary regime which had never proven adequate and now was defeated, or to believe in the promises of a new regime whose power was paramount. This was not really a choice at all, and my sympathies began to turn toward the Communists.

Li-li inadvertently contributed to my change in outlook. When I first arrived in the U. S., she had written to me frequently but irregularly and her letters had been so warm and personal that I looked forward to them eagerly. After a few months, however, she began to write regularly—about once every three weeks—and her letters grew stilted and impersonal. In fact they contained little else but admonishment for me to study hard. By the end of 1948, my degree was assured and only the formal confirmation of it in February 1949 remained. When I sent Li-li this news, she ceased writing to me altogether. At first I was worried and I wrote frantic letters to her. As the weeks passed without a reply, however, I forced myself to believe that she had found a lover or perhaps a husband and was no longer interested in me. It was not easy to accept this idea. It took months and cost me much in anguish. When I did accept it, however, I felt that a large part of my life was empty. I tried to fill the void by dedicating myself completely to the new China.

This does not mean that I became an ardent Communist. I admired much in the Chinese Communists, but I had doubts about their ideology. Many of the Chinese students felt the same, and yet each of us had to make an irrevocable decision for or against the Communist regime.

For the noodle-eaters, the choice was tragically simple. Their passports had been issued by the Nationalist Government and were stamped with student visas. By early 1949, the retreating Nationalists could no longer provide funds for these students.

37

The American Government, under the E.C.A. program, offered limited aid, but only to Chinese students taking technical courses. Under the immigration regulations, no one here on a student visa was eligible for employment. The Chinese Embassy honored its obligations by paying the return passage for students who no longer could be maintained in the United States. Under these paradoxical circumstances, most of the brilliant young nontechnical Chinese were shipped back to a now-Communist China.

A student like me, however, had four choices. I could go to Taiwan and join the defeated Nationalists whose regime had never earned respect and would exist only while propped up by other countries. I could go to overcrowded Hong Kong and attempt to compete with the foreigners who dominated an outmoded colonial society. Neither alternative promised a future worth working for.

I also could apply for American citizenship and try to make a life for myself here. The immigration rules, however, would make this difficult; also, it would be expensive because I would have to live on an allowance from my father until my student status was altered. Moreover, although I cannot say that I personally suffered from discrimination, I saw enough of it to feel "not at home." The American way of life was admirable, but it seemed restricted to Americans, and therefore offered me no hopeful future.

Finally, I could join the Communists in China. They were working to build a new Chinese social order. I was dedicated to the same endeavor. If they were really reformers, my training would be valuable to them, and my future possibilities were limitless.

In early May 1949, I received from Communist-occupied Shanghai a letter that contributed much to my decision. Dr. Stewart Yui, the professor whom I admired so much, had become the head of the entire Shanghai University but he also still managed the Political Science Department. His letter contained the thrilling offer of a post as his assistant in that department. Dr. Yui was no Marxist, but he wrote glowingly of the changes taking place under the new regime. He said that men like me were badly needed, that we would receive the full support of the authorities, and that we would have the opportunity to influence and train the country's future leaders. Such a career was more than I had dared to dream about. Nevertheless, I cautiously wrote to Dr. Yui asking for more information about the conditions in Shanghai before I accepted his offer.

At the same time, however, I wrote to my father in Hong Kong telling him that I intended to return to Communist China. To my consternation, he replied immediately, begging me to stay in America. He said that the Communists were "evil people," and he implied that I would be in danger if I went to the mainland.

Two days later, I received the second letter from Dr. Yui. He wrote nothing to suggest that I would have anything to fear in Shanghai. I now reached my decision to join the Communists. I considered that my father was becoming old-fashioned and was losing touch with the realities of the modern world. As much as I loved and respected him, therefore, I disobeyed him about staying in America and booked passage for Hong Kong.

I arrived late in September 1949. From the ship, I saw my father in the crowd at the pier. I was shocked at how he had aged in the two years I had been away. I saw his face light up when he recognized me on the gangplank. A moment later he was gripping my hand with both of his. We were speechless with emotion. Finally he looked down at the cigarette which I had forgotten was still in my other hand. He had never seen me smoke, and now with mock sternness he took the cigarette from my fingers and threw it away. The intervening years seemed to

39

vanish, and I was a small boy again with my gentle and loving father. I felt an overpowering rush of affection and hugged him. He laughed at this, but he said, "My son, you are very thin."

"It was the voyage," I said. "I was seasick."

He took my arm. "We must begin to fatten you up right away," he said.

At home, a large celebration with many relatives and an elaborate tea was waiting for me. That evening he took a group of younger people to the Repulse Bay Hotel where we dined and danced until midnight. It was all very gay—and completely unlike my father. After a few days of continuing celebration, I perceived that my father was doing everything he could think of to tempt me to stay with him in Hong Kong. He kept avoiding a serious talk alone with me. One night, however, I went into his room just after he had retired.

"I have to tell you," I said gently. "I'll be leaving within four days." I sat down on the foot of the bed. He did not answer, but he reached over to turn on the table lamp. "I have reservations on the steamer *Hunan*," I said. "We'll go to Tientsin first."

My father's face seemed to grow older. "Tell me the truth, my son," he said. "Are you returning because of that girl Li-li?"

The question was so unexpected that I was confused. The possibility of seeing Li-li again was in my mind, I suppose, but I could honestly say that she had nothing to do with my decision to return. I began an impassioned defense of the new regime. My father had always dreamed that I would one day become a great statesman in a strong free China; thus I argued that by going to Shanghai I would be working toward the future he wanted for me. I saw that I was not convincing him, however, and I ended lamely by asking him what he had against the Communists.

"They want only power," he said bitterly. "The rest of us are tired of fighting and wrongdoing. We want peace and decency. The Communists use these desires against us. They will make our country into hell."

His words, in Chinese, were quaintly old-fashioned, and when used to describe something as modern as Communists they sounded almost ludicrous. How could I accept my father's judgment over Dr. Yui's? My father knew nothing about politics, and he had never lived under the new regime; his antagonism to the Communists therefore had to be irrational. My professor, conversely, was an expert in political science and had firsthand knowledge of what the Communists were like. Surely I was right, therefore, in taking his advice. I could think of nothing more to say; I squeezed my father's hand and stood up to leave.

But he caught my arm. "My son, I beg of you, don't leave us," he said. "If you go there, it will be as though you fell into a bottomless well. I shall never see you again."

I had never seen my father lose control of his feelings to this extent, and it made me sick with anguish. "I'll think about it some more," I finally stammered.

His grip on my arm loosened. He turned away from me suddenly, but I saw tears on his cheeks. I spent a sleepless night.

I did not, of course, change my mind. At the pier, I insisted to my father that our parting was only temporary. His last words to me were, "I can only pray that you are right and I am wrong."

This was in September 1949. The Nationalists still held Canton, and from Taiwan they continued air attacks on Shanghai. Thus the coastal steamer service to Tientsin was the only practical way of getting to the Communist-held part of the mainland.

On board the small British freighter were two friends, Sun and Lui, whom I had met on the ship from America. Sun had studied law at the University of Indiana and also had been given a post at Shanghai University by Dr. Yui. Lui, although our age, had been a vice-consul in Boston for the Nationalist Government; he had resigned, however, and was returning to offer his services to the new regime. Like me, both men were idealistically enthusiastic about the changes taking place on the mainland. By the time we reached Taku Harbor, therefore, we were greatly excited. None of us had ever seen a Communist before, and we were infinitely curious about these controversial people. As the ship approached Tientsin we crowded to the rail, drinking in the sights; we felt both apprehension and the thrill of anticipation.

A launch detached itself from the shipping at the docks and knifed through the water toward us. It was filled with soldiers in sand-colored uniforms. They clambered quickly aboard, handling their rifles with practiced ease. We now saw our first Communists.

My immediate impression was that they were absurdly young. They looked like simple, open-faced, teen-age farm boys. But then what really surprised us was their dignity and courtesy. Although they were polite to everyone, they gave special consideration to Sun, Lui and me—the only passengers who had come from the United States. Obviously, these disciplined youngsters were trying to be as helpful as possible. Our spirits rose; in fact, I think we were a little hysterical with relief.

On shore, the customs officials were equally polite. They did not even examine our luggage. They spoke pleasant words of welcome to each of us. Outside, we found a bus waiting for the three of us. We had never dreamed that we would be expected. We were taken to the Astor Hotel, one of the best in town. We were told that our accommodations and whatever food we wanted—either Chinese or European—were free. We also received an invitation to be the guests of honor that night at a dinner given by the city's deputy mayor. We were too excited to settle down for the rest of the day in hotel rooms. We wanted to see what a modern Chinese city looked like under Communist rule. We therefore left almost immediately to explore Tientsin. The city itself was orderly and spotless; it had an air of industriousness. The people seemed busy with important work to do.

Among the people, those who were known as "cadres" stood out easily. These "cadres," who are omnipresent in China, are generally thought to be Communists, but actually comparatively few of them are Party members. They are, in effect, the government workers of the Communist regime. They all wear the same uniform, a drab two-piece kind of coverall in either blue or khaki. They are invariably young, thin and intense; they look sexless and fanatic. They all carry pens and diaries in which they note down everything they see and hear.

Nevertheless, what I saw of Tientsin filled me with new pride for my country. By the time we returned to the hotel, I was more sure than ever that I had been right to go against my father's wishes.

A car came for us that evening, and we were driven to an official guest house. The deputy mayor, a fat, affable man, greeted us himself. He introduced us to ten other guests, most of whom were officials in the municipal government. The majority wore the simple Communist Party uniform. They called each other and us *ton-tse*, which means "one who has the same objectives you have"; in other words, "comrade." Everyone expressed approval of our having left America to return to our mother country, but no one questioned us about our experiences abroad. Instead, our hosts wanted to know our first impressions of the New China. Our answers seemed to please them.

The dinner was surprisingly elaborate. At the table, the deputy mayor asked us about our plans. Sun and I had positions waiting for us at Shanghai University. We were told that train tickets to Shanghai would be obtained for us as quickly as possible. Lui, who had left the Nationalist Consulate in Boston, however, had no plans. Arrangements for his future were made immediately, through another official sitting near by. Lui was to be enrolled in the Graduate School of the North China Revolutionary College where he would have six months of training and indoctrination before being assigned to a permanent post.

Of the three of us, the Communists were impressed the most by Lui, who had voluntarily left a good job with the Nationalist Government. In a toast to us, the deputy mayor praised Lui's "great courage" in "casting aside darkness to seek the light." "This kind of action," he said, "should set a good example to other KMT [*Kuomintang,* or Nationalist] officials now serving abroad," and he added, "I am sure Comrade Lui will find his true destiny here in the New China." We were all told that we were "welcomed back to our mother country," and the toast ended with the words, "It is to be hoped that thousands of other Chinese now living and studying in foreign lands will follow in the footsteps of these bright young comrades."

After breakfast the next morning, our train tickets arrived and we found that our reservations were for three days hence. A cordial note from the city's official entertainment committee suggested that, in the meantime, any amusement we could think of would be arranged for us. What we wanted most was to see Peking. None of us had ever been to this famous city, and we felt that to be so close without visiting it would be a shame. We were sure that our overgenerous hosts would arrange an elaborate excursion if we even hinted at our wish, but we were embarrassed to take advantage of their hospitality to such an extent. We therefore went to the station on our own, and we reached Peking that afternoon. We registered at a small hotel in the western part of the city and set out at once on a sight-seeing jaunt. By nightfall we were exhausted, but what we had seen whetted our appetite to see more.

While we were having our breakfast noodles the next day and planning a trip to the Forbidden City, three armed policemen approached our table. The leader curtly demanded to see our papers. As always, I was astonished that the Communists seemed like rawboned farm boys; but their seriousness belied their age. We handed them our passports, which had been issued by the Nationalist Government when we had gone to the United States. The policeman looked at these documents with contempt and threw them back on our table. He wanted "identity papers" which, of course, we did not have. When the policemen learned this, they unslung their rifles. The leader raised his voice; he demanded an explanation of our presence. Lui did the talking; the moment he mentioned America, the policemen became excited. The leader motioned with his rifle and told us to come with him.

We were marched to a nearby district police station where we were shown into a shabby room with a battered desk and a few rickety chairs. Armed guards were placed at the door and we were left alone.

Fifteen minutes later, a police official entered. He was about our age, but short and thick. He sat down at the desk and began to bark questions without looking at us. He asked us our names, where we were staying and when we had arrived. Then he wanted to know why we had come to Peking. I began our story, but he kept interrupting me. Finally, exasperated, I told him that if he wanted to get to the bottom of this matter he should listen quietly until I had finished talking. He looked up at me for the first time. I saw that his face was dark with fury. I realized also that he was not merely uneducated, he was stupid as well, and I felt a tremor of fear. After I had made my explanation, he again demanded to know why we had come to Peking. I began all over, this time using simpler words.

But he still was not satisfied. I slowly perceived that he was

45

incapable of understanding the tourist pleasure of sight-seeing. He could not believe that people would actually waste money and time to travel solely for the purpose of visiting a new place. I was trying to enlighten him on this subject when he suddenly stood up. "Enough of this!" he said. "You are stubborn. Very well. You sit here and wait." He stamped out of the room.

This time we nervously waited for two hours. Finally, a tall man of about thirty-five entered. He sat down, lit a cigarette, and stared at us coldly, silently. Then he read some notes. At last he leaned back. "All right," he said. "What are you doing in Peking?"

I had had time to think out our explanation carefully, and this time I made it more detailed. I emphasized the fact that we had been embarrassed to allow our generous Tientsin hosts to spend public funds on our entertainment. Also, I happened to mention that we were returned students.

The two words seemed to electrify the officer. "You're *returned students?*" he asked, leaning forward. "Can you prove it?"

I opened the passports on the desk and showed him our student visas. He studied them carefully. He stood up then, and I saw something like fear in his eyes. "Comrade returned students! How can I apologize?" he stammered. "The inconvenience we've caused you! A terrible misunderstanding." He told us that we had acted correctly and that the whole trouble had come from the failure of the Tientsin police to notify him of our arrival. He insisted that we allow him to see that we were provided with better accommodations and given a really fine tour of the city.

By now, however, we had lost our desire to see Peking. We said that we had to get back to Tientsin. The officer protested that we could not leave without being properly entertained, but we insisted and finally he drove us to the station in his own jeep.

Right up until our train pulled out, he continued to apologize and to try to persuade us to stay.

I know now that he had good reason to be afraid. In those days, the Party Line was that returned students were to be extended every possible courtesy upon their arrival. If we had complained about our treatment, therefore, he could have been charged with "failure to implement Party policy," a serious offense. I also realize now that the hotel clerk in Peking had reported us to the police for not having the proper papers. At the time, however, we were confused and upset; we did not know what to think of the experience.

We were met at the Tientsin station by members of the official entertainment committee. For the next 48 hours we were kept so busy with parties and plays and concerts that we had no chance to think. When the time came to say good-bye to Lui, and for Sun and me to take the train to Shanghai, we no longer were worried about our Peking adventure, and our enthusiasm for the New China was greater than ever.

Shanghai was unchanged. Some of the theatres were even showing recent American films. Our house in Yu-yuen Road near Jessfield Park was exactly as I remembered it, and our beloved old servants made me feel that I had left home only the day before. I spent the night at our house and the next day moved to Shanghai University in the suburbs.

This was the exciting climax of my return. I had spent ten years of my life in the schools and colleges of the university and now I was coming back as an important teacher. I was given quarters with three other bachelor professors in a fine house on the campus. My friend Sun had already moved in, and he introduced me to the other two occupants. One was Mr. Wong, a chemist who had studied at Columbia University in New York. The other was Dr. Tan, who had a Ph.D. from Chicago Univer-

47

sity and who taught in the Education Department. I especially liked Tan; he was big, awkward and homely, but he was good-hearted and he shared my intense idealism about a glorious future for China.

That evening I had a reunion with Dr. Yui. He was now the Chairman of the University Committee, which was like being president; he was also Dean of the University and of the College of Letters, as well as the head of the Political Science Department. He was a tall, distinguished man with elegant manners. The other guests that night included several professors whom I remembered, and four American missionary teachers.

The Americans were especially interested in the news I could bring them of their own country. As soon as I had the chance, however, I asked if the new regime had made any changes in the university.

One of the professors replied that the Communists had dismissed the former president, Dr. Henry Ling, but had done nothing else. The authorities, he also told me, had promised that the Christian universities would not be changed and in fact would be helped to expand.

Another guest, however, said that no *apparent* changes were being made. This brought on a lively discussion. To me, the essential point was that the courses were being taught as before; the same textbooks, most of which were American, were still used. Nevertheless, one innovation mentioned was a "reform movement" that had begun among a small group of teachers. The group was made up of those who taught Chinese language, history and literature. None of them had studied abroad, and for this reason their status was inferior. They did have some cause for dissatisfaction, and their agitation for a change therefore seemed reasonable. I asked if these people were Communists, but no one seemed to know.

"Actually," Dr. Yui said, "the Communists still seem to be underground."

None of this conversation perturbed me. I went to bed that night, tired but happy, full of hope and expectations for an exciting new life.

CHAPTER 3

Our song is ended.
Sighing, we look toward heaven.
Our eyes are washed with tears.

—TU FU

ONE OF the delights of returning to Shanghai was to see Charlie Chan again. I spent my first weekend at the Chan mansion. Charlie seemed unchanged; he had the same crooked grin and the same half-humorous, half-cynical outlook. For the whole Saturday, I listened to him relive some of the "binges" we had had in America.

Just before dinner, however, Charlie's older brother, Chan Jen-ping, arrived home, and Charlie dropped his frivolous talk. "J.P.," as everyone called him, was the remaining son of the concubine and therefore Charlie's true brother. J.P., better-looking than Charlie, was more serious and reserved. Although he seemed humorless and spoke little, he was thoughtful and generous; people liked him better the longer they knew him.

At dinner, J.P.'s wife and five children joined us. Now for the first time, I pieced together the story of how the Chans had fared under the new regime.

By 1949, the elder of the family, the famous industrialist, was too old to work, and for several years his four legitimate sons had been in control of the business. The concubine's sons had lived by what they could wheedle from their begrudging half brothers. The four legitimate sons were smart enough to know that they would have no chance under the Communists, and when the Nationalist collapse became imminent, they wanted to leave, moving their industrial equipment out of the country. In fact, they loaded several ships with the machinery from some of their factories. At this point, however, the old man came out of retirement long enough to order the ships unloaded and the machinery returned. The underground Communists had persuaded him that they would not confiscate the Chan property and, on the contrary, would help the family to increase the holdings. Before the Communists captured Shanghai, the legitimate sons left hurriedly, taking with them only the movable property. The concubine's sons found themselves in charge of the family's industrial empire. J.P., with Charlie as an assistant, became China's most powerful industrialist, a situation which a year before would have seemed incredible.

The fact that J.P. and Charlie had grievances against their half brothers under the old society made them trustworthy to the Communists. J.P. was even invited to Peking for an interview with Mao Tse-tung, who said to him, "I hope you will bear more little ones for the good of the people." By this, Mao meant that he wished J.P. to increase the Chan holdings. Also, Mao had previously stated in a speech, "China suffers from too little rather than too much capitalism." J.P. was declared a "national capitalist"; this meant that he was accepted as politically reliable by the Communists and regarded as useful to the regime. J.P. believed that he and the other "national capitalists" would be encouraged rather than harassed; he thought that landlords and speculators would be abolished and that holdings of Nationalist-connected businessmen would be confiscated, but that the Communists would not introduce socialism for another 25 years.

Thus J.P. now lived in security and splendor. The magnificent family mansion was his. The old father lived with the concubine in Wusih, about 70 miles away. Paradoxically, the old man's wife, the mother of the legitimate sons, lived with J.P. and Charlie in the town mansion.

I became a regular weekend guest at the mansion. Charlie was still full of humor and wit, but he had become more discreet. He was behaving himself. In fact, he fell seriously in love and got married. His wife was the daughter of another national capitalist and was considered the most beautiful girl student at Aurora College; Charlie was considered the luckiest man in Shanghai. In typical Charlie fashion, he thought that I might feel somehow deprived in this situation and he "fixed it up" for me to meet another girl student, Fan Su, who also was a beauty queen and the daughter of a national capitalist. When the four of us went out we attracted much attention.

The important part of my life during those first months back in Shanghai, however, was at the university. I had the contentment of working hard at a job I liked. I enjoyed my association with Dr. Yui, whom I admired, and I got on well with Tan, Sun and Wong, the other young professors with whom I shared a university house. We seldom saw a Communist. In order to understand and serve the new regime, however, we attended lectures on Marxist-Leninist theory. Also, through the press, we followed the descriptions of Communist policy, but because the

53

policies did not concern us directly we believed that the authorities would leave us alone to work out our own problems.

Only one small circumstance marred the pleasure of those first months. One evening early in 1950, I was called upon formally by three students and a young assistant teacher from the "reform group." They questioned me on my opinions concerning Dr. Yui and the American missionary teachers, whom they mentioned in not quite respectful terms. I considered that my opinions were none of their business, but I politely evaded their queries. To my surprise, they called on me again three days later and thereafter I had to put up with them several evenings a week for the next two months. They wanted me to disassociate myself from Dr. Yui and the American teachers. They accused the distinguished head of our university of being a "lackey of the imperialists." I told them that I felt he was patriotic and that he was working hard for the good of the university. My visitors argued, however, that he was an "innocent dupe of the imperialists" and all the more dangerous for being well-meaning. The smugness of my callers irritated me. They never mentioned Communism or even the new regime, but they spoke in slogans and clichés; some instinct warned me not to lose my temper with the persistent "reformers."

And then suddenly the reformers stopped calling on me. Even though they seemed to have no official status, I became uneasy that the new regime might now regard me as a "backward element." Moreover, in early 1950 we began to hear rumors that the Communists were using excessive brutality in implementing land reform. In mid-1950, when these rumors were persistent, I was included in a group of ten professors invited to witness a "struggle meeting" against a landlord in a village three hours' drive from Shanghai, and I had my first chance to see the Communists in action.

In the village square, about 200 obviously excited people were gathered. In front of the crowd, five Communist cadres sat at two tables. We professors were seated a short distance behind them. The landlord, a haggard man of forty with his hands tied behind him, was brought forward by two policemen who forced him to his knees in front of the tables; his head sank until it almost touched the ground. A cadre now made an angry speech, describing the injustices that the peasants had suffered. He told the villagers that this was their day to redress their wrongs; he encouraged them to air their grievances. Finally, showing reluctance, they began to come one by one to the tables and to describe the wrongs committed by the landlord. From their stories, the landlord seemed a monster of villainy, greed and lechery. The villagers were encouraged to scream abuse at him. They slapped him, pulled his hair, pounded on his back with their fists and spat on him. When the fervor of the "struggle" began to diminish, the cadres exhorted the crowd to renewed effort. I noticed one man who needed no encouragement. He seemed consumed with hatred for the landlord, and I felt he must have suffered terribly.

The struggle went on for four hours, until dusk. The prisoner did not once raise his head or make a sound, but I could see his lips moving as though he might be muttering to himself. Once he retched violently and vomited. When the meeting was over, he was dragged away, unable to walk. His sentence was ten years of labor reform.

After the meeting, the cadres invited our comments. I said that although I believed land reform was essential, I wondered if the methods we used were a little rough. I was answered by a Mao Tse-tung quote: "Lenience to the enemy is cruelty to the people."

That night I stayed in the hut of an old peasant who talked about the village. I was astonished to learn that the man who had showed such animosity toward the landlord was the landlord's elder brother. Originally the father of the two sons had divided his land between the two brothers. The older son had drunk and gambled away his inheritance. He then became almost a beggar living off the grudging charity of his younger brother. The wastrel resented his brother's success. When the cadres came to the village and asked who had the most grievances against this landlord, the villagers pointed out the older brother. The cadres then trained him for the "struggle," and he became the "hero" of the local land reform movement.

Nevertheless, the peasants were pleased with the results of the campaign. At the land distribution ceremony the next day, their gratitude was evident. I remember an old woman who clutched her deed to her bosom and kissed it as though it were a baby. Between sobs, she said that for generations her family had toiled ceaselessly for others, always trying to save enough to buy at least one *mou* of land, but they had never managed to earn anything more than the food to keep them alive. Now, because of the Communist Party and Chairman Mao, her dreams had come true. I was deeply touched. I approved of the results achieved by the Communists even if I was a bit doubtful of the methods used.

I also had doubts about Communist propaganda tactics. In early 1950, the press had become anti-American to an extent that, to me, seemed pointless. Then suddenly in June 1950, we heard that the South Koreans, "instigated by American imperialists," in an "act of flagrant aggression" had attacked the "peaceful North Koreans." The fact that the "peaceful North Koreans" were advancing rapidly into South Korea quickly became obvious. We professors at the university asked ourselves openly: If the North Koreans had been so peaceful, why was the campaign into South Korea proceeding with such efficient military planning and dispatch? And if the South Koreans were the aggressors, what were the North Koreans doing in their country? Our criticism was not leveled at the Communist authorities or regime, but at the ineptitude with which the information about the Korean conflict was being presented.

With the beginning of the Korean war, the intensity of the anti-American propaganda was greatly increased. We understood that the authorities were trying to whip up violent emotion among the Chinese people. In the hysteria, our American missionary teachers were accused of being spies. The evidence against them was too flimsy for belief by a rational person, but the teachers were hounded out of the country. The rest of us rationalized this injustice with the idea that the Communists were inexperienced and were trying to achieve quickly a great deal, so that they were bound to make a few mistakes.

One morning in November of 1950, our cook at the university excitedly roused all four professors in our house. Cadres had arrived; the faculty and the entire student body were given ten minutes to dress and assemble at the university square. Printed banners were thrust into our hands. They carried such messages as Down with the soft-worded, cloak-and-dagger lies of the American imperialists and Protest against Austin's shameless lies. Everyone was asking what it was all about, but no one seemed to know. We were told to shout the slogans printed on the banners. Thereupon we were marched for five hours all through Shanghai. We were joined by the students and faculty members of the other Christian universities. We shouted the slogans until we were hoarse, and still the cadres exhorted us to greater effort. Finally, back at the university, still not having eaten, we were made to listen to a fiery speech from the Party Secretary. Only now did we learn that we had made a "spontaneous" demonstration against a speech by Warren Austin, then the American representative to the United Nations Security Council, on the long record of friendship between the peoples of China and the United States. Austin had mentioned the universities and hospitals which Americans had established in China. Naturally, Shanghai University, which had been built and supported by Southern Baptist missionaries, was included. We Chinese, students and professors alike, had immediately risen in "spontaneous protest" to the supposed lie.

Thereafter we were called out at frequent intervals to "protest spontaneously" other "imperialist lies." We rarely knew what the issue was until we read the story of our "voluntary demonstration" in the papers. The press was going full blast against American influences in China. The American contribution to Chinese universities was described as a sinister plot to make Chinese students the "running dogs of imperialism." China's foremost research and training hospital, the American-supported Peking Union Medical College, was depicted as a laboratory where American doctors performed fiendish experiments on Chinese women and children. Even U.N.N.R.A., through which many Chinese lives had been saved by American food and medical gifts, was designated as an American plot to plant disease among the Chinese.

Looking back now, I can remember the impatience I felt with the authorities for permitting such absurd lies to be spread. I told myself that the leaders were deluded and were using mistaken tactics. I thought that their errors could and must be corrected quickly; otherwise, the regime would lose the respect of the rest of the world.

At the end of 1950, the obvious falsehoods and the anti-American propaganda were again increased in the drive for volunteers to fight with the North Koreans. At the same time, the drives to collect funds for the Resist America—Aid Korea Campaign began. The first time I was approached, I voluntarily agreed to contribute the amount of a half month's salary. I learned quickly that this was regarded as insufficient; the collector kept after me until I had pledged three months' salary. I found that the other professors pledged the same amount, but the collectors never once dropped the fiction that our contributions were voluntary.

Along with our "contributions," we professors were asked to make "original" recruitment speeches to our students, who were especially wanted in the army. The arguments we were advised to use were based on the propaganda fabrications, and if our speeches were insufficiently persuasive, we were "advised" until our revisions and improved delivery were acceptable.

By this time, the propaganda lies, plus our "spontaneous" demonstrations, "voluntary" contributions and "original" speeches might have made me revise my opinions about the regime, but I was preoccupied with a completely separate problem: Li-li.

When I had first returned to Shanghai in September 1949, Dr. Yui had warned me about her. He said that the puritanical Communists grouped taxi dancers with prostitutes, whom they regarded as "degenerate elements"; anyone who associated with these "elements" was guilty of "degenerate living." Thus my future would be jeopardized if I began seeing Li-li again.

At first I had had no intention of seeing her; I assumed that she had found another man. Nevertheless, I thought about her, and I was excited by the idea that she was near by. Then one evening when I was in a restaurant with the Chans, Li-li came in with another party. She paled when she saw me but made no sign of recognition. She was even lovelier than I remembered, and my desire to see her became almost irresistible. I asked Charlie to find out what he could about her.

A week later, Charlie reported that she was living at the same place and still worked as a taxi dancer.

"Has she married or become anyone's concubine?" I asked.

"Apparently not," he answered.

Now my curiosity, as well as my desire, was aroused, and I could resist no longer. I found out where she worked and telephoned her. She seemed surprised to hear my voice, but nothing in *her* voice indicated that she was pleased. I insisted that I had important things to tell her, and she reluctantly agreed to meet me at her place the next afternoon.

I spent a sleepless night. The next day when I entered her room, her parents discreetly withdrew; Li-li and I stared at each other.

"You've not changed," I said finally. "You're still beautiful."

She thanked me. "I understand you've changed into a progressive," she said.

I reached for her then, but she stopped me. "If you want to talk, we had better go out," she said.

We went to a restaurant where we could dance and have tea. We both found we were too nervous to dance. Finally, I blurted, "Why did you stop writing to me?"

She looked surprised. "Because your father made me," she said.

It was my turn to be surprised. I learned now that, shortly after I had arrived in America, my father had gone to her to ask her not to contact me. He was respectful to her, and she therefore could not resist his request. She felt, however, that if she stopped writing suddenly, I might become so upset that my studies would suffer. She promised my father that she would discuss only my studies in her letters and would stop writing when my degree was assured.

My throat ached; as always, Li-li had acted in my best interests, and she had been completely honest with both my father and me. I felt that my anguish was communicated to her, and she softened a little. Later, she took a packet of letters from her bag and handed them to me; they were the ones I had written to her from America. "I think you want these back," she said.

Li-li, now, had underestimated me. She had heard that I had become an ambitious Communist fellow traveler and assumed that I would want to hide my past indiscretions with a "degenerate element" by destroying my incriminating letters. When she finally accepted the sincerity of my protests, she softened completely. Back in her room, she allowed me to kiss her. She was unresponsive at first, but then she sighed deeply and melted against me. I insisted that I must see her again soon. She hid her face in my shoulder and wept a little, but she agreed.

Thereafter, we met regularly. Our relationship was the same as before. Also, as before, I did not make love to her. Her position as a taxi dancer had changed drastically. Few real taxi dancers remained; most of them had become "party girls," and obviously both groups would soon be liquidated. Li-li's only hope for the future, therefore, was to find a husband. A suitable marriage would require her to have an unblemished reputation. Thus, we had to be discreet. I told Charlie and J.P. that I was taking French lessons on Saturday afternoons. If the weather permitted, Li-li and I would drive into the country with a picnic lunch. We would find a secluded corner in an old temple garden. We might spend hours in serious discussion, or we might sit silently, holding hands. Just being with her was bliss, and I asked for nothing more. If we had to stay in the city, I took her to the dance halls where a man interested only in dancing might take a girl like her.

Late in 1950, our meetings became known. Charlie told me that J.P. knew about them and was worried for me. From a sudden change in Dr. Yui's attitude, I realized that he also had found out. Li-li herself warned me that I would not be allowed to continue my university career if I insisted on seeing her. Worse, I

61

knew that I was jeopardizing her chances to make a suitable marriage. One sad day in early 1951, therefore, we faced the truth that the future for both of us depended upon our separating forever.

"Forever" seemed so horribly long, however, that we decided we owed each other one last fortnight of being together completely. Thus, during the winter vacation in early 1951, Li-li and I went to the scenic resort town of Hanchow.

The best accommodations were reserved for only high Communist officials and their foreign guests, but we found a pleasant room in the West Lake Hotel. At dinner we giggled like two happy children, but we were too nervous to eat. Later, when the soft night closed around us in our room, Li-li responded to my kisses with deep sighs and little moans. When I tried to remove her dress, however, she stiffened and hid herself from me. Many soft caresses and words of assurance were necessary before her trembling ceased, and she turned to me at last. She pulled me to her, and in our embrace she cried out sharply. My lovely Li-li had been a virgin. I should not have been surprised; she was always honest and had never made any pretense with me. In any case, I now had the delight of teaching her the intricacies of love.

The next two weeks were the happiest of my life. We rowed on the lake. We explored the quaint little hillside temples. We wandered blissfully through lovely gardens. And we visited the historic spots, telling each other their stories and legends.

We discussed neither the past nor the future. One morning, however, I was overcome by the thought that our last moments together were slipping by so quickly, and I tried to make her agree to marry me. Li-li refused to consider it. She said that my marrying her would mean disaster for me, and she admonished me gently to accept the fact that this interlude must be our last.

She also told me that, as a taxi dancer, she still had a few clients with whom she was popular and respected. She had had several marriage offers. Thus she begged me not to worry about her; after we returned to Shanghai, I was to think of her as a married woman and forget her.

I could not forget her after we returned, however, and I could not face the prospect of never being with her again. She compromised by promising that I could contact her on a certain date two months later; if she had not arranged to be married by then, I insisted that I would make myself responsible for her future.

At the university, two days after we parted, Dr. Yui talked to me sternly. I learned that someone had seen Li-li and me together in Hanchow and had told Dr. Yui. He said that we could no longer hope the Communists would allow us to manage our own affairs. He reminded me how the American teachers had been driven out during the Resist America—Aid Korea Campaign. He emphasized that we American-trained professors were in an increasingly doubtful position. "You must not take chances," he said. "The authorities could use your association with this girl as an excuse to take strong action against you." I saw that Dr. Yui was genuinely frightened, and I also became afraid.

Despite the agony of being separated from Li-li, therefore, I avoided contacting her until the morning we had agreed to meet for one last time. The day was warm and scented with spring. Li-li looked calm and beautiful; only her eyes showed the emotion we were both hiding. She told me she had accepted a proposal and that she would be married six weeks later. She refused to tell me anything about her fiancé.

On impulse, because the day was so perfect, I suggested we drive into the country. She hesitated for only a moment. I drove aimlessly, and for several hours we spoke little. I sensed that Li-li was not disturbed about her pending marriage, and I was

63

relieved that her problem was solved. Nevertheless, I was deeply depressed. On a deserted back road, we came to a canal, and I stopped the car under a blossoming tree. I turned to Li-li and took her into my arms, but she stiffened against me. I suddenly felt that I wanted desperately to make love to her. She did not resist, but she cried with such genuine anguish that I had to stop. I realized that she felt strongly the need to be honorable for her fiancé. This was the moment when I knew finally that our affair was finished.

It was now late afternoon. Neither of us had eaten all day. The next town we came to had a small restaurant in which I ordered a meal. While it was being prepared, a boy offered to guide us through a nearby temple. When we returned I offered him three JMP as a tip. To my surprise, he refused the money and asked instead that we save him the scraps from our meal. I could not understand the request because the sum I had offered him should have fed him for an entire day.

The boy told me, however, that local people were not allowed to buy restaurant meals. This seemed unbelievable, but when I tried to take him into the restaurant with us, the proprietor refused him entry. The proprietor said that the government regulations allowed him to serve meals only to visitors. He did agree, however, that we could save a part of our food and take it with us, ostensibly to eat during our trip. Li-li kept aside a good selection of food and we took it to the boy, who had been watching our car. He brightened when he saw the food and began to devour it at once; between mouthfuls he told us a shocking story of local conditions.

People were finding themselves worse off than before, he said. As landowners, they now paid no rent, but had taxes. The taxes were paid in kind, as the rent had been, and the tax rate was about the same as the former rent rate. The tax calculation, however, was based on the yields of the most productive and most efficiently cultivated land in the area. Those who had received less fertile plots or who were less efficient found that they were giving so much of their produce that not enough was left to feed their families. Again, the farmers traditionally had cheated a bit before "reform" by adding a little sand to the grain; also, in emergency, the landlord usually could be persuaded to grant a few days' grace in the rent payments and give a reduction if the family was really in distress. The cadres, however, under pressure from their absentee superiors, permitted no such leniency and any farmer who cheated or who made late or even minutely short payments was guilty of "violating the people's interest." Thus most of the people of the district were in distress; many were selling their land to the few relatively successful cultivators and were looking for jobs in Shanghai.

As we drove away, I was troubled by what the boy had told us. Until now, I had thought of the land reform movement as an achievement of the new regime, and if I disapproved of the way the Resist America—Aid Korea was handled, I could still credit the Communists with basic integrity concerning the vital agricultural problem. If the peasants now were worse off than before, however, my evaluation of Communist tactics would need more thinking about.

Back in Shanghai that evening, Li-li and I parted without further emotion. I think we were resigned at last to the inevitable; we turned away from each other to face our own separate problems.

This was on April 21, 1951. Exactly a week later, my problem of evaluating the new regime became more difficult. April 28 was a Saturday, and I spent the weekend at our house in the city. That night, I worked late correcting student papers. For hours I heard the screaming of sirens and the roar of trucks speeding through the streets. I was uneasily aware that something momentous was happening, but I was not alarmed.

The next morning, however, the servants reported in consternation that thousands of people had been arrested. They said that all those who had held positions in the Nationalist Party under the previous regime were taken by the security police. I doubted the rumor, but my uneasiness increased.

I returned to the university that afternoon. I was about to enter my room when I noticed the door next to mine. I gasped and stared at it in horror. The door was sealed with a large red paper *X;* it meant that the occupant was under arrest and that his possessions were not to be disturbed until the police had examined them. My good friend Dr. Tan—the bumbling idealist who could not even stand to hurt anyone's feelings and who had believed sincerely in China's future under the new regime— was gone. At one time in his past, he had held a minor post in the Nationalist Party, and because of this we would never see him again. From the moment I saw the red *X*, I began to be afraid.

The number of people arrested throughout the country on the night of April 28, 1951, is not known. Nevertheless, almost everyone had some relative or acquaintance who simply disappeared. In Shanghai many public buildings, including two schools, all of which had been taken over by the police weeks before, were used as prisons. One of the execution grounds was near the university. Every day we would see the truckloads of prisoners. While we were in our classes we would hear the terrible shooting. The trucks carrying away the corpses dripped streams of blood into the road that ran past the university buildings. Within the next few months, all the ex-Nationalists were wiped out.

We at the university were confused—stunned, perhaps—with shock. Part of the shock came from the realization that the regime had been guilty of treachery. In December 1950—four months before the night of the arrests—the Security Bureau had requested all those who had held positions with the Nationalist Party to register. The stated purpose was to give those who had made "political mistakes" a chance "to start life anew." They were to submit autobiographies, emphasizing their past Nationalist activities. They also had to write "social relationships reports" in which they listed the known details of every acquaintance, whether a friend, relative or an associate. Guaranties were made repeatedly that no matter what one's "evil doing" had been or what position one had held with the Nationalists, everyone who "confessed everything to the people" would be treated leniently. Only those who failed to register would be punished. Those knowing someone who had been connected with the Nationalist Party were urged to persuade him to register.

I attempted this persuasion on several ex-Nationalist friends, but they were already convinced. When the ex-Nationalists did register, they seemed greatly relieved; they had been worried about their past political connections, and now were happy to have the burden lifted. Tan, one of the professors who lived in our house, was among these. They laughed now at the people who had left the mainland in fear of the Communists.

In short, we believed that the Communists would keep their promise. By the end of April 1951, all the ex-Nationalists had registered. Without warning, then, the authorities arrested them all. Most of those arrested were executed or punished secretly. Relatively few were held for trial.

Those brought to trial were always actual gangsters or corrupt politicians. The trials followed the same pattern as the "struggle meetings" of land reform. The cadres assembled a crowd by ordering the residents of an area to appear in a specified public place. Planted activists led the people in shouting

67

abusive slogans. Handcuffed prisoners were brought out and made to kneel before the "masses." Communist officials opened the trial with a speech denouncing the accused and listing his crimes. Previously arranged accusers then came forward to tell, vividly and often sincerely, their grievances. The crowd, harangued by the activists, were worked up to frenzied screaming: "Kill the counter-revolutionaries! Kill! Kill! Kill!" Thereupon the officials, "in response to the will of the masses," ordered the prisoners to be killed. Usually, the sentence was carried out at once in front of the crowd.

I was made to attend these sickening exhibitions frequently. I remember especially the trial of a factory foreman who had extorted money from his employees and had seduced women workers under him. When found guilty, he was shoved off the platform. He rolled grotesquely because of his tied hands. While he was still on the ground, a policeman shot him through the head. I was about ten paces away. I saw the splatter of the victim's brains, and the obscene twitching of his body.

Not all of the ex-Nationalists were killed outright or executed secretly; many were sent to "labor reform" and died slowly. I have never seen a "counter-revolutionary" who was released from this punishment. The prisoner received no pay and was given barely enough food for subsistence. If shelter was provided at all, it was the absolute minimum. The prisoners did not even have a clothes ration, so that their only covering was what friends or relatives dared send them. They worked in gangs at manual labor 14 hours a day, seven days a week. My friend Lui, who had been a Nationalist consular official in Boston and who had voluntarily returned to serve the new regime, was sent to labor reform. His work gang was assigned to the Sikang-Tibet Highway Project, and I never heard of him again.

Another type of punishment was given to those whose "crimes" did not call for execution and who were too old or respected for the dreaded labor reform. It was called "surveillance," and I saw its effects on a lawyer friend of mine.

The friend had graduated from Stanford University and became the dean of a Shanghai law college. Like me, he enthusiastically supported the new regime, and he had been made the Secretary-General of a Communist-sponsored trade association. Nevertheless, he was picked up one morning and taken at once before an already assembled crowd. He knelt for three hours before the officials while the crowd was made to scream abuse at him. The only charges brought against him were that he was a "lackey of the rich and an oppressor of the poor" and that he had a brother in the Taiwan government. For this, my friend was sentenced to be kept under surveillance for three years.

He was made into a janitor at the trade association he had previously headed. He was paid JMP18 a month and could live only by selling his household furnishings. His employers addressed him only to give him orders and wrote weekly reports on his behavior. He himself had to go once a week to the police with a written expression of his gratitude to the Party for the leniency of the people's justice; if his gratitude was not expressed in terms sufficiently abject, he was made to rewrite his paper until it was found acceptable. No one else dared speak to him, let alone try to help or comfort him. After 16 months he threw himself into the river.

I had had no direct connection with the Nationalists, but I was endangered by having friends who were arrested for the crime. For each, I had to write a long report suggesting that I had been aware of his evil association and had disapproved of it. Moreover, my reports were intended to incriminate my friend and were returned for rewriting until they were acceptably damning.

Because of my friendship with Tan, the security police interrogated me several times a week for three months. They apparently wanted to find out if Tan had tried to make me pro-Nationalist, even though I knew that Tan had sincerely supported the new regime. Also, I was once questioned daily for 13 days about a Mr. Wu, whom I had seen only once in my life. He had brought me a tennis racket from a mutual friend in Wisconsin. Each interrogation began with the same question: "You say you were not acquainted with Mr. Wu. Then why did he bring you a tennis racket without knowing who you were?"

The arrests and trials went on for six months, until late 1951, and became known as the Suppression of Counter-Revolutionaries Campaign. By the time the campaign was over, a breakdown in normal human relationships was noticeable. During the persecution, friend had been made to betray friend; family members had been forced to denounce each other. The traditional warm hospitality of the Chinese, therefore, disappeared. We learned that the more friends we had, the more insecure our position. We began to know the fear of being isolated from our own groups and of standing helplessly alone before the power of the State.

While the campaign was going on, the power of the State was also felt at the university. During the Resist America—Aid Korea Campaign of the year before, in mid-1950, the constant propaganda pressure created confusion and restlessness among the students. A Students Union was formed; its leaders seemingly were elected by the students but actually came from the Communist Party or the New Democratic Youth League, which later was made into the Communist Youth League. The Students Union leaders were in the forefront of the contribution drives and the demonstrations; they increasingly took over the job of "educating" the students.

When the semester started in early 1951, the government's

Higher Education Bureau sent a new man for the top post at Shanghai University. He began a drastic reorganization. The old and respected professors were either demoted or transferred away from the university. Their posts were given to young assistant professors from the reform group or to a few ex-graduates who, we now learned, had been underground Communists. Dr. Yui's titles were stripped from him one by one. His courses were taken over by men who often lacked the qualifications of even their students. I was taken off my own courses and assigned to others for which I had no training.

Training, however, was no longer necessary. The American texts and methods had been discarded and now translations of appropriate Russian lectures were merely read aloud to the classes. A gramophone would have worked just as well.

Also, in the spring of 1951, a batch from the old group of professors was sent for an indoctrination course at the East China People's Revolutionary College in Suchow. Here they wrote thousands of words of self-criticism and abject apology for past "evil thinking." Their places at the university were taken by new young assistants whose qualifications grew less with each new arrival. When the trainees at Suchow finished their course, however, they were not returned to the university. Instead, these men who held high degrees from some of the world's best universities were sent to such posts as assistant clerk in a village library, cashier in a district bank, etc. None of them received assignments of any real dignity or service.

I realized now that I would be sent away for indoctrination as soon as a half-educated "progressive" could be found to take my place. I also faced the bitter truth that under the new regime my education and training were considered not merely useless, but actually dangerous; I knew I would never be permitted to hold an educational post of any responsibility. I therefore decided I

71

must leave the university before action against me could be taken.

By now, however, no one in a university post was allowed to leave his job without official permission. I discussed the problem with J.P. Chan. He badly needed "progressive" executives to replace the older men whom the Communists were already forcing him to dismiss. J.P. offered me the managership of three of his flour mills if I would promise him not to see Li-li again. He then contacted a high official, requesting that I be allowed by the Higher Education Bureau to leave the university to work for him.

When I knew that the application was going to be accepted, I went to Dr. Yui to tell him that I would be leaving. The moment he understood that I was resigning, his face showed panic. "You mustn't do that," he said. "It's too dangerous to bring attention to yourself now." He told me that I was on the list to be sent to Suchow for indoctrination ten days later.

Dr. Yui was relieved, however, when he learned that my permission to leave the university would come from high official sources. "I am sorry to tell you this, my son," he said, "but you made a serious mistake. When those youngsters from the reform group came to you criticizing me, you should have joined them at once in denouncing me. The Communists gave you your chance for several months, and you refused it. Now they will never forgive you. . . ."

Dr. Yui's words aroused my fears less than they did my sympathy for him. Neither he nor the other old professors had been given even one chance by the regime, and they would never be forgiven for being what they were. Dr. Yui was wrong, however, in thinking that my mistake had been simply my loyalty to an old and beloved professor. My mistake was more fundamental. I had had plenty of evidence that the regime was capable of extreme dishonesty; what I had failed to perceive was that the Communists disposed of anyone who refused to participate in their dishonesty.

My university friends had been unable to learn this truth, and they were finished. I was lucky however, because in effect I was getting a new start. When I joined J.P., I would no longer be classed with the intellectuals; instead I would become a "national capitalist."

This time I would be careful to behave as the regime demanded. I no longer trusted the Communists, and I would try to match their cunning with my own.

CHAPTER 4

Ravenous tigers threaten us by day,
And in the night venomous snakes
Wait with fangs ready...
To cut us down like hemp.

—LI PO

ALTHOUGH I knew nothing about managing flour mills, I felt I could qualify in one essential: I would cooperate with the Communists and follow the Party Line. I was not sure how this was done, but I was confident I could learn it in time. Meanwhile, a good first impression was important. J.P. Chan told me that the previous manager had been a dictatorial old conservative who had antagonized everyone at the mills. I considered this an advantage for me. In contrast to the old manager, an eagerly cooperative youthful "progressive" should seem a satisfactory change.

The employees, apparently, were glad of any change. When J.P. took me to the mills the first day, the 1,500-odd workers

75

had sent a delegation to greet us at the gates with firecrackers. In the mills' dining hall, the staff welcomed me with a tea party. I watched J.P. for clues on protocol. He introduced me first to the Communist Party Secretary, next to the Chairman of the Trade Union, then to the Secretary of the New Democratic Youth League, and finally to the five department heads. The other 80 staff members were introduced en masse.

I now made the speech which I had carefully prepared and which I hoped would make all of them think well of me. "I am too young and inexperienced to be familiar with the problems of running these mills," I began. "Nevertheless, Chairman Mao has taught us, 'from the masses and to the masses.' I intend therefore to adhere strictly to the mass line and to learn from all of you in order that we may serve the people well."

To prove that I was adhering to the Party Line, I deliberately admitted that I was serving the mills' private owners whose interests "might not always coincide with those of the workers." I added, however, that through the Party's correct policy of "Public and Private Interests both taken care of—workers and capitalists mutually benefited" we would be able, through discussion and compromise, to operate the mills for the benefit of all. I ended my speech by saying that, under the former old-style managership, real progress had been impossible, but that now we had a new opportunity to make these mills a praiseworthy model of private enterprise in the New China.

After my speech, the Party Secretary accompanied me to my office. He was about my age, but he was not well educated. His face was totally without expression. "The old manager never spoke as you did," he said. "I'm sure that now the mills will run smoothly."

I took this as high praise, and I felt relieved. Perhaps my job would not be too difficult after all.

Fortunately, I had no difficult decisions to make during my first days at the mills. I signed payrolls, authorized machinery repairs, reapplied for increased electricity allocation and acted upon other routine matters that required little exercise of judgment. Nevertheless, I was careful to consult the Party Secretary frequently. He never actually expressed an opinion on the decisions he preferred me to make, but gradually from his attitude and choice of words, I learned to tell what he wanted, and I always acted upon it. I felt that he appreciated my effort.

The Party Secretary, in fact, showed his appreciation a few weeks later by seeing that I was made a member of the District Political Consultative Council for the area in which the mills were located. The Council consisted of representatives from the district's various groups—trade unionists, students, workers, et cetera. Its real function was to disseminate Party directives among the groups, but the pretense was carefully maintained that the Council members themselves arrived at their own interpretations and decisions.

The first Council meeting I attended concerned a Roman Catholic youth group, the Society of Mary, which the Communists were determined to eliminate. The District Party Secretary described the Society as an evil tool of imperialist espionage and then presented the matter for discussion. Most of the speeches denounced the Catholic Church in strong terms. I noticed that the District Party Secretary looked increasingly displeased as he listened. As a new member, my turn to comment came last. "We must remember, first, that the policy is to protect freedom of worship," I said. I cited the appropriate article from the Common Program (which served as a temporary Constitution before 1954), and continued: "The Society of Mary, however, has been used by the imperialists for their evil ends. Thus the Society must be exterminated, not because it is a religious organization

77

but precisely because its evil is done under the cloak of religion and thereby threatens religious liberty. We must act vigorously to stamp out this Society in order to protect Catholicism and to further the policy of religious freedom...."

The District Party Secretary brightened. Although this approach had been made only in my speech, he adopted it in his summation of the "people's will," even using many of my expressions. This success increased my self-confidence immeasurably. I believed that Communist thinking, although complicated and devious, was stereotyped and needed only careful study to be understood. I began to lose some of my fear.

The fear, however, returned stronger than ever after I had been at the flour mills about a month. In October 1951, Mao Tsetung stated, "Thought reform, especially thought reform of the intellectuals, is one of the most important prerequisites for the realization of democratic reform and industrialization." With this, the Thought Reform Campaign was launched; it was directed at the intelligentsia and was concentrated on the universities.

Preparations for the campaign had begun at Shanghai University even while I was there. One day we found that the university's Party organization had been suddenly strengthened. A new ruling specified that a member of the Party or the Youth League should sit at every table in the dining hall and should occupy a place in every dormitory room. These Communists took notes on the day and night behavior of every student. Even the words of a student talking in his sleep were recorded and considered for political significance. Another ruling provided that every graduate would be required to go anywhere and to accept any job, as directed by the regime. The reports of the "watchdogs," therefore, were vitally important to the students' future; in fact, the students referred to their dossiers as "destiny

78

papers." The stated purpose of the close scrutiny of the students was to increase the efficiency with which the educated youth were assigned to jobs. The obvious result, however, was to enforce acceptable behavior from the students. A highly acceptable and rewarded form of behavior was informing on "backward" and "reactionary" thinking or activity among the faculty.

Thus, when the Thought Reform Campaign began against the Shanghai University faculty in late 1951, accusations from the students supplied the basic ammunition. Preparations for the attack came with the arrival of specially trained cadres. In the first step, the faculty members were required to write long autobiographies covering their lives from the age of eight. As these were completed, the cadres organized group meetings in which the papers were criticized. In a series of speeches to these meetings, the university's Party Secretary pointed out that the Chinese intellectuals were guilty of harboring three types of "wrong ideas": anti-Soviet Union, anti-Communist Party, and anti-People. Such ideas were to be weeded out in group struggle.

In theory, the autobiography of each member of a group was searched by the other members for the roots of wrong ideas. In practice, however, only one or two members were singled out by the cadres for concentrated struggle. These unfortunates were called the "heavy points." They symbolized the evil of the whole group, and their fate served to warn the other members what to expect if their own thoughts were not promptly and completely reformed.

The heavy points were accused of having wrong thoughts which they had not disclosed thoroughly in their autobiographies. Thus in the group meetings they were struggled against to reveal these thoughts and to atone for harboring them. In addition, a loud-speaker truck was often parked in front of the house

79

of an accused to pour out at him a shrill stream of invective, threats and demands for his "confession."

Few heavy points stood the pressure for more than a few days. Usually by then they were frantically writing confession after confession in the desperate attempt to find one that the cadres would accept. A stubborn professor who insisted on his innocence for as long as a week, however, was usually locked in a room and was harassed continually by relays of cadres until he had submitted an acceptable "confession."

Several of the heavy points escaped confession by committing suicide. Those who did confess faced the "people's justice." Some were sent to the work gangs of labor reform. A few were sentenced to "surveillance." But the rest, including those who had submitted autobiographies but had not been designated heavy points, were reassigned to inferior positions. Moreover, a professor who had been well known and liked by his students generally was made to give his confession before a mass meeting in which he was publicly ridiculed, vilified and degraded.

Dr. Yui suffered this indignity. He had been made the heavy point of his group, and the pressure for his confession had been especially hard. Fortunately, I was spared attending the mass meeting at which he was publicly humiliated and made to wallow in self-abasement, but I read about it in the press. Because he was old and had been much respected, the "people's justice" was lenient with him. He was sent to Fu Tan University, also in Shanghai, where he taught a beginner's English class as a sixth- or lowest-grade professor.

I also remember well the case of my friend Professor Long. He had returned in 1950, *after* the outbreak of the Korean war, from Baylor University in Texas. He had been sincerely and actively pro-Communist, but because he had been sent to America on a missionary scholarship, he was made a heavy point. He withstood the pressure until one night the cadres broke in to ransack his rooms on the pretext of searching for a classified document that had allegedly disappeared. Professor Long became hysterical. "I am blind, blind!" he shouted. "In the States, people warned me not to return, not to trust the Communists. But I wouldn't listen. I believed in the Communist Party. I *must* be blind." And then he jabbed at his eyes with his two index fingers until blood ran down his cheeks. Thereafter, he made long and abject confessions.

Up to this point, Long's case was typical. It became unique, however, when higher Communist authorities declared him innocent of the charges. Nevertheless, he was now blamed for being "unable to stand the test." In Communist thinking, a politically "pure" person welcomes a test of his purity. In failing the test, Long proved that he was politically impure. He was punished by being sent to a lowly assignment in another university.

At first, I considered the Communists stupid for alienating Long. After the betrayal, persecution and humiliation he had received from the Communists, he undoubtedly hated them, and they therefore had turned a valuable pro-Communist into an anti-Communist. Only later did I perceive that the Communists had been fully aware of Long's loyalty to their cause and were equally conscious that after the "reform" he was disaffected. They had succeeded, however, in terrorizing him so thoroughly that henceforth, regardless of what he *thought*, he spoke and acted during every waking moment exactly as the Communists wanted. In this state, the Communists felt safer and more secure about him.

The stated purpose of the Thought Reform Campaign had been to correct the "backward and reactionary" thinking of the intelligentsia. The immediate effect of the campaign was to break up the unity of the intellectuals, to remove them from positions of authority, and to debase them before the people. Only when the campaign was over in early 1952, however, did the final real purpose become evident. The authorities announced that, for increased efficiency, the higher educational system needed "readjustment."

In the readjustment, the colleges of various universities were reshuffled and merged. Under cover of this activity, the Christian universities throughout China were eliminated. The facilities of Shanghai University, for example, were taken over for an Agricultural Machinery School. Thus, merely between semesters, the way having been prepared through Thought Reform, the whole higher education system of China was altered beyond recognition. No trace of intellectual prestige remained, nor any of the spirit and tradition which had distinguished one institution from another. The Party organizations now completely controlled education.

The tragic experiences of the professors in the Thought Reform Campaign frightened me badly. I realized that I had had a narrow escape. Moreover, my fear was increased by the results of another campaign which had been carried on simultaneously with Thought Reform and which at first had seemed far removed from me.

The other campaign became known as Three-Anti. It had the seemingly worthwhile stated objectives of eliminating bureaucracy, waste and corruption in *government*. Early in the campaign much publicity was given to the case of two high Communist officials who were found guilty of accepting bribes and of using the bribe money to set themselves up in private enterprise. They had to face the "people's justice" and were promptly shot. This news was exhilarating. The general belief was that the regime really was going to clean up its ranks. I also believed this, and I approved of it. The usual techniques of mass struggle and confession were used. Soon "confessions" began to pour out of every government office, and we were surprised at the extent of bureaucratic corruption. Then we realized that under cover of popular approval and high-power publicity about outstanding cases, the authorities were quietly liquidating many others without trial. "Disappearances" became common, and from these we finally learned the real purpose of the campaign: the liquidation of a whole group.

When the Communists had first come into power, they had urged all the civil service employees to remain at their posts. Since then, these employees had been repeatedly assured of the regime's protection and even gratitude. Thus the transfer of power to the new regime was made smoothly and the essential services continued to operate. By late 1951, however, sufficient Communist cadres had been trained to take over the administration, and now the former employees were liquidated.

I realized this fact by early 1952, but I did not fully appreciate its significance. Two old civil service men I had known disappeared, and J.P. knew many more whose fate was the same. In addition, we had a mutual friend, a courageous civil official who finally committed suicide under the pressure to confess crimes of which he was innocent. Later, higher authorities cleared him and dismissed the cadres whose zeal had caused his suicide; no public exoneration was made, however, and J.P. and I had to console his embittered widow. These experiences, plus the fact that I no longer believed the Communists, should have made me more astute. I failed to reject completely the Three-Anti Campaign news, which mentioned only the struggle against government corruption. In short, I was still confused by what the Communists *said* and what they *did*. By this time, I was also very frightened, partly from realizing what would have happened to me if I had stayed on at the university and partly because a close friend, falsely accused, had been driven to suicide. I no longer had any confidence in my ability to match wits with the Communists, and it was confusion, rather than fear, that explained my dangerous naïveté in the next campaign.

The next campaign overlapped Thought Reform and Three-Anti, beginning in early 1952 just after the climax of the other two. The new campaign became known as "Five-Anti," and its stated objectives were to eliminate five major sins of the bourgeoisie: bribery, tax evasion, stealing government property, cheating on contracts, and stealing State secrets. The last "sin" referred to the act of discovering the government intention, for example, to buy up certain commodities and then to use that knowledge to make excessive profit. A number of businessmen had profiteered in this fashion during the Korean war, and up to now most businessmen were managing to make adequate profits despite extensive government controls.

To me, these five bourgeois sins seemed worth eliminating, and when the campaign was announced I suggested to the Party Secretary at the mills that we stage a formal investigation to ensure that our operation was completely free of the specified sins. The Party Secretary indicated his affirmation of the plan, and I called in the various department heads. Twice we all worked hard to find evidence of present or past malfeasance. Everyone was cooperative, but no one could recall any unethical past practices at the mills. As for the present, we worked under a contract which had been drawn up by the authorities and signed by J.P. We processed wheat for the government at a fixed fee. The Party Secretary and Trade Union Chairman checked every aspect of the operation. I had been a bourgeois businessman only a few months, and I had already proven that I was cooperating to my fullest extent with the regime. I could not imagine that I had anything to fear.

84

During this period, groups of department heads and other employees began to take leave in rotation, but I thought nothing of it. Then, when I called a third meeting to examine our record for the bourgeois "sins," I suddenly found that everyone refused to attend.

I am still amazed at how naïve I was in having those meetings. I already knew that the authorities in Thought Reform had *said* they were attacking wrong thoughts among the intellectuals but in fact they were attacking the intellectuals; and they had said, in Three-Anti, that they were eliminating corruption among civil employees whereas their intention was to eliminate the old employees. Now they said that they were against sins of the bourgeoisie. Why did I not realize, therefore, that the campaign would be against the capitalist class and that at the mills *I* was the target, not any sins that had been committed in the mills? The extraordinary aspect of the meetings I had called, however, was the fact that in the first two the Party Secretary himself obviously had believed the officially publicized purpose of the campaign; by the third meeting he had received the proper instructions from the usual specially trained cadres sent from the Party Headquarters.

These cadres were called "tiger beaters." They entered a business firm and from the employees selected "activists" whom they organized into teams of "beaters." The beaters were taught to gather the information and evidence which would flush out the capitalist tiger. The beaters had been active among the mill employees for at least two weeks, and I had heard nothing about it. Thus, I was caught completely off guard when the blow fell.

When I entered the mill that fateful morning no one spoke to me, not even in answer to my greeting. For generations Chinese employees had always shown deep respect for executives and as long as the fiction of private enterprise under the new regime was maintained, the employees continued the old habit. Moreover, I had been friendly and informal with them so that our relationship had become close. Their sudden coldness therefore was a shock.

The Party Secretary was standing stiffly at attention with two rough-looking cadres in my office. He disregarded my greeting. "Loh, I have to inform you that henceforth you will not be permitted to leave this office until you have written out a full confession."

"Confession?" I stammered.

Visibly exasperated, the Party Secretary quoted me the official pronouncements about the Five-Anti Campaign. It was as though a notorious criminal were being reminded by a judge of the laws he had broken. But the Party Secretary knew me, knew every detail of my activities in the mills and knew also that, under the control exercised by the regime, I could not possibly have committed any of the five sins in our mills. I simply could not believe that he was serious.

The Party Secretary did say that because of the Party's leniency, I was being granted three days to prepare my confession instead of one. But he warned me that only a full confession would be acceptable and that any attempt to hide my crimes would be dealt with severely. Then he went out, leaving the two tough tiger beaters to guard the door. They watched me as though I were the country's number one enemy.

I sank down into the chair at my desk. I picked up a pen, but my hands were trembling too much to write. I know that I was terrified, but I was conscious mainly of confusion. I kept thinking that it was all a mistake. I sat for at least an hour, my head in my hands, trying to make my thoughts seem rational. For the first time, I knew the incredulous desperation of a campaign victim. The suicide of my friend was still vividly real, and I decided

at once against any such heroics as trying to protest my innocence. The simple truth was, however, that I still did not know
enough about the mills' operations to have any idea concerning
what I could confess.

Later that morning some staff members entered and, without
speaking or looking at me, put up some posters on the wall where
I could see them from my desk. On the largest was a caricature
of me. I was shown with the thick upswept hairdo that was then
peculiar to young American hoodlums, and my tie was covered
with dollar signs. This typed me as an American-educated capitalist. I was shown holding a paper marked CONFESSION, but the
paper contained only an onionskin and a feather; this indicated
that my confession dealt only with unimportant matters and
evaded the important points. And I still had no idea what to
confess. The other posters contained such slogans as CRUSH THE
VICIOUS ATTACK OF THE CAPITALIST CLASS, SURRENDER, YOU VILE
CAPITALIST, A COMPLETE CONFESSION IS THE ROAD TO SURVIVAL—
ANYTHING LESS WILL LEAD TO DEATH.

Just before noon, technicians entered and installed a loud-
speaker in one of the office windows. A few minutes past noon,
it sputtered once and then burst into an ear-splitting racket. I
gathered that a mass meeting of the employees was being held in
the main dining hall. It went on for the entire lunch period. Most
of it was a harangue against the unscrupulous capitalists. I realized that activists were working up the crowd to a frenzy, and
now I was aware of nothing but fear. I did not know what might
happen at the next moment.

When the mass meeting was over at 2 P.M., individual beaters
took over the microphone to address me directly. They shouted
abuse, insults and threats, and they admonished me constantly to
make my confession full. Occasionally, the loud-speaker would
cease, but before my nerves could loosen in the blissful silence,

the shouting would begin again. At 5 P.M., I listened to another mass meeting and again felt the terror of unleashed mob violence.

At 6, the mill cook brought me a blanket, which he dropped on the floor, and a bowl of noodles which he put gingerly on the edge of my desk; he ran as though I were a dangerous animal. I requested then to be allowed to go to the toilet, but my guards accompanied me. They would not allow me to close the door to the cubicle. Later, back in the office, my guards were changed for another pair of tiger beaters who stared at me with visible hatred. When I tried to sleep, wrapped in the blanket on the floor, the guards would not allow the light to be turned off and they sat silently only a few feet away, never taking their eyes off me.

On the morning of the third day, a beater entered and ordered me to follow him to the Party Secretary's office. I had tried desperately to imagine what was wanted of me but had been unable to think of anything to confess.

As I walked through the building the employees jeered and called such insults as "capitalist swine," "unscrupulous dog" and "counterattack the vicious capitalist class." Those whom I passed closely spat at me and some tried to strike, but my guards prevented them. The employees who were loudest and most vehement in their insults were those with whom I had been the most friendly. At first, this cut me deeply, but then I realized that precisely *because* they had been friendly to me, they would be the ones threatened the most and for their own safety they would strain to show that they no longer had anything but hatred and contempt for a capitalist criminal like me. Oddly enough, this thought made me feel better. It was the first evidence I had had that the whole nightmare was being staged. I understood now why so many employees had taken leave. They had been given "training" in how to behave toward me.

88

I entered the Party Secretary's office, realizing that this was the first time I had been made to come to him; previously, he had always maintained the pretense of my authority and had come to my office. Now he did not even rise from his desk. He held out his hand without looking up. "Your confession," he said.

"I am sorry. I have tried hard but so far I am unable to think of anything to confess," I said. I tried to sound calm but humble. "Perhaps it is because I am stupid—"

"Stupid!" he interrupted. "When the people ask you to confess you suddenly become stupid. Yet when you were exploiting the people you seemed to be very smart." He suddenly got up from his chair. I could see that he was trying to control what seemed to be real anger. Pointing his finger at my nose, he said, "You capitalists seem to think you can commit endless crimes against the people and pretend you have done nothing..."

"I want to confess everything, but I just don't know how," I answered.

The Party Secretary sat down again. "You had better stop pretending," he said. "I warn you, Loh, the people's patience has its limits. We will give you two more days, and if you do not have a full confession by then, we may not be able to prevent your arrest."

I spent two more days of torment—wearing the same clothes, going without shaving or washing, enduring the constant scrutiny of my guards and listening to the blasting loud-speaker while I wracked my brains for some crime that I might logically confess to. But it was still no use. When I was taken again to the Party Secretary's office I really felt I would not return. Although my failure infuriated the Party Secretary, however, he gave me one more chance: a full confession within 24 hours. I was in com-

89

plete despair as I was escorted through the crowd of jeering employees back to my office.

An hour later, one of the accountants entered with his books. I was shocked, because no employee had been allowed to enter my office since the day of my detainment. The accountant banged an account book down on my desk and pointed to an inventory entry. "Did you ever realize where your property came from?" he asked. He tapped his finger against an entry which showed 30,000 gunny bags. Before I could answer, he had thrown open another old account book from the days of the Japanese occupation and pointed out a similar number of gunny bags. While I was trying to gather my wits enough to find meaning in all this, the accountant kept up a stream of accusations and questions—"How can you run a business if you do not know what is going on? How can you pretend to be blameless when you are guilty of stealing the people's property?" Finally I realized that these 30,000 gunny bags, which had been absorbed into our inventory in 1946, had originally come from the Japanese. Thus they should have belonged next to the Nationalists and then to "the people" under the present regime. This was my crime!

I felt a rush of relief. This was not because my danger was any less, but because this whole drama was being carefully staged, I thought I knew now the part I was expected to play. I wrote up my confession quickly and that afternoon I asked to see the Party Secretary to give it to him.

The Communist glanced at my paper briefly. Then suddenly he wadded it up violently and threw it on the floor. "How dare you insult the people by pretending that you were guilty of such an insignificant amount?" he shouted at me. "I warn you for the last time, Loh. You will make a *full* confession or suffer the fate you bring on yourself."

Now, however, the Party Secretary's bluster did not frighten me as much, but I was depressed by the realization that my role was to be long and drawn out. I understood that my "confession" was to be squeezed out of me piecemeal. I was to play the stubborn hardened criminal while the Communists were clever, thorough officials who worked tirelessly in the people's behalf to uncover all my crimes. Back in my office, I had to endure another full day of agonizing suspense before the accountant appeared to point out another vague item which enabled me to confess to a further act of embezzlement.

Six times my "confession" was rejected, and each time the number of my acts of embezzlement was increased. These crimes now totaled more than a hundred, and not one of them would stand up under even a casual scrutiny of the mills' affairs.

The last felony, added to the list for my seventh and final "confession," was the most ludicrous of all. In 1950, the Communist authorities had submitted to J.P. a contract which he had signed with them and which had stipulated that the mills were to grind 80 million catties of wheat into flour. The officially specified ratio required the mills to produce 65 catties of white flour for every 100 catties of wheat received; any amount of flour or by-products milled in excess of the 65 catties was to be the firm's fee. The Communists now charged that the ratio should have been 70 catties of flour per 100 catties of wheat, and that originally the cadres had been unscrupulously lured into signing what was supposed to be an unfair contract. Thus, they charged that I owed "the people" for four million catties of flour. This amounted to JMP800,000 (US $335,000). The casual way in which they repudiated a contract they themselves had submitted and signed was bad enough, but I could hardly believe that they wanted me to make myself culpable for an in-

cident of this magnitude that had happened almost two years before I came to the mills.

Nevertheless, when the Party Secretary received my seventh
confession he remarked, "At last, I believe your confession is
relatively thorough." He passed the papers around to his subordinates, who glanced at them and nodded sagely as though they
also had arrived independently at the same judgment. "But the
final verdict, of course, is with the masses," I was told. "You will
now write out an expression of your attitude concerning your
crimes."

By this the Party Secretary meant that I should "beg the masses
for forgiveness," throw myself on their mercy and thank the
Communist Party for its help in guiding me toward a true understanding of my evil and its consequences. I had read and heard
the accepted "expression of attitude" often enough so that I was
able to write one myself without effort.

A few hours after finishing it, I faced the climax of my
"struggle." The tiger beaters propelled me roughly into the mills'
dining hall, which was filled with every one of our employees.
My entrance was the signal for a tremendous uproar. The screams
of rage, the shouted slogans and insults, were deafening. I was
made to stand with humbly bowed head before the small stage
on which the Communist officials sat at tables. I had lost 13
pounds. I was filthy, unshaven and exhausted. My knees trembled
with both weakness and fear. The shouting behind me was turned
off suddenly. The Party Secretary rose and read off the list of the
people's charges against me. When he finished, he commanded
me to "face the masses"; I had to turn and bow with complete
humility to the crowd. The shouting began once more.

When the noise was turned off again, the Party Secretary asked
if anyone had accusations to make against "this capitalist." One
by one, now, representatives from each of the employee groups—

the old workers, the young workers, the electricians, the separate departments, etc.—came to the stage to denounce me. The worst accusations were made by those whom I had known best, but now I understood and sympathized with these people. I could see the pain in the eyes of some as they stumbled over their memorized speeches. I imagined what I would feel if I had been one of Dr. Yui's close associates who had publicly vilified him.

Nevertheless, I listened carefully to the accusations, believing that in the stories they told of my evil deeds I would have a clue to my fate. All of the accusations, however, were only of crimes associated with my class. In a typical story, for example, an old worker said that ten years previously his wife had been ill and he had begged the manager for 5 yuan for medicine. He had not only been refused, he had been temporarily fired from his job, and his wife had died. He now pointed dramatically at me. "You thieving unscrupulous capitalist," he shrieked, real tears on his face, "my wife's blood drips from your hands."

Another old man occasioned the moment I remember clearest. He mounted to the platform, bent and feeble. He paused for a moment, his eyes closed, trying to remember, I think, his prepared speech. "Mr. Manager . . ." he began. All the others had addressed me only with epithets, of which "capitalist dog" was perhaps the mildest. Decades of habitual respect for "the management," however, prevented the old fellow from addressing me in the new unfamiliar terms the tiger beaters had taught him. He got no further with his speech. Two beaters jumped up to the platform, grabbed him by the shoulders and shoved him toward the stairs. The old man stumbled down them and would have fallen if members of the audience had not caught him. The look of pain and confusion on the old man's face haunts me still, and at this moment I came the closest to breaking down completely.

The beaters covered the awkward moment by leading another outbreak of slogan-shouting.

The accusations took almost three hours. Thereafter, I was made to mount the platform. I read my confession in a weak voice. Then I begged the masses to forgive my sins and to give me one more chance to serve the people. I also thanked the great Communist Party which, under the wise and benevolent leadership of Chairman Mao, had instigated this great campaign. Because of the campaign, I had learned to recognize the evil in me and thus had a chance to make a new man of myself before it was too late.

When I finished, the Party Secretary again addressed the crowd. "Can any of you bring to light further crimes committed by this capitalist?" he asked. I sensed that this was the climactic moment for me. If the authors of this drama intended my role to be tragic, an actor or two from the audience would now accuse me of crimes that had not been specified for me to confess. I closed my eyes and held my breath.

But the masses were mute. Finally, the Party Secretary said, "I assume, then, that the masses regard the confession of this capitalist as relatively thorough." He cautioned the crowd, however, to continue to look for further of my misdeeds which would necessitate reopening my case.

The Secretary turned to me. "Loh, you have confessed the sins you committed and you have promised not to commit such sins again," he said. "Do you mean this? Are you sincere?"

"I am completely sincere," I said.

The Secretary turned back to the crowd and raised his hand. Finally, I would know my fate. "I now declare," he said, "that the great Five-Anti Campaign for our mills has been completed with 100 percent success." This was answered by a burst of joyous cheering from the crowd. I was too dazed for a moment to realize that it was over and that I was free. Of course, I owed the government JMP1,200,000 which I did not have, but at least I had been spared sudden death from a policeman's bullet or slow death from labor reform. An hour later, I was home. I shaved, bathed, drank a bowl of soup and went to bed for ten hours of sleep.

"Home" since I had been working at the mills was in the mansion of J.P. Chan. I had become practically a member of the family. While I was sleeping, Charlie also arrived home. His ordeal in a different group of the Chan factories had been almost identical to mine and had even lasted the exact same length of time. His "embezzlement," however, had amounted to 2½ million JMP, and the effect of the experience on him was worse than on me. Charlie was a changed man. Thereafter, I seldom saw him smile and he never made jokes or even spoke much. He simply did as his older brother told him to do.

J.P.'s trouble, naturally, was infinitely greater than ours. He was in charge of more than thirty separate mills and factories in China and the amount of "embezzlement" on his Shanghai interests alone came to the astronomical figure of US $8 million. Because of his already-established international reputation as the No. 1 "national capitalist" and also his connections with high Communist officials, he was spared the indignity and discomfort of being locked in an office and harassed by semiliterate tiger beaters. In fact, I have no doubt that I escaped as easily as I did only because I was "under his umbrella." Nevertheless, he was confined to his house and the process of going through mountains of ledgers to find JMP20 millions' worth of embezzlement for confession was a job that took weeks. I helped him continually, writing his book-length "confession" until the early hours of the mornings.

While I had been confined in my office, I had been allowed

no contact whatever with the outside, and in the subsequent weeks I was so busy with J.P. that I had little chance to learn what was really going on. Thus the details of the Five-Anti Campaign came to me gradually. I was spared the shock that it was to most of the others in the Shanghai business community, for this campaign was easily the most violent of all that had been waged so far.

Shanghai, being the nation's industrial and commercial center, bore the brunt of the attack. More than half of all China's private investment was in Shanghai, which alone had 165,000 separate private enterprises. Not all of these could be investigated at once, and the campaign was waged in three phases. During the first, the largest concerns were attacked and J.P.'s industrial empire, being the country's largest, received special attention. In this we were lucky, because those who received special attention usually were leniently treated. The others were not as fortunate.

Three types of pressure for "confession" were used in the Five-Anti Campaign. The first came from the employees of a firm. Just as in my mills, the workers were trained and worked up to a frenzy against the management. In my case, however, this pressure was light because I had the protection of J.P.'s influence. In firms where the managers had really been arrogant or heartless, however, the workers were much more violent. Many managers suffered actual physical abuse. At best, they endured much more harassment and humiliation than I had.

Another type of pressure used by the Communists was called "dog-eat-dog." At the very beginning of the campaign, several really unscrupulous businessmen in each branch of industry and commerce were apprehended. After these men had confessed, they were told that their crimes deserved "more than one death," but that their actual fate would depend upon the contributions they individually made to the campaign. Thus, these businessmen were turned into tiger beaters themselves, and terror drove them to become even more ferocious than the cadres. Moreover, because they knew well their own branch of business and the other men in it, they were the most capable of devising crimes to which the others were pressed to confess. The morale-shattering aspect of this situation was that an honest and decent businessman found himself confronted by a despised member of his own trade and pressed to confess to crimes that his accuser, and not he, had committed. To me this was the most disillusioning aspect of the campaign. True, the unscrupulous businessmen were liquidated later when their usefulness in the campaign was finished, but for each of them, many honest men were punished for their misdeeds. Quite aside from the injustice, this Communist trick was an indication of the regime's complete dishonesty, and the entire business community fell into deep despair.

But the third type of pressure was even worse. The Communists used the families, usually the wife and children, of the victim to help wring the "confession" from him. Few Chinese women ever knew anything about their husbands' business affairs. When the wife's anxiety at her husband's disappearance was sufficiently high, she would be approached by a sympathetic beater. He would explain that her husband had been guilty of serious misdeeds. Nevertheless, if her husband would only confess, the people would be lenient and he would be returned to her, but if he continued to refuse confession he was sure to die. The wife, then, frantic to save her husband, would be taken to him, usually with the children as well, and would beg him on her knees to confess. At this, the innocent man usually was really broken; if not even his own family had faith in him, to whom could he turn? He had only two alternatives: he could "confess" or die.

And now the number who chose death rather than participation in the regime's dishonesty began to mount. The suicides came in waves; they would strike a district or a branch of industry. The sight of people jumping out of windows became commonplace; I saw it twice even though I seldom left the house during this period. The coffin makers were sold out weeks ahead. The funeral homes doubled up so that several funerals were held simultaneously in one room. The parks were patrolled to prevent people from hanging themselves from the trees.

Moreover, the simple act of killing oneself was far from easy. Most businessmen being struggled against were under the constant guard of the tiger beaters; windows were kept closed, and no implements or materials that could be used in suicide were permitted near the victim.

Nevertheless, ingenious methods were found. As despair and hopelessness settled onto the business community, the victims began to plan their suicides before the struggle against them began and to use their death as an act of defiance against the regime. A relative of mine, for example, was in the pharmaceutical trade. He obtained cyanide pills for himself and his acquaintances. When his turn came before a mass meeting, he shouted at the Party Secretary that the Communists were the real enemy of the people. He said that their end would be worse than his because friends and relatives would weep at his funeral but no tears would be shed when the Communists were killed. With that he swallowed his pill and was dead even before the Party Secretary had finished calling the security police.

The father of Charlie's wife managed to hide a rope and was able to hang himself with it in a closet. In Shanghai, there were eight flour mill managers with jobs comparable to mine; two of them committed suicide. One slashed his wrists with a watch crystal while he was wrapped in a blanket at night on his office floor. The other fought with his guards and succeeded in jumping out of his window; he apparently tried to drag one of the tiger beaters with him.

In addition to suicide, some victims defied the Communists by refusing to "confess." At the public meetings, they would deny that they had committed any crimes, and often they would shout down the beaters, accusing *them* of crimes against the people. This took great courage, because it meant immediate arrest and brutal treatment from the police.

The climax for us came when the older Chan was subjected to harassment. The old man was seventy-eight and had been retired years previously. He was a self-made man who had started from humble beginnings to become the richest man in China, and he was much respected for his philanthropy. It was he, also, who had overruled his sons when they tried to take industrial equipment out of the country, and who ordered the equipment returned to the plants because the Communists had convinced him that his business empire was needed and wanted. The regime, therefore, did not inflict the full "struggle" on old Chan. Nevertheless, they took his servants away so that the feeble old man was made helpless. Worse, they denied him access to the sources of his income, so that he was without funds. No capitalists were allowed to leave Shanghai during the campaign and thus we could not go to the old man. Finally, at great risk, we managed to get a messenger to him secretly in Wusih with what little cash we ourselves could get our hands on. The messenger reached him just in time, because the old man was already beginning to starve. Finally, the Communists sent several hundred factory workers to enter the old man's house and "educate" him with a violent anti-Capitalist demonstration. The humiliation and shock of this brought on a collapse from which he died three months later.

After the demonstration, J.P. reached the end of his patience. The messenger who brought the news of his father's collapse was prevented by two tiger beater guards from entering the house. We were forced to go outside and listen to the message in front of the guards. After hearing the messenger's story, J.P. was thoughtful for a moment. Then he said, loudly enough so that the tiger beaters could hear, "If the Communists come one step closer to me—*just one step*—they will find me dead." We knew he meant what he said, and we were shocked into silence. J.P.'s suicide would be a real blow to the regime, and he knew it. From that moment on, we at least had no more trouble with the Five-Anti Campaign.

The Communists had gone too far. Hopelessness and terror were spreading rapidly throughout the country. Some inkling of conditions on the mainland began to reach other countries, and revulsion against the regime grew. The remittances from Overseas Chinese, one of the regime's important sources of foreign exchange, dwindled. The Communists had made a bad mistake, and now they knew it.

Later, we were able to judge the real objectives of the campaign. The intention was to destroy the social prestige that the capitalist class still held, increase the official control over commerce and industry, and to milk free enterprise of its profits. The authorities did not intend, however, to eliminate the national capitalists completely; the semiliterate cadres were still far from sufficiently trained to take over management of industry. Also, the regime's reputation abroad would suffer drastically if the middle class were wiped out so soon and in such a manner.

The biggest mistake of the Communists, however, was the one that they make the most often. They failed to understand the true nature of human beings. According to their dogma, a businessman was supposed to be a cringing coward motivated solely by avarice; the idea that such a large percentage of them would prefer death to dishonor was incomprehensible to the Communists. In addition, the regime miscalculated the reaction of human beings to terror. Fear can make a man subservient only as long as he still has some hope of survival or escape. If the suppression is so severe that he loses this hope, he also loses his motive to be subservient.

The Communists did not admit that they had made mistakes, but by late spring of 1952 the regime's policy began to change. The change was introduced through an important speech by Chen Yi, then Shanghai's mayor. In the speech, five degrees of culpability for confessed "criminals" under the campaign were defined: 1) law-abiding businessmen; 2) basically law-abiding businessmen; 3) semilaw-abiding, semiguilty businessmen (which we called "the double semi"); 4) guilty businessmen, and 5) seriously guilty businessmen. Henceforth only men in the last two categories were to be brought to trial. The Chans and I were put into the first category of law-abiding businessmen, which meant that we were considered to have committed most of our sins unintentionally. Nevertheless, we were expected to "pay back to the people" the sums to which we had confessed.

At this time, stage two of the campaign was under way. Actually, the end of stage one had been the worst part. Thus, although the policy had softened, the effect was not yet felt and the morale of the business community was at its lowest ebb. To my surprise, I was now called upon to help the Communists. The tiger beaters were becoming almost powerless for the simple reason that the smaller businessmen were so senseless with terror that they could not be reasoned with. Even a slight increase in pressure now was apt to touch off new waves of suicides. My function was to show these businessmen that I, although a convicted embezzler of JMP1,200,000, a sum vastly greater than any crime they could possibly confess to, was nevertheless free and unharmed and that they therefore had nothing to fear. We dealt with these small men in groups—all the cloth merchants in one district, for example, were collected for group confession. Each had learned that to save himself he had to betray someone else, and because they all knew each other as competitors, they were able to work up effective confessions for each other.

The tiger beaters could not even appear at these meetings, because the businessmen became incoherent with fear merely at the sight of one. Thus when I had gathered up the confessions, I took them in to wrangle over them with the beaters. The policy now was to squeeze from the businessmen the absolute maximum without driving them over the brink to suicide. The businessmen, on the other hand, were long past hoping to save anything but their lives. Between these two extremes was an area for compromise, and I learned quickly to fulfill my role of go-between effectively. I saw many pitiful cases, but I now witnessed repeatedly proof of the fact that the law-abiding honest businessmen invariably suffered the most. Until this time, I had believed that in a capitalist society only unethical businessmen ever really achieved success, and that under Communism, decency was rewarded. I now felt that whereas an honest merchant under capitalism probably made less profit, his loss was only money. Conversely, an honest Chinese under the Communists was unable to survive at all.

Nevertheless, I was able to help a few of the more deserving cases and at the same time satisfy the beaters. I was designated a "model national capitalist" and was rewarded by being appointed one of the deputy chief justices of the People's Special District Court, which tried the smaller cases of the "confessed" businessmen of the fourth, or "guilty," category. The panel of judges consisted of 15 men, most of whom were prominent tiger beaters in the campaign. I did not attend the trials; I merely sat in on the meetings in which we all rubber-stamped the sentences which were read to us by the District Party Secretary who was the Chief Justice as well.

One day we had a case with an unusual aspect. Every sentence passed always stipulated the right of appeal, but no one—until now—had dared to question the "people's justice." The owner of a small bicycle shop had been fined JMP3,000, which obviously was more money than he had ever previously earned, and he had entered an appeal. It happened that the Chief Justice was not present that day, and a deputy who was a Trade Union Chairman of little education or intelligence was in charge. The panel's opinion was that the bicycle shop owner had not learned sufficiently what the Five-Anti Campaign was meant to teach him. His fine, therefore, was to be doubled and he was to be sent to one year of labor reform.

I, however, dissented. I had been keeping up the study of Party policy and I felt that I was correct. I argued that the right of appeal was unequivocally stated, but that if we carried out reprisals against the one man in hundreds of cases who exercised the right, we would discourage any more appeals. I ended by saying that in thousands of cases, who is to say that the People's Court might not make a mistake in one, or even two? If that should happen and no one dared appeal, then injustice might occur. The others on the panel shouted at me in disapproval and even accused me of "protecting the unscrupulous businessmen." Nevertheless, in the vote I held out. The verdict was 13 to my 1 for reprisals against the bicycle shop owner. The next morning, however, the Chief Justice telephoned me. He told me that he had reversed the decision of the court to agree with my suggestion. I was cynically amused at the "democratic" process of the People's Court, but I was pleased that I had been able to interpret policy correctly. I began to hope that I still might have a chance of survival in the New China.

CHAPTER 5

The chicken-thief now is posing as a pillar of the community.
He has not stolen a chicken for three days.

—CHINESE PROVERB

THE ELDER Chan died in July 1952. J. P. Chan was told that the government would arrange the funeral. The Governor of Kiangsu Province was appointed the head of a committee to handle the details. The sum of JMP25,000 was appropriated for the expenses. Special trains were scheduled to take the bereaved from Shanghai to Wusih. The funeral procession itself was more than a mile long. Prominent in it were the Secretary of the local Communist Party and the Trade Union leaders whose "education" of the old man had caused his death; they also had hired at government expense dozens of professional mourners to give the occasion a suitable air of melancholy. At the People's Auditorium, where the procession ended, high officials read long and flowery eulogies. And the press throughout China devoted pages of praise to old Chan; he was officially described as a "model of China's patriotic national capitalists who had fought against imperialism, feudalism and bureaucratic capitalism all his life."

We were astonished by this sudden burst of official affection for a famous capitalist who, three months previously, had been on the point of starvation because of the regime's animosity. The elaborate funeral and the flattering publicity dramatized the reversal of the regime's policy toward private business and businessmen.

The main reason for the drastic change in policy was not difficult to understand. The excesses of the Five-Anti Campaign had left businessmen so terrified that they would do nothing for fear of making a mistake. Commerce and industry, therefore, were nearly paralyzed, and production was dangerously low. The regime did not have its own trained personnel who could take over the running of private concerns. Thus, the capitalists were still needed, and the authorities tried to restore confidence within the business community. The businessmen were called to attend public meetings at which they were addressed reassuringly by high officials. They were praised for their past contributions, and encouraged to make future effort. The tax burden, for example, was eased; the authorities did not go so far as to reduce the tax rates, but property evaluations were "reconsidered" so that the tax amounts were less. Even more important, the fines imposed during Five-Anti were "rechecked" and most of them drastically reduced. The fines of J. P. Chan's enterprises were cut in half, and we were given 20 years in which to pay them. Firms near bankruptcy because of the fines were offered government low-interest loans. Merchants were helped by new regulations which restricted sales in some State-operated stores so that business was diverted back to private owners. Industrialists were told that their future was bright because the now-scheduled Five-Year

Plan would mean such heavy government buying that immediate production increases were necessary.

A requirement for increased production was the reestablishment of discipline among the workers. During Five-Anti, management had been degraded so thoroughly that it no longer had the authority to demand efficiency from the workers. Moreover, the campaign had dramatized the idea that the workers were the new ruling class; labor, therefore, had become impervious to all authority, including the authority of the Communist Party. To remedy this situation, in late 1952 the regime undertook a campaign of "democratic reform" within the working class.

The officially stated purpose of the campaign was "democratic reform through the elimination of feudal exploitation among the workers." I had doubts about this largely meaningless aim, but I did believe that the campaign would be helpful. If the workers were to be the rulers in the new society, they needed to learn their responsibilities and to be taught that they could not be permitted the unbridled license that had made them useful to the Communists during Five-Anti. Furthermore, I believed that the regime really did want to "educate and to raise the political level of the proletariat."

The education of the proletariat began with the arrival, at each industrial establishment, of the usual specially trained cadres. The workers were called together in meetings to which management also was "invited." In the campaign's first stage, called "speaking out on sufferings," each worker related details of the ill-treatment he had endured under the old society. Those whose experiences had been particularly grievous were given much publicity; they had been trained to tell their stories in such a way as to wring the utmost emotion out of their listeners.

The next stage was called "the digging up of bitter roots," and was also open to management. In the meetings now, the emphasis was on *why* the workers had suffered so much before the Communist victory. As I listened to the discussions and observed the high-pressure tactics of the activists, I began to have my first misgivings. I sensed that a bitterness was being worked up against the Nationalists, a bitterness that was out of proportion to the requirements for merely educating the workers to new standards and responsibilities. Finally, in a mass meeting, the workers reached the "unanimous conclusion" that the sole cause of their suffering was "the reactionary Nationalist regime." I was now definitely uneasy, and I knew that the campaign was not over.

In fact, the real campaign was only beginning. I was not invited to observe its third stage, but of course I knew what went on. The group meetings became the usual violent struggle meetings. All the workers who had been trade union leaders or activists in the old society were forced to "confess"; their fellow workers were made to turn on them and attack them mercilessly. In response, then, to the "demand of the masses," the former labor leaders began to be arrested, and within only a few days they all vanished. In our mills alone, 53 out of about 1,500 workers were sent to labor reform.

These labor leaders were the men who had been the backbone of the labor movement in the old days. They had done much of the organizing; they had led the strikes and had fought for such benefits as labor had been able to achieve. Some of them had had official recognition from the Nationalist regime, but in the Suppression of Counter-Revolutionaries, the Communists had left them alone. This old association of some of the leaders with the Nationalists was now used as the excuse to liquidate all of them. Under the Communist-controlled Trade Unions, the old labor leaders had no voice, of course, but they had cooperated fully with the regime, and many of them had been tiger beaters during Five-Anti. Their real crime was that they still enjoyed prestige and influence with the working class. Thus the workers were made to betray and repudiate the one group who had really protected their interests. After the mass arrests which followed the same pattern in every industry throughout China, the Communists no longer needed to fear any possible obstacle to their complete control over the proletariat.

The fact that the Communists intended to use their control to suppress the proletariat became clear immediately. Apart from the labor leaders, a number of workers stood out from their companions by being strong and stubbornly individualistic. Often they were men with pride and honesty who were not afraid to argue with and even to criticize the cadres. Some of them, as acknowledged members of the proletariat and thus of the new ruling class, objected to the arrogance of the cadres. Such men were admired by their fellow workers and were bothersome impediments to full Communist control over the proletariat. Nevertheless, they had had no connection with the former labor unions and in fact were so politically pure that they could not be liquidated even in the extensive purge of Democratic Reform.

For these men, therefore, the Communists devised a special treatment called the "Honor Roll." At intervals, the Honor Roll was posted on the factory's bulletin board, and the names inscribed were chosen by the Party. The recipients of the honor were given a farewell celebration with gongs, firecrackers, flowers and speeches in praise of their heroism. Thereupon, they were taken from their families and sent to the work gangs in the desolate border regions where, for all practical purposes, they suffered the slow death of labor reform. In my mills, during the years I was there, about a hundred of our best workers were "honored" in this way.

All the workers now were crushed. Their position was no better than ours, and their fears were as great. Nevertheless, by their very numbers they possessed a strength which we relatively few capitalists could never have. Gradually the workers learned to offer passive resistance which, although never on a planned or organized basis, nevertheless became a serious problem for the regime.

Basically, the passive resistance was expressed in a kind of slowdown. Outwardly, the workers seemed animated with the zeal demanded by the authorities, but both the quantity and the quality of production fell noticeably.

The most noticeable aspect of the resistance was absenteeism. Taking advantage of the stipulation in the Labor Insurance Regulations that only a small reduction in pay would result from medically approved sick leave, the workers now formed long queues outside the clinics. Most of the "patients" had undiagnosable symptoms which the doctors dealt with by authorizing a few days' leave. The authorities placed the blame for the situation on the doctors, who thus were caught between two pressures. If a genuinely ill patient were denied leave and suffered an accident at work because of it, the doctor was held responsible. When in doubt, therefore, doctors tended to grant the leave. Absenteeism rose to as high as 20 percent in most factories; it averaged 16 percent in my mills.

The authorities, obviously, were disturbed, and before long a countermeasure to absenteeism was devised. "Comfort missions" were organized by the Health Committee of the Trade Unions. In our mills, the mission consisted of five men who were exempted from regular labor and assigned the sole duty of visiting every sick worker to find out if his case was genuine. Almost immediately our absenteeism dropped from 16 percent to 5 percent. Within a few weeks, however, it was back to a steady 16 percent again. One day, the man in charge of our Workers' Health Committee came into my office, visibly depressed. "It is unbelievable that comrade workers can be so unconscientious," he said. He told me that now the sick worker had his wife or children keep a lookout for the "comfort mission" and warn him of its approach. "Thus by the time we arrive," he said, "the patient is always having a severe attack of pain."

The Communist attack on the workers disaffected labor and brought about passive resistance, but it never again permitted the workers to enjoy the previously held status. It is important to understand, however, that the degradation of the workers gave no corresponding rise in the status of the capitalists. During Five-Anti, the capitalists had been beaten down so thoroughly that the only question was their survival, not their status. The result was now that in every private enterprise, regardless of the elaborate Communist charade, the only people with any authority and status were those directly responsible to the Communist Party. In this situation, labor and management were drawn together silently in a relationship of sympathy and understanding that hitherto was unimaginable.

Thus, although Democratic Reform did not touch me personally, it did affect me in one respect more than all the other campaigns. After the attack on the workers, my eyes were opened finally to the real nature of Communism. Until this moment, I had been horrified by the brutality of the Communists and revolted by their dishonesty and treachery, but I still believed that they were organizing a society which would be dominated by and would benefit solely the proletariat. I might disapprove of the methods used to eliminate obstacles to this end, and I might be dismayed because I personally was denied a permanent place in the new order, but I could find no real objection to the stated objectives of the regime.

When the regime, however, attacked and suppressed the workers—the supposed ruling class for whose benefit the other classes were eliminated—the Communists proved that they were not serving the people as they claimed; instead, they were intent on making the people serve them, and their objective was nothing more than political power.

The differences, now, between the stated objectives and the real purposes of the regime's campaigns became clear. I remembered how genuinely I had approved of agricultural reform, and how confused I had been to learn that the peasants were worse off afterward than before; I saw now that the campaign had succeeded mainly in breaking the landlords' hold over the peasants and in bringing the peasants under direct control by the State.

The Suppression of Counter-Revolutionaries, obviously, was intended to eliminate the possibility of united political opposition from remnant groups of ex-Nationalists. Thought Reform was not meant to "correct reactionary thinking" among intellectuals, but to destroy the intelligentsia itself so that the one group whose members could think for themselves and who would eventually see through the regime's façade would be prevented from ever uniting in opposition. Similarly, Three-Anti was not intended simply to eliminate government corruption; its main purpose was to eliminate all government administrative officers who had served under the former regime. Again, Five-Anti was not primarily for the purpose of correcting the sins of the capitalists; it was meant to destroy the unity and influence of the class itself.

And finally, Democratic Reform was not intended to raise the political level of the proletariat; its objective was to make the workers also completely subservient to the Party.

I realized that each of the campaigns had been carefully planned and efficiently executed. Regardless of its officially stated objectives, each had accomplished its intended purpose. The regime had methodically and ruthlessly suppressed every recognizable group within the population. Previously, the idea that a small clique could seize and maintain absolute power over 650 million unwilling people would have seemed impossible. Now I perceived that it was not only possible, but not even particularly difficult. The trick was to use the people's desire for peace, security and dignity against them. The Communists *said* they intended to fulfill these desires, but all they *did* was to subjugate the people, in the name of the people, by using terror.

I was at last completely disillusioned about the regime, but paradoxically, now that I understood it, I got along better. In the mills, the atmosphere had changed drastically. Because of Five-Anti, the workers were not expected to show any respect for a convicted capitalist embezzler like me. At the same time, because of Democratic Reform, they were not permitted any show of class superiority or privilege, especially now that the regime was encouraging the capitalists to take back some limited initiative. Both the workers and I understood the roles we were to play, but we also understood that the authority of the Party Secretary in the mills was absolute.

Nevertheless, I did have some vague nominal authority. The Temporary Regulations for Private Enterprise, which had been recently issued, stated that capitalists in their own firms were permitted control over "general management," over finance, and (subject to Trade Union approval) over personnel. Outwardly, therefore, my position seemed unchanged, but actually it was completely different. Previously I had chosen diplomatically to discuss most problems with the Party Secretary; now I was made to understand that the decision on every matter, regardless of how trivial, must come from him. To maintain the pretense of my nominal authority, he communicated his decisions to me in a kind of code. If, for example, the question was whether we should accede to a certain Trade Union demand, he would say to me, smiling, if he approved, "Oh, it's your decision. It sounds all right." If he disapproved, he would say without smiling, "I have no comment. The decision is yours."

I was not expected to think, only to obey. The Party Secretary's one qualification for making the decisions on running the mills, however, was his political purity. He was sure, therefore, to make mistakes. I had already learned, however, that the Party must never be made to appear fallible. Any success achieved in our mills was to be credited not even to the Party Secretary, but solely to the Party itself. My real function, therefore, was to take onto myself the blame for any errors made in the mills by me, the Party, the Youth League or the workers.

An example of this situation concerned a nurse whom the Party Secretary "instructed" me to hire in response to a request from the Trade Union's Health Committee. I chose the nurse whose application was approved by the Party Secretary, and also, in accordance with his decision, I hired her on the basis of three months' probation. The nurse apparently performed her duties satisfactorily, but she began to have an affair with the mills' married doctor. Because the nurse belonged to the Youth League, her immorality was considered to detract from the Party's perfect purity. Thus, members of the Party, the Trade Union and the Youth League tried to make her desist. When they failed, the Party Secretary, together with the heads of the other two organizations, called on me informally; they said that the mills' administration really should not tolerate the nurse's behavior, and they suggested that I use the authority conferred on me by the private owners to discharge her. I agreed at once to carry out their suggestion, thanking them for their concern in improving the operations of the mills. As soon as they left, I called in the nurse; I told her that her service was unsatisfactory and because she was at the mills only on probation I was relieving her of her duties. I thought that the matter was closed.

The next day, however, the same group called on me formally, this time with the girl. They all looked solemn. The Trade Union Chairman spoke first. "Mr. Manager, to safeguard the interests of the working class," he said, "I must protest your unreasonable discharge of this comrade nurse whose service we have found wholly satisfactory."

I was dumfounded.

The Party Secretary then stated his view. "Mr. Manager," he began, "under the leadership of the Communist Party and the working class, you capitalists can no longer treat the workers as you did during the reactionary period. If you have made a wrong decision concerning this comrade nurse you had better correct it at once."

I was confused, but I remembered to thank them for their interest, and I promised to look into the matter, giving them my decision the next day. Discreet inquiries uncovered the fact that the official opinion on the nurse had changed completely in the 24 hours immediately following my dismissal of her. I did not know what had brought about the change, but at least I knew what to do. When the delegation appeared the next morning I said at once, "I have investigated the work of the nurse, and I am satisfied with her record. I reverse my previous decision and now will officially re-employ her. I am grateful for your timely advice in righting a wrong. . . ."

The Party Secretary replied, "Mr. Manager, you have been rash in this matter, but you realized your mistake and you corrected it in time. This is a good sign."

The nurse was kept, and she continued her affair with the doctor. Later, from an old employee, I learned that the nurse had a relative who was a senior Party official. When I had fired her, she had pleaded in vain with the Youth League, the Trade Union and the Party Secretary, all of whom had rejected her. She had then gone to her relative who had simply ordered our Party Secretary to reinstate her. I was used to cover up this bit of nepotism within the Party.

By performing such services, I received the unspoken approval and even cooperation of the Party Secretary. I speak of him as though he were one man; actually the Party Secretary for my mills was changed frequently in order to prevent the possibility of a personal relationship developing between us. Nevertheless, they all looked the same, and my relationship and problems with each were identical. I had no animosity toward them. Their status was much higher than mine, despite my nominal title, but like me they lived in fear of disfavor from their superiors. Any mistake credited to them discredited the Party, and this their superiors would not countenance. If, for example, in the case of the nurse, I had either by intention or accidentally forced a revelation of the true situation, the Party Secretary would have been transferred—and soon after I would have been accused of some "crime" and arrested. This, or at least the threat of it, happened to enough of my acquaintances so that we knew perfectly well what to expect.

Conversely, when I protected the Party Secretary and therefore the Party itself by taking the blame for his mistakes, he at least saw to it that I was not punished for them. I was perfectly willing to do this—my survival depended on it—but I lived in constant fear that I would misjudge or misinterpret a situation and thus make a wrong decision.

Just as bad as the fear was the fact that I now lived only to debase myself. The sheer dishonesty of what I was doing sickened me. The humiliation was indescribable. Each of the other national capitalists accepted or adapted to this situation according to his own temperament, but all of us suffered from despair that was expressed in a kind of deep apathy. To make matters worse, I was not the only one who saw that, by attacking the workers in the Democratic Reform Campaign, the Communists had proved that their real objective was absolute political power. Capitalist, intellectual, peasant or worker made no difference; we began to see ourselves merely as machines which were designed to serve the regime and which were meant to be discarded the moment they ceased to be useful. Thus, despite the seemingly generous encouragement given to the businessmen, commerce and industry still moved lethargically. The authorities, therefore, were forced to make further concessions. Early in 1953, many of the petty regulations and restrictions were suddenly removed, and the regime permitted a slightly freer social life, apparently in an effort to raise morale. These measures resulted in what came to be remembered nostalgically as "the good year of 1953."

The small businessmen especially benefited by the "good year." For many of them, it brought the only taste of prosperity they had had in their lives. Artisans and craftsmen such as blacksmiths and machinists expanded their activities and became, in effect, small factory owners. Even some of our own machinists at the mills accepted government subcontracts or sub-subcontracts on which they worked at home. A saying at the time was: "Socialism in the daytime; capitalism at night."

The night life also took on a pale reflection of its former glitter. The few remaining night clubs were full constantly. The taxi dancers and prostitutes had long since been banned, but many were permitted to exist as "underground party girls." They were now booked far in advance, and their ranks were increased by part-time amateurs. Girls who worked in factories and previously had lived drably seemed to find the new gaiety irresistible. This came to my attention when the Trade Union Chairman requested me to dismiss one of our girls who was found to possess 15 pairs of fancy high-heeled shoes and several colorful sheath dresses. Another of our workers, a seventeen-year-old girl, became pregnant, and the Union tried to help her; she told us, however, that she had had affairs with at least twelve men and thus had no idea which one was the father.

The older and more established bourgeoisie as well as the newly rich small businessmen tended to burn the candle at both ends. Nevertheless, the gaiety was tinged with hysteria, and even a little sadness. There was definitely a feeling that this was the last fling. People were spending what they had while they had it, trying to enjoy themselves while they could.

The Chans and I relaxed a little during this period, but because of our increasingly prominent positions we never participated in the city's feverish night life. Instead we merely entertained friends and high Communist officials at home. J.P. was careful to maintain his contacts with high Party officials. He went to Peking frequently to attend meetings and to confer with the top leaders. I remember that Pan Han-yin, Shanghai's deputy mayor, was a frequent guest for dinner and bridge.

The most elaborate entertainments in the Chan household were Chinese Opera parties. Musicians would be hired, and we and our guests would sing our favorite selections. I rarely participated, because I did not really understand Peking Opera. One evening, however, J.P. invited Mai Mee, the famous star from Peking, to a dinner party at the house. She was then about twenty-three, a tiny little thing and not especially attractive, but she was vivacious and irrepressibly gay and witty. Mai Mee was the opposite of Li-li, but I found her captivating. Mai Mee began to teach me about the opera, and despite the fact that Li-li still occupied my thoughts, I might have become romantic about her except that she had a husband; she was married to a young student in Peking.

The Chans obviously wanted me to get married, and they still hoped I would choose the beautiful Fan Su. I tried to find her attractive, but the truth was that she lacked intelligence, and after Li-li, she seemed vapid. Moreover, I did not feel that this was the time to think of marriage. Even though it was "the good year of '53," the whole atmosphere was poisoned with suspicion and mistrust. Neither the Chans nor I had any feeling of security about the future, and we dreaded what new disasters the regime might bring upon us.

Oddly enough, Fan Su was responsible for increasing our dread of the regime's tactics. After she graduated, she was assigned to a job in a municipal government office. One day, she was seen there by the head of Shanghai's Security Police, and a day later she found that she had been made his secretary. Despite their antagonism to the bourgeoisie, the Communists—including Mao Tse-tung and the other top leaders—were known to have a weakness for bourgeois girls. Fan Su was flattered by the attention of such a senior official, but she became shocked by what she saw of Communist police methods. One night she told us in wide-eyed innocence that huge dossiers were kept on everyone; she said that each dossier contained all the necessary evidence, whether real or fabricated, so that the person could be arrested and eliminated immediately if the regime ever wanted to get rid of him. To our horror, we realized that Fan Su was not bright enough to be adequately discreet. Such talk could get her into serious trouble, which could spread with equal disaster to us. J.P. tried to shut her up, but thereafter we were so frightened by her that all of us—including Charlie's wife, who was her close friend —tried to avoid her.

Nevertheless, through another indiscretion of Fan Su's, I

learned in late 1953 that disaster had struck Li-li and her husband. She had married the owner of a small factory, and until now I had been pleased to think that she was living in comfort and respectability. The police discovered, however, that although the factory was in her husband's name, the real owner was a Nationalist who had escaped to Taiwan. Li-li's husband was arrested, accused of "hiding enemy property" and suspected of "maintaining secret relations with the reactionary clique"; i.e., of keeping in touch with the real owner. The husband was sent to labor reform. I dreaded to think what Li-li must be going through. I knew that the police would be hounding her to determine whether she herself had any "secret relations with the reactionary clique." In fact, even I endured the interrogation of the police, who tried to establish that I had seen her after her marriage. I had not seen her since April 21, 1951—more than two years before—but the police did not give up until J.P. assured them that I was telling the truth.

It was agonizing to know that Li-li was in trouble and that I could do nothing to help her. All I could do was to make sure that I had no contact with her; even an accidental meeting with only a few words exchanged in greeting would be excuse enough for the police to turn all her testimony and mine into lies. Her husband's crime was serious, and she would never again be free of suspicion. I heard that she had returned to live with her parents and had found a menial job in a sewing cooperative.

Li-li's tragedy marked the end for me of the "good year." In December 1953, the authorities suddenly announced the so-called "General Line," and from then on the fate that the regime had in store for us was no longer in doubt.

"The General Line and the General Task for the Transitional Period," we were told, would be to complete the "foundations for a socialist society." This was the first time that the word "socialism" had appeared as an aspect of official policy. Previously, whenever the question had been raised as to why socialism was not mentioned in the Common Program, the answer had been that socialism was too remote for consideration. In the present period, we were supposedly building the New Democracy which would need to be perfected before the plans for socialism could be made. Now, however, Mao announced that we *had* been building toward socialism since October 1, 1949. This was such a complete contradiction of what had been stated previously that much of the material published on policy during the past four years had to be withdrawn from circulation. Meanwhile, the top leaders were making marathon speeches to proclaim and explain the new Line.

Now began the tiresome effort of attending endless meetings on the subject of the General Line. It is important to understand that from the beginning of the regime, the entire population had been divided into groups which were subdivided into "mass" organizations. Every person was forced to belong to a mass organization of his group. Thus, for example, professors had to join the Educational Workers Union. Students had their own union. Every peasant belonged to a branch of the Peasants Association. Housewives came under their respective Residents Associations, which were divided into district, street and lane branches. Normally, everyone was made to attend meetings of his organization once a week, but during special campaigns the number and length of the meetings increased greatly. At the meetings, the pretense was scrupulously maintained that the regime's current policy was discussed by the people. The inference was that through discussion the people arrived at their own conclusions about the policy.

Actually, however, the Communists introduced their own conclusions in advance. Thereupon, the people went through the motions of discussing the policy; they praised it and finally gave it their "unanimous support." No one was allowed to avoid giving his comment, which might have to be rephrased many times before the organization officials were satisfied. The individual's response, behavior and attitude were under constant scrutiny. If he earned the disapproval of the officials, the other members of his group were made to turn on him; the others feared the same treatment if they did not.

Thus, although the individual belonged to a group, his greatest danger came from the group—from the only people who normally would be expected to understand, help and protect him. The result was that he knew the terror of being utterly alone and vulnerable in a hostile society. In the neighborhood where he lived, the census police kept a constant check on his movements. In his place of employment, the Communist officials ensured that he made an adequate contribution to the regime. But the control over his behavior, exercised by the officials of his mass organization, was absolute. The meetings therefore were a fearful strain.

At the same time, they were stultifyingly dull, and the idea of the number of them you would have to attend down through the years made the future difficult to face. I can remember only one amusing incident associated with these meetings. At a lane meeting in 1954, an old servant of ours was made to express her opinion on the draft of the new Constitution. The poor woman was senile and illiterate. In the Shanghai dialect, the words for "constitution" and "magician's trick" are pronounced the same. To the old woman, the whole discussion seemed to concern "supporting the new magician's trick." Finally, she managed to say, "During my seventy-three years I can recall having seen only one magician's trick. The People's Government which is now about to perform a magic trick, therefore, has my support. I am determined to witness it." The cadres were furious; no one dared to laugh, but the officials sensed the ridicule of the others. In punishment, the meeting was not allowed to break up until, hours later, the old lady had been taught to say something acceptable about the Constitution.

I belonged to two mass organizations. One was the Democratic League which I had joined while still at the university. It was for intellectuals. It was Communist-sponsored and -controlled, but was intended to create the impression that the regime democratically permitted political parties other than the Communist one to function. After going to the flour mills, I had joined in addition the local branch of the All-China Federation of Industry and Commerce, a front organization which had replaced the old Chamber of Commerce. In December 1953, when the authorities presented the new policy of the General Line for "discussion," I had to attend meetings on this subject sponsored by both organizations. We learned that private trade, industry, agriculture and even handicrafts would be taken over gradually by the State. Henceforth, the Party policy toward private enterprise would be to "utilize, restrict and remold." Private enterprise would be fitted into the framework of the overall national economic plan. The present owners eventually would become "self-supporting laborers." Meanwhile, pilot projects would be set up as models from which we could learn what to expect.

Most of us expected the worst. We were confused only by the fact that the regime appeared to be trying to warn us in advance, whereas their usual tactic had been to cover up their real objectives with false promises and assurances. Some took this new approach to mean that the regime had learned its lesson from Five-Anti and now was attempting to be honest with us; they hoped that our fate might be no worse than the authorities described it. Others, however, felt that the regime considered us

so beaten down that elaborate deception was no longer necessary.

Charlie and I had our first premonition of what the regime now
planned for us at a mass meeting for prominent businessmen addressed by Shanghai's mayor. After describing the meaning of
the General Line for the Transitional Period leading toward socialism, the mayor said, "You national capitalist friends are now
approaching your first and most important barrier—the socialist
barrier. It will not be easy to cross. . . ."

All we had gone through previously, we were to understand,
had been nothing. Only *now* were our difficulties in preparing
for the "first barrier" beginning. I remember the look on Charlie's
face. He had been badly shaken by his experience in Five-Anti,
but now I saw him sink into utter hopelessness. I think my feelings were the same. The mayor added that although we would
have to manage the climb over the barrier ourselves, he would
see that no one died in the attempt. He reminded us that the
Party was always ready to extend us help and advice. Our past
experience with the regime's "help and advice" allowed us no
illusions about our new status.

The fact that our status had changed drastically was immediately apparent in my job at the mills. The Communists were
openly contemptuous of me as well as of the workers. With me,
the Party Secretary began a kind of cat-and-mouse game designed to humiliate and demoralize me to the extent that I would
never for a moment forget the power held over me.

By this time, the mills were operating entirely on a fee basis.
The authorities sent us wheat and paid us a set amount to grind
it into flour. In early 1954, however, the fee was lowered and
the amount of wheat sent to us was cut until our labor force had
only five or six days of work a month. Nevertheless, we had to
pay the workers for full time, and we were not permitted to

dismiss any of them. Our income now would not cover our payroll, but we were not permitted to go out of business. The whole situation was blamed on my evil capitalist ways; all I could do was to apply for bank loans and hope for a change.

Thus, in addition to the dishonesty of the life I led and the degradation of the job I was doing, I also was made to act out a pantomime on the evils of capitalism. I spent most of my time pretending I was a businessman engaged in the private enterprise of applying for a loan. While I humbled myself before the arrogant Party Secretary who acted as Manager and ran the bank, the Party Secretary who ran my mills knew whether I would get the money, but I did not. On the days when he knew I would return empty-handed, he would have the workers stage the sort of reception he considered best calculated to demoralize me. Sometimes I would face their scorn and derision as though I were a stupid and miserable failure. Again, I might contend with their sorrow and pain as though I were a heartless brute whose indifference was responsible for their children's hunger. And worst of all, I might face their unleashed fury as though, because of my criminal greed, I denied them their hard-earned pittance; many times I feared that the mob of my workers would get out of the cadres' control and that I would be thrown bodily into the river. Nevertheless, at the last minute the bank always provided just enough funds to put off the crisis for a few days; frequently the amount I received covered only the payroll—without my own salary.

We did not need many months of this treatment to know that our position was hopeless. We could feel the power of the regime settle on the country like a massive weight. In every segment of society, gaiety now was considered "degenerate living" and was a criminal offense. The simplest indulgences were frowned upon. The people were to live like puritans, their one pleasure in serving the socialist cause. In fact, we were all made to feel that we would be allowed to live at all only as long as the regime considered us useful. Like everyone else, I understood that when the Communists talked about serving the people they really meant that the people were to serve them. I faced the fact that the Communists would not—could not—release the suppression; if they did—even for a moment—the resulting explosion from a betrayed people would destroy them.

Each day seemed longer than the last, and harder to face. I never had enough sleep, and what I had was torn apart by nightmares. One sultry night in June 1954 when I was writing to my father, I suddenly found myself wanting to pour out my anguish to him. I tried to tell him how right he was and how wrong and foolish I had been not to heed his advice. I wanted to beg his forgiveness. I wanted to say that I would never doubt his wisdom again. I did not dare express such feelings openly, but I knew that the censors were seldom well educated. I therefore quoted from classical poems. One couplet read, "A wrong step, once taken, can never be retraced." And another said, "To retrace one wrong step takes 100 years"; i.e., it cannot be done in one's lifetime. In Chinese these quotations expressed powerfully to my father the magnitude of the mistake I had made.

Ten days later, I had spent an exhausting day at the flour mills and at an endless group discussion meeting, and I did not get home until midnight. A telegram from Hong Kong was waiting for me. It was from my brother, and it said that my father had died that afternoon of a heart attack. For a long moment, I was stunned with shock. I stood motionless, and the only sound was the crinkling of the paper in my trembling hands. Something in my face must have startled the *amah*, because she came in a few minutes later with the rest of the servants. Then the house was full of people, relatives and family friends. I tried to speak, but

126

I could make no sound. I felt that the world had come to an end and my only hope was that my father had died before reading my letter; the anguish I had expressed in it would have hurt him deeply.

For three days I was too distraught to go to the office. On the afternoon of the third day, I took a walk in Jessfield Park and when I returned, a letter was waiting for me. The handwriting was familiar, and to my horror I saw that it was my father's. Even worse, when I opened the letter I realized that he had written it the morning of the day he died. Moreover, the first lines indicated that he was replying to my message of despair. For a moment, I suffered the hell of thinking that my letter to him might have been the immediate cause of his death.

My father's message, however, was full of life and hope. He had understood my feelings and was trying to give me courage. Taking my poetry cue, he quoted a couplet which read, "As long as the blue mountains stand, one need not doubt that trees will continue to grow." In English, one might express something of this meaning with, "Where there is life, there is hope." He was telling me that although I could not retrace my wrong step, I might be able to direct my future steps so as to take me away from the horror with which I now lived.

At first, my father's letter made me feel even worse. The control exercised over us was so complete that escape from it appeared impossible. My father's optimism therefore seemed as naïve now as once I had thought his beliefs about Communism to be. Thus I returned to my grim routine in a kind of daze, and I was indifferent to my fate.

This was July 5, 1954. Two nights later I saw Li-li in Bubbling Well Road, and life seemed to flow back into me. I was conscious of a great swell of hot anger at the people who had tricked and captured me. My father had begged me not to go

127

to Communist China, and his final message had expressed the hope that I could get away from it. If I *could* get away, I would be fulfilling his last wish, and even if he would not be there to see me, I would feel that I had somehow made up a little for the suffering I had caused him by not listening to him before.

To me, living in Communist China seemed worse than death. My only hope for life, therefore, was in fighting for a chance to escape.

CHAPTER 6

Somewhere they say there is another world,
And we shall have another life.
But I know only this world and this life.

—LI SHANG-YIN

AFTER July 7, 1954, I thought about escape constantly, but the more I thought about it, the more difficult it seemed. I could imagine only one possibility. The government had begun to send "cultural" and trade delegations abroad. Most of the delegations stayed within the socialist bloc, but some visited the Asian neutralist nations. If I could be sent as a delegate to a neutral country, I might find a chance to defect.

I therefore began a discreet investigation of how the delegations to neutral countries were selected. It did not take me long to learn that all delegates who had so far had a chance to leave the country had two qualifications in common: first, they were either Party members or had a long record of service to the Party; and second, they were vulnerable to "remote control" by the authorities, usually because they had close family members left in China to serve as hostages. In addition, the fact that I had lived abroad for two years in a free country was against me. I was thus depressed to find that I entirely lacked the necessary qualifications.

Although I was discouraged, I did not give up. I would have to search much further, I knew, for my opportunity. Meanwhile, at all cost, I would avoid acquiring a wife and children who could be used by the authorities to establish a real hold over me. For the first time, I was glad that I was not married to Li-li. At the same time, I realized that not having the means for such a hold would increase the authorities' suspicion of me. My first effort, therefore, had to be toward establishing an exceptional record of enthusiastic support of, and real service to, the regime.

This was extremely difficult now that the Party policy was again antagonistic to businessmen. Under the General Line of the Transitional Period, we were in the "softening-up" phase during which, in the manner of Pavlov's dog, the reflexes of the capitalists were to be conditioned for socialism.

The softening-up became apparent in late 1954 when the first pilot projects for Joint State-Private Enterprise were inaugurated. One or two firms from each branch of trade were chosen. The pilot projects were always the best equipped and most profitably operated firms. The State acquired part ownership of these firms by taking over the shares of such "counter-revolutionary elements" as the big investor T. V. Soong, by taking shares in lieu of the fines assessed under Five-Anti, and even, in a very few cases, by actual investment.

These pilot Joint State-Private Enterprises were given every possible advantage. Their assets were evaluated fairly. The tax levies were just. Government low-interest loans were easily available. Adequate quantities of raw materials were supplied promptly. Labor problems were solved without bother or friction. Priority was given to these firms' distribution and transportation facilities. In fact, the government saw to it that the pilot projects operated smoothly and showed a healthy profit.

In short, the capitalists who had the State for a joint partner did very well indeed. Each of them was made into a rosy picture of socialism's glorious future.

On the other hand, the horrors of "free" private enterprise were depicted even more graphically. We "national capitalists" whose firms were not chosen for Joint State-Private Enterprise were "softened up" by being denied all of the advantages given to the pilot project owners.

My experiences at the flour mills were typical. The contempt and animosity I had been receiving from the mills' Party Secretary became worse. The amount of wheat sent to us by the government had not been enough to keep our mills operating a quarter of the time; now we were sent less. Moreover, the fees paid for our work were reduced. Our losses therefore became even greater. We were still not permitted to go out of business, but bank loans became even harder to get. And, of course, the workers were made to demonstrate more frequently and violently against me.

Further means of harassing us were introduced. The Tax Bureau became a powerful political weapon in our "remolding" and softening-up for socialism. The tax rate on company profits was reasonable—34.5 percent—but the Tax Bureau cadres' computation of our "profits" was not. Thus, for example, despite the fact that our mills were operating at a loss and had done so for three years, we were taxed on our "profits." Such profits were arrived at by the cadres in several ways. One way was an arbitrary refusal to allow for depreciation. Our power-conveyor belts, for example, were counted as assets at their full value when new. We were not allowed to dispose of any worn-out belts, and thus our "assets" in this type of equipment alone were inflated hundreds of times over.

Again, at our mills the machinery was as much as 30 years old and thus consumed electricity at a high rate. More modern machinery could operate on little more than half of our requirement. Thus our electricity expense was high. When the Tax Bureau cadres checked our operations, however, they cut down the electricity expense charge to the minimum required for modern plant equipment. When I protested, I was asked by the cadre, "Why should the State suffer for *your* capitalist inefficiency?"

The tax cadres even exercised police powers, and all businessmen were terrified of them. One night, an old friend of mine was dragged out of bed along with his wife and two children. They were made to stand outside in the cold, facing up against the wall of their house, while it was ransacked by the cadres for evidence of tax evasion. The search was fruitless, but instead of apologizing, the cadre said, "You think you are smart, you unscrupulous businessmen, but just wait. Sooner or later we'll get the evidence we want." The worst effect of this experience was on the children, who were so hysterical with fear that they had to be kept in bed for several days.

The cadres also used physical torture. A relative of mine who owned a grocery store was once interrogated for 28 hours continuously by relays of tax cadres. For a half hour he would be shouted at and abused while the muzzle of a pistol was held against his temple. These cadres then would leave, suddenly to be replaced by another who was all smiles and helpful encouragement. He in turn would be replaced by a group who used physical violence. My relative was pistol-whipped so severely that his mind was never the same again.

It is important to understand that such treatment was pure extortion. Every business was controlled by the authorities so thoroughly that the owner could not possibly hide income. The use of violence, however, helped to demoralize the businessmen and also wrung from them any additional money they might have.

The tax cadres probably were responsible for the new wave of suicides that began in early 1955 among the businessmen. As before, many of the men driven beyond endurance performed acts of defiance before killing themselves. The case of a fish peddler in Shanghai's Cha-pei section was well known. He had been forced to sell everything he owned in order to meet the demands of the tax cadres. His wife had left him because he could no longer support her, and still the cadres demanded more. The peddler took a heavy fish knife and publicly split the cadre's skull. He then slit his own throat.

Financial troubles alone would have been enough to cause many men to beg that their businesses be taken over as Joint State-Private Enterprises. Many did appeal for this "privilege," but they were refused. In addition, however, the regime also softened us up with endless labor troubles while we watched the pilot projects operate peacefully.

These troubles are not to be confused with the practice of inciting workers to demonstrate against owners. In my case, for example, the workers' union would present me with demands. If I acceded to them, on instructions from the mills' Party Secretary, then my "capitalist mismanagement" would be blamed for worsening the mills' financial position. If I refused the demand, also on the Party Secretary's instructions, then I would endure the workers' wrath and be accused of "grinding the faces of the poor" and of "exploiting the working class."

In practice, the Party Secretary rarely instructed me to accede to the workers' demands. This was partly because the Communists always preferred to have me in the position of seeming to

133

be antagonistic to the workers, partly because by refusing the
demands I helped maintain the pretense that I possessed man-
agerial authority, and surprisingly partly because the Communists themselves did not have absolute control over the workers.

After Democratic Reform, the workers were crushed so thoroughly that they were completely subservient to the cadres, but
the regime carefully maintained the fiction that the workers were
the new ruling class. The poor workers, therefore, had to *act* as
if they were the rulers but at the same time *submit* to rule by the
Party. Many of them were too ignorant to play this complicated
role well, and they made mistakes. I am convinced that the main
reason private enterprise was not taken over completely by the
Communists before this time was so that we capitalists could be
blamed for the workers' ineptitude.

My experience with rats at the mills illustrates this situation.
During the softening-up period, the government also was waging
the Elimination of Four Pests Campaign against flies, mosquitoes,
sparrows and rodents. Of these pests, rats were our biggest problem. We therefore bought a thousand traps and placed them
throughout the warehouses. A worker was assigned to buy and
affix food as bait in the traps. Each day fewer rats were caught.
At first we thought we were catching them all, and we notified
the Food Bureau that our establishment would soon be rodent-
free. Rat damage to the bags of flour continued, however, and
a check revealed that the worker had been embezzling the funds
for buying bait. When caught, the worker's attitude seemed to
be that as a member of the new ruling class he was entitled to
anything he could get his hands on. The Communists quickly
disabused him of this idea, and the mills' Party Secretary instructed me to call a meeting to review the case. The worker was
ordered to make a public confession. He read a statement apparently written for him by the Trade Union. "I was influenced

by decadent capitalist ideas," he said, "and I wished to embezzle some money so that I could become a capitalist myself. Fortunately I was discovered, and with the help of the Communist Party I was made to realize my mistake. From now on, I am determined to put up a sustained fight against decadent capitalist ideas. . . ."

The Trade Union Chairman, the Youth League Secretary and several representatives from the workers made speeches on the evils of capitalist thinking and implied that, locally, I was the source of this evil. When my turn came, I criticized myself humbly for having failed to supervise the baiting of the traps and especially for having been an evil influence on the worker. I ended with a statement that at the time had to be included in every speech made by a national capitalist: "Through the case of Comrade B——, I have come to realize more clearly the decadent and dangerous ideas of the capitalist class. Henceforth, I am determined to intensify my alertness, speed up my self-reform, struggle for the early abandonment of exploitation and become a self-supporting workingman. . . ." The meeting ended with denouncements of the capitalist class in general. The worker's name, however, appeared on the Roll of Honor a few weeks later.

I was so used to taking the blame in cases like this that I played the role automatically and unconcernedly. My one real concern in the case of the rats was that, as an aspect of the Elimination of Four Pests Campaign, everyone including me was to catch, kill and deliver two rats a day. The rats at the mills were the prerogative of the mills' campaign activists and cadres and were therefore not available to me. It is important to understand that during the campaign, fulfilling this demand was a serious obligation. My house, however, had no rats. One of my servants saw that I was troubled and drew me out about it. He then solved my problem. A brisk black market business in dead rats had sprung up. The servant had a special container made and he obtained the necessary dead rats for me. Thus I merely had to carry the repulsive but neatly packaged cargo to the office each day.

Much more difficult was my effort to deal with a touchy labor problem. Our mills were on the river's edge; barges delivered wheat and took away the flour. In the old days we had unloaded and loaded the barges with automatic equipment. Enough electricity to operate this equipment was not now available. Therefore the barges were unloaded and loaded by 800 transport workers. These workers had their own union. They were not our employees and we were not responsible for them in any way except to provide a dining place and rest rooms. Nevertheless, one day they "demanded" that my mills provide an enamel cup and two towels for each of the transport workers.

The request itself was not unreasonable and the cost of fulfilling it would not have been excessive; moreover, every national capitalist by now automatically acceded to all worker demands until his Party Secretary instructed him otherwise. In this particular case, the question was simply whether we should go beyond the obligations of our contract with the Transport Union. A matter of principle was involved; if I acceded, a precedent would be established and I would be accused of being "unprincipled in luring the workers to extravagant demands." I checked the matter with the mills' Party Secretary. I interpreted his instructions to mean that I should reject the demand.

I did reject the demand, and of course faced "struggle." The transport workers sent daily delegations to my office to argue and harangue. Whenever I went outside, I had to endure their abuse and threats. This went on until finally I suggested that we take the matter to the Bureau of Labor for arbitration.

Arbitration for labor disputes was carried out in the Labor Bureau's large building on Avenue Joffre. The unions seldom won a case brought to arbitration. The fact that a dispute got this far meant that the owner had been instructed by his Party Secretary to refuse the labor demand; the arbitration therefore was merely the performance staged to put the blame for the refusal on the owner rather than on the Party. I arrived at our appointed arbitration room at 8 A.M. I found that eight of our transport workers plus four of their union's higher officials were already there to present their side of the case. I alone represented management. Four Labor Bureau officials were the arbitrators; they read out to me a formal statement of the transport workers' demands. I replied politely, "I am sorry, but I cannot accept this request."

Thereupon, the twelve union representatives, joined by the four "arbitrators," began the usual abuse, insults, threats and haranguing. The table-pounding and shouting went on for hours. It was only what I expected and I regarded it merely as an unpleasant chore to get through as best I could. According to the standard procedure, I was to maintain my refusal while the Communists made their point that they sided entirely with the workers. Thereupon, with a final show of "what can you expect from the heartless capitalists?" the union's demands would be rejected, and the show would be over.

As the hours went by, however, I slowly realized that this particular show was not following the standard procedure. The haranguing, instead of running down, was getting more intense. At lunchtime, the others went out two at a time, but I was not allowed to eat or even to have a glass of water. Moreover, the insults to me in this attack were beyond those normally used. One cadre, for example, said once, "How could such a fine national capitalist as Mr. Chan have employed a *gangster* like you?" Another cadre said that I was "as *reactionary* as a rock." A third even accused me of being a "lackey of the *imperialists*." These remarks may seem of little consequence, but the Communist insults fitted into a rigid pattern. When the arbitrators went outside this pattern, I knew that either they or I were making a serious mistake. I now became really frightened; I thought that I had somehow misinterpreted the instructions of the mills' Party Secretary or that the policy in this case had been switched since I had spoken to him last. By six in the evening, the haranguing still had not let up although everyone was near exhaustion. I did not know what was expected of me, and I was sweating with fear. I finally obtained permission to telephone J.P. "I have been here since eight this morning without food or water," I said in front of my tormentors. "Let them arrest me, but I cannot take any more. What shall I do?"

I could tell from J.P.'s voice that he was furious. He thought for a moment and then said, "Accept their demands and leave. This is something I'll have to look into. Meanwhile, you get out of there as quickly as you can."

I put down the receiver and turned to the arbitrators. "All right," I said quietly. "I'll sign the workers' demand. Give me the paper." My words had a dramatic reaction. The simple transport workers began to cheer jubilantly for their victory. The higher officials of their union and the four Labor Bureau arbitrators looked stunned. One of the Bureau cadres had had his arm raised to shake his fist at me; now he slowly opened his hand. "Now, now, Mr. Loh," he said. "We shouldn't be hasty. Let us bring you some tea . . ."

"No thanks; let me have the paper," I said.

"Mr. Loh, a fine progressive national capitalist like you will understand that we have our problems. I am sure that if we sit down and talk a bit more . . ."

What he was really saying was, "Please don't get us into trouble." Nevertheless, I reached over, picked up the paper, signed it and walked out. At home, even though I was almost sick with fatigue, I wrote out a detailed report of what had happened. This was dangerous, because in any conflict between a capitalist and the "ruling class" of workers together with the cadres, the capitalist was foolhardy to do anything but hope that the matter would be dropped as quickly and quietly as possible. When I had given in to the workers' demands, however, I had gone against Party policy, and I had either to push on and prove that I was right in doing so or suffer the consequences.

What had happened was that the Labor Bureau arbitrators had made a bad mistake. Whenever cadres like these, or workers, made a mistake that might reflect on the Party, we national capitalists took the blame; when a cadre erred in implementing policy given to him by his superiors, however, *he* was in trouble. The arbitrators were meant to put on a show of siding with the workers and they were to abuse and demoralize me, but they were not to push me so far that I would give in to the workers' demands. After all, my mills were operated for the regime's benefit, not mine, and the acceptance of the transport workers' demands would set a precedent that would increase the regime's difficulty with the mills.

I lived through several days of fearful suspense, but when J.P. brought my report to the attention of the mayor of Shanghai, I was exonerated. The four Labor Bureau cadres were transferred to lesser positions outside Shanghai. I even received an unofficial Party apology. The situation could not have turned out better for me. I had been brought to the attention of higher-ups as a man who really understood Party policy and had the stamina to endure 10 hours of "struggle" in its defense. I felt that I had moved an inch toward the goal of earning enough trust from the authorities to make escape possible. My morale was raised imperceptibly.

My morale was raised a bit higher late in 1954 by another totally unrelated incident. Immediately after my father's death in June, I had moved out of the Chan mansion back to my own house. This was because of the Chinese custom that decreed a bereaved person must not live in the house of anyone outside his family during the 49-day period of mourning. After the mourning period I stayed on in my house although I usually ate with the Chans. Nevertheless, during the especially demoralizing period of the "transition" under the General Line, I was much alone, brooding about means of escaping; occasionally I was optimistic but usually I felt hopeless and depressed. I thought of Li-li often and that increased my restlessness. One night when I was discouraged, I happened to see that Mai Mee, the witty and vivacious opera star from Peking, was playing at Shanghai's old traditional opera theater. On impulse, I went to the theater and tried to get a seat for the night's performance. The house was full. I went back to the stage entrance in hope of seeing Mai Mee. I intended to tell her that I would try to see one of her performances later.

Mai Mee seemed pleased to see me and she obtained for me a front row seat for the evening's performance. Afterward, I went back again, this time to thank her. The theater was the old-fashioned type that had living quarters for the performers within the building itself. Thus I had tea with Mai Mee in her apartment. She arranged for a seat to be available for me every night of her two-month engagement, and she said she hoped I would attend her performances often. I began to go almost every evening and to visit her in her rooms afterward. I had known that she was popular, particularly with the masses, but I was astonished to find out how much she was adored. Under her tutelage I became quite familiar with Peking Opera, but most of all I learned Mai Mee's story.

Mai Mee came from an opera family; in America, one would say she had been "born in a wardrobe trunk." The custom had been that only the star performers traveled; each theater had its own permanent cast of extras and character actors in residence. Mai Mee's father had played the traditional "fighter" parts and had lived in the very theater where I visited her. By the age of six, she knew everything about the opera and everyone in it. She had little formal education and could write only a few characters, but she was quick and intelligent, and she understood her audiences perfectly. By the age of twenty, her experience in the roles was wide, and she had developed a distinctive technique. She modified and sometimes went beyond the highly stylized gestures of the traditional parts. She made the parts more understandable; her interpretations had more vigor and particularly more sex in them. The common people loved it, and her fame spread rapidly. Now, at twenty-four, she was earning a fortune and was ready to form her own troupe.

Mai Mee herself tended to be bored with actors. She was impressed by people who had education, manners and social prestige. Thus she had married a Peking college student who was two years younger than she. Apparently he fawned over her like a puppy, and she seldom took him on tour.

As Mai Mee confided increasingly in me, I found that I was able to confide equally in her. The importance of this cannot be understood by anyone who has not lived under Communism. The Communist technique of using those who were closest to a person as a constant threat over him meant that each individual had a terrible feeling of isolation. To find someone in whom one dared confide was an indescribable delight. This did not mean that I told her my opinions about the regime or that I intended to try to escape. It meant only that I could relax with her instead of being constantly on guard. I could explain my problems and get her sympathetic understanding. Also, the fact that she was completely unlike Li-li was helpful in that she offered me female companionship without reminding me of the one woman I could not get entirely out of my mind. For me the relationship was perfect. It was a boon to my morale.

I was also able to help her. Mai Mee's position in the new regime was unique. She herself did not understand it, but she knew that the authorities were antagonistic to her, and she was frightened about her future. One day she sent me a frantic note asking me not to attend her performance three nights hence because the first two rows had been commandeered by a delegation of cadres from the Culture Bureau. We both knew what that meant and I went to her the moment I could get away.

The basis of Mai Mee's trouble was that she had genuine popular support. She had been asked repeatedly to join a State-operated opera group, but she had always refused. This was partly because in a State group she would be forced to abandon her own interpretation of the roles and partly because she earned much more money on her own. The Communists, however, always regarded with suspicion someone who had the real support of the masses but who did not come completely under Party control. So far, because of Mai Mee's popularity, they had not dared move openly against her, but sooner or later they would attack her. We could be sure that the purpose of the Culture Bureau's delegation would be to find everything that could be used in a tirade against her.

I therefore advised Mai Mee to play her role that night as nearly as possible in the traditional manner and still give some evidence of her own style. Above all, she was to avoid any sexiness that would offend the Communists' prudery. Mai Mee, thus, would give the cadres as little as possible to criticize. Nevertheless, the papers next day carried scathing descriptions of her performance. It was described as "yellow"; this implied that it was vulgarly salacious. (American jazz, for example, is described as "yellow music.")

Mai Mee was upset, but I outlined a plan for her whereby she might win the regime's support and still maintain her independence. I drafted a letter which she could send to the authorities requesting permission to produce some of the new "progressive" operas that had been written under official sponsorship. Most of these avoided the more blatant forms of propaganda, but Mai Mee had refused to play them because they were not very good. Nevertheless, if she could use her skill to make one or two of them more popular, the authorities would be pleased.

In addition, I wrote out several statements using the approved phraseology which she could give publicly and which would suggest that she supported the regime. And finally, we worked out a means whereby she could implant with the proper authorities the idea that by permitting her to operate independently, the fiction would be maintained that the regime was not antagonistic to "cultural free enterprise." Under my direction, Mai Mee began her campaign at once, and a lessening in the authorities' antipathy was immediately noticeable.

My friendship with Mai Mee had an unexpected result. The workers from my mills were ardent fans of hers and they would see me almost every time they went to a performance. Their reaction was a kind of respect mixed, I suspect, with envy. In fact, I became something of a hero at the mills. Even the cadres were impressed. Thus, although the Communists continued to show their contempt officially, and the workers continued, officially, to demonstrate against me, I could tell that both pretenses were slightly less sincere.

It is even possible that my friendship with Mai Mee and its reaction on our workers enabled me to win an "elective" post in the government. In any event, shortly after she left Shanghai I was selected by the Party as a candidate for representative to the District People's Congress. Despite Communist propaganda stories about "free democratic elections," I was the one and only candidate, which of course meant that I would win the election. The election itself was merely another aspect of the elaborately staged pretense that the people had a voice in government affairs.

The National People's Congress is the highest "elected" body in the government. Elections for the Congress begin at the lowest level and work upward. My first post was at the District level.

The mills of my enterprise were one of three enterprises in our District, and the 9,000 workers of the District "elected" three representatives. For candidates, the Communists chose a Party Secretary from one enterprise, a Trade Union Chairman from another, and the national capitalist from mine. Posters appeared in the mills with the biographies of the three candidates. My biography was a far cry from the description of me made public during Five-Anti.

On election day, the mills' assembly hall was decorated and the workers arrived in their best clothes. After many speeches, ballots were distributed by group leaders to each voter. Below the names of the three candidates were three blank lines in which the voters could write in any name they desired. Because the election was carried out under the close scrutiny of group leaders, however, the three candidates won 97 percent of the vote. One write-in got slightly over 200 ballots. These votes were far more significant than the 8800 votes for the Party-appointed candidates because they represented the real choice of the voters. This unlisted "candidate" was highly respected by his fellow workers for being outspoken, even to the cadres, in defense of the workers' interests. For his effrontery to the Party in winning

200 votes, he was put on the Honor Roll six weeks after the election. He was transported to the Sinkiang desert and for at least the remaining three years I spent at the mills he was not heard from again either by us or by his wife, who came to us constantly hoping for news of him.

Later, I was also "elected" to the higher Shanghai People's Congress. Even in this post, we still merely "discussed" Party policy and approved it unanimously, but my political status with the regime was increased and for the first time I was invited to parties given by high Communist officials. I was astonished at the extravagance of these parties and at how thoroughly the normally fearsome Party leaders abandoned themselves to wild merriment when they relaxed. Only the most attractive actresses, the most expensive food and the finest imported liquor were served to them. The parties often lasted until dawn and usually by the end most of the dignitaries were so drunk they had to be carried to their cars by their guards. I remember one night, for example, when Yang Van, the head of Shanghai's Security Police and the man who had made Fan Su his secretary, became uncontrollably drunk. Waving a bottle of brandy, he sang for us an obscene but popular "yellow" song called "18-Touch," which the police had banned. Afterward, he announced that that morning his police had arrested some scoundrels who made their living by cheating at cards. He then bragged, "But I can do it better than they can." Thereupon, he proceeded to demonstrate his skill with a pack of cards, and he told us that at one time he also had made his living as a card cheat.

I did not enjoy these parties; they terrified me because I never knew what one of these powerful men might do next, but I did appreciate the chance to have some decent food. Ever since the new regime had started, the food shortage had been slowly getting worse. Rationing was now inaugurated and rice and sugar

145

were in especially short supply. We realized that the reason our mills were sent so little wheat was that the quoted figures on grain production were astronomically inflated.

One day, however, salesmen from the China Food Company entered our mills; they erected stalls and put up posters reading, COMRADES, BUY ORANGE MARMALADE TO DEMONSTRATE YOUR PATRIOTISM. The Party Secretary, over the loud-speaker, also urged us to buy the marmalade. His statement was: "Comrade workers, our Party and government always take thought for our health. Therefore they have instructed the China Food Company to prepare this nutritious marmalade for the workers. We must respond to the concern shown for us by buying more of it." Few of the workers were able to buy sufficient food for their families, but they knew that to escape being branded unpatriotic they would have to buy a few tins of the completely unfamiliar food whether they could afford it or not. They had to be given directions on how to eat it and at the inevitable group meetings they were made to express their "unanimous praise and gratitude."

A few weeks later, however, we learned the true story of the marmalade. Soviet Russia had placed a large order for the jam. The contract specifications stipulated that the skin of the fruit should be included. The translator, however, inadvertently omitted this part of the contract, with the result that the entire order was refused for being substandard. The Foreign Trade Bureau therefore had the Shanghai Trade Union dispose of the stock to the city's workers. The regime lost nothing on the transaction and the working class paid for the mistake.

As the food shortage became more acute, the regime began to encourage birth control. The population increase was now threatening to outstrip food production on a scale that could well mean danger to the regime's control of the mainland. The

Marxist-Leninist theory, however, was diametrically opposed to birth control. The propaganda stated that birth control in Communist China was basically different from that in "imperialist countries." The difference was not explained but no one ever dared question Party policy and we were all accustomed to the peculiar logic of the Communists.

The drive began with extensive press articles on the subject of birth control. Previously the papers had condemned it often and vehemently as an aspect of "reactionary thinking," but they now praised it. The China Pharmacy Company on the ground floor of the Wing On Building in Shanghai devoted a large space for the display and sale of contraceptives, and then all other large stores did the same. The Communists had young salesgirls explain the illustrated charts on birth control and describe how the contraceptives were used. Large crowds usually collected for these lectures but the effect on the population was insignificant. The authorities therefore attempted to enforce the measure directly onto the workers through their places of employment. Thus at our mills we were supplied with quantities of contraceptives which were distributed to our employees, the cost being deducted from their wages. During the lunch period, the clinic doctor lectured on birth control over the loud-speaker. Because both sexes ate in the dining hall, this caused agonizing embarrassment. I was told that at home, the workers suffered even more embarrassment. As an economy measure, they had been told to wash out and re-use the contraceptives; when the new articles appeared on the washline, children tended to steal them, thinking they were balloons. Birth control probably achieved some results, but I think that the workers generally disregarded the drive because for once the Party could not make a detailed check on their cooperation.

They also disregarded the regime's attempt to make the Chinese like the Russians. The workers never did really understand the relationship between the two countries. They had even more difficulty in understanding why one group of foreigners had been thrown out only to let another in. Moreover, this new group had the same advantages as the old. They were paid, for example, ten times the salary of a Chinese with equal ability. Worse, for several years they were given Hung Jao, Shanghai's most exclusive residential area which previously, even under the Japanese occupation, had not been closed to Chinese. It was now not only closed but was fortified and guarded. The Soviet experts could be seen everywhere in the Shanghai shopping area; they avidly bought up all the American and European watches, pens, cameras and other luxury imports which were still available but which no Chinese could afford.

In my mills, the workers were especially bitter because none of them was allowed to buy the white flour we milled; almost all of it went to Russia. To make matters worse, we were inflicted with a twenty-year-old Russian girl, an "expert" who was sent from Moscow to check our shipments for insects. We were supplied with fine tea and cigarettes for her refreshment and special plainclothes policemen were provided for her protection. We were ordered to treat her respectfully as "elder sister." Meanwhile she was rude in the orders she gave to our workmen. When an insect was found in the machinery, all of it had to be dismantled, cleaned and reassembled. The process took a full week. On the morning that the mill was once again ready to operate, she found another insect and again ordered the whole cleaning process to be repeated. This was too much. An experienced old technician grabbed the offending insect, put it in his mouth and ate it. "Let me see if I die from eating this one insect," he shouted. "We have been toiling night and day cleaning these machines for you. You are this exacting, but we have to eat potato flour while making wheat flour for your people to consume. We have not seen you greedy Russians bringing any food for the Chinese to eat. What is this so-called 'selfless assistance'? Who is assisting whom? I am ready to give up my old life . . ."

The girl could not understand Chinese, but evidently she understood that something was wrong. She left immediately and we did not see her again. Nevertheless, we were severely reproached by the Food Bureau. The mills' Party Secretary and Trade Union Chairman were transferred for "failing to educate the workers adequately." For a whole month, our mills held self-criticism meetings in which, as usual, I played the leading role. The sympathy of the workers for the old technician was so high that the authorities dared not punish him for almost a year. Thereupon he was put on the Honor Roll.

During the worst part of the transition period, the Chans and I felt that we had one small measure of security in J.P.'s contacts with high Party officials. His closest contact was with Pan Han-yin, first deputy to Chen Yi, Shanghai's mayor. Pan was an excellent orator; he was well educated and always well dressed and well mannered. He lacked that air of cunning and menace which most of the Communists had. We had become really friendly with him. He even asked J.P.'s children to call him "godfather." Chen Yi, we knew, was being groomed for a really high post in Peking and everyone believed that Pan would be made the mayor. Pan, therefore, received much deference from all quarters in Shanghai. Just when the appointment of the new mayor was due, Pan was called to Peking. We assumed that the trip would be for the purpose of conferring the title on him. The night before he left he had dinner with us at J.P.'s house and he seemed relaxed and happy.

Two days later, however, we were shocked to learn that he had been arrested for treason the moment he arrived in Peking.

149

No more details were given, but Pan was never heard of again. For our own protection, we now made a lightning-quick readjustment. We who had been his best friends spoke of him the most scathingly. The other officials and civic leaders, who only a few days before had been fawning over him, led the chorus of denunciation. I stated for the press: "I will be more vigilant in the future in recognizing traitors and in drawing a clear line between them and me. . . ." I remember watching J.P. go through a photograph album, his hands shaking. He took out every picture that included Pan and burned it.

Only a week later, the head of the Security Police, Yang Van, was also arrested. The charges against him were not made public, but he also disappeared. Tragically, poor Fan Su, who was beautiful but dumb, also suffered through her association with him. She was sent to prison for a year. When we saw her next she was unable to speak coherently and she looked like an old woman.

These experiences destroyed what little feeling of security we had. No one could deny that we had been close friends with Pan, who was now a traitor. If officials who had been as powerful as he and Yang Van were unable to command security in the new regime, what chance had we?

I decided that my plan to escape must be devised as quickly as possible. The most likely exit from Communist China, I decided, was Hong Kong. The thought that only three years ago I could have gone there whenever I wished tortured me. An exit permit now would seem like a reprieve from a death sentence.

After several weeks of painstaking thought, I hit upon a means of sounding out the mills' Party Secretary, with a minimum of risk, on the possibility of obtaining permission to visit Hong Kong. I told him about my father's death; my father's tomb, I had been informed by my brother, was nearly constructed and the burial ceremony would take place within a month. "I don't think I ought to go," I said to the Party Secretary, "but I would welcome your advice."

"You are quite right," the Secretary said. "The dead are dead. Turn your sorrow into energy to serve the people better."

This meant an emphatic "no." I still had far to go in building a place of "trust" for myself within the regime.

CHAPTER 7

Diligence is a treasure beyond price;
Caution is the talisman for survival.

—CHINESE PROVERB

My BEST opportunity for winning the authorities' trust stemmed from a chronic weakness of the Communists. Invariably, Communists assume that the truth about their social order cannot be revealed and that a falsified image of it must be presented to outsiders. The process of deceiving the foreigners resembles theatrical production. Each little play is carefully staged and rehearsed. The actors are required to be so skilled and trustworthy that suitable talent is always in short supply. Successful performers, therefore, can expect some small measure of security within the regime.

At first, no English-speaking, non-Communist "progressive" was trusted enough to be given a real part in the deception dramas. I became a performer only after I had proven helpful

153

in other lesser capacities, and also after the authorities had learned that unless people like me were used, the dramas could be fiascos.

I witnessed, for example, one of the early entertainment fiascos which unquestionably detracted from the regime's prestige. On this occasion, J.P. and I together with two other national capitalists were "invited" to meet a group of important British industrialists at the Shanghai railway station. We were under the tutelage of two Communist officials. One of them knew English, but not well enough to follow a general discussion in it. We therefore were instructed to pretend that we could not speak the language; the Communist then would act as our interpreter and thereby retain control of the situation.

When the substantial-looking foreigners descended from the train, saw our well-dressed delegation and were told that we had come to welcome them, they approached us with outstretched hands and friendly comments in English. We could only shake their hands, looking blank and bowing—and feeling mute, miserable and foolish. Matters were made worse by the boorish manners of our "interpreter." I still remember the baffled looks of the British visitors. One turned to a companion and said, "I can't understand it. Shanghai men like these always speak English." He then asked the interpreter who we were. The interpreter, however, did not know the word "industrialist" and said lamely that we were "merchants." The distinguished visitors were obviously not flattered to be met by a group of shopkeepers with a semiliterate interpreter. They withdrew into a kind of haughty reserve, and even the Communist officials understood that the visitors had been given a less than favorable impression of the regime.

Even the Russians could acquire an unfavorable impression in the early days of the regime. Once, for instance, a high Soviet official was met at the station by a delegation that included

Shanghai's best band. When the visitor appeared, the band burst into the well-known Russian song "You Are the Beacon." Later, when the Soviets entered a protest, the chagrined authorities learned that the song was the funeral march which had been played at Lenin's funeral.

Blunders like these forced the authorities to appoint more and better-trained men to the official Committee for the Entertainment of Foreign Visitors. By 1954, when Shanghai was receiving increasingly frequent and important foreign visitors, the entertainment was staged with a high degree of efficiency. The performers, although still under the watchful eyes of "interpreters," were permitted to speak English and were allowed more leeway in the interpretation of their roles. The interpreters, usually pig-tailed girl cadres, became simply reporters. Before each entertainment program, the performers were briefed on the background of the guests and were told how to answer the questions they could expect to be asked. The performers and the entertainment officials together worked out the acts and arranged for the props that would create the planned impression on the visitors.

From the beginning, J.P. was the star performer among the ten chosen showpiece capitalists. This was partly because he was China's biggest national capitalist, but also because he brought exceptional talent to his role. Moreover, after Pan Han-yin's arrest, J.P. no longer dared depend upon friendship with high officials for security; instead, he concentrated on making himself more valuable to the regime by further improving the performance he gave for visiting dignitaries. The result was that he was used almost too frequently; the authorities apparently feared that some foreigners might get the impression J.P. was the only important capitalist who supported the regime. I had often helped J.P. in his entertaining, and for once my American education was regarded as an advantage. Thus I also was able to establish myself in the profession of preventing foreigners from seeing an accurate picture of life in Communist China.

My life with the Communists now took on a new dimension. In the mills, the Party Secretary and I were on opposite sides, but the entertainment officials and I had to work together, each supporting the other, if we were to deceive the foreigners successfully. Even a small slip made by either of us could have international repercussions which could bring us both unfavorably to the attention of the authorities. Thus, whenever I was chosen to entertain a group of foreigners, I would be informed at least a week in advance. I would then attend meetings in which I would receive "guidance." Nevertheless, I was permitted to make suggestions which would be discussed fully before being either rejected, modified or accepted.

During the actual entertainment, the "interpreters" noted down everything that the visitors and I said and did. I myself had to write a full report on what had transpired between my guests and me. All the reports on what I had said and done were searched for discrepancies which, if found, were investigated immediately. Nevertheless, I felt safer in the presence of the interpreter cadres. They were anxious to report that the entertainment had achieved its planned objectives; any success therefore would be credited to me, and thus strengthen my position in the regime.

Moreover, the entertainment was not without pleasant aspects. My house, for example, was often supplied for the occasion with additional elegant appointments such as objets d'art, books, gramophone records, etc. Specially trained servants would always be sent by the officials. At least one extra motorcar would be put in my garage to make me seem more affluent, and I would be permitted to buy more gasoline than usual. I would be supplied with luxury food and imported cigarettes and liquor which normally were difficult to obtain. Even better was the fact that I was allocated fuel to heat my house if the entertainment was in winter; the fuel shortage was so severe that we had to do without heat except when we had foreign guests. But best of all was the feeling that if my entertainment was successful I would have moved a short distance toward the time when escape might be possible.

Conversely, if I gave only one unsuccessful performance or made an unintentional mistake, I would not be asked to participate in the entertainment again. Among my acquaintances were two showpiece capitalists whose performance had proven inadequate; the fact that they were denied further parts in the show was merely the first indication that they were out of favor with the regime. The chances of survival for anyone who had incurred the Communists' animosity were lessened considerably. Thus I valued highly every indication that the authorities continued to consider my performance satisfactory.

The sheer dishonesty of what I was doing, however, depressed me badly. It sometimes made me despise myself, and it increased my loathing for the Communists. Nevertheless, the worst aspect of the entertaining was the constant fear of a slip-up which would cost me the favor I was building up so carefully with the authorities.

Slip-ups, of course, did happen frequently. One I remember particularly occurred in early 1955 when the General Line was being implemented. By this time, my meetings with foreign visitors were often staged so as to seem spontaneous and unplanned; in other words, the officials would pretend to choose a businessman at random and bring the foreigners to talk to him unannounced. This called for even more careful planning by the cadres and skillful acting on my part.

Thus when a group of touring South Asian journalists called

on me "unexpectedly" one afternoon, I played the part of a surprised but delighted host. The questions they asked were the ones
that had been expected, and I answered them according to my
instructions. When we were having tea, however, one of the
journalists suddenly said to me, "Your servant. I knew I had
seen him before. He was one of the waiters at lunch today."

I tried not to panic. I knew that the foreigners had lunched
with officials who could not be connected with me in any way.
If the journalist thought about the situation, he would be sure
to realize that my tea party was staged. And if he wrote about
it as such after leaving the country, my career as a showpiece
capitalist was likely to be finished. I explained to him that, under
the new regime, I was financially more secure than previously
and thus tended to keep more servants than a bachelor really
needed. I therefore sometimes allowed my butler to earn extra
money by serving at special functions. Because I had not expected guests that afternoon, I had permitted him time off during
the lunch hour.

Happily, my guest seemed to accept this explanation and even
to be impressed. Nevertheless, my mind was racing with the
problem of how I would word my report, and I began writing
it the moment the visitors left. In my report, I blamed myself for
the doubling-up of the servant, but I suggested that henceforth
the officials should check on the assignment of the special servants with greater care. I emphasized, however, that I had been
able to turn into an advantage a situation which might have
been embarrassing. I was complimented on this two days later at
a meeting with the entertainment officials, and I was told that
my suggestion of checking servant assignments was accepted. I
felt that my efforts in this case were appreciated, but that I had
had a narrow escape.

The truth is, however, that the Communists rarely blundered

once they had perfected their means of deceiving foreigners. They took infinite pains to see that the entertainment went smoothly. Emphasis was placed on making it seem casual and spontaneous. This was easier than it may sound, because almost all visitors wanted to see the same things; rarely did a foreigner ask to see something for which a showpiece had not been carefully prepared. When this did happen, the visitor's request was refused so apologetically that he seldom felt anything was being hidden from him.

Moreover, each visitor was studied with such care that generally his behavior could be anticipated. He was shown only what would impress a person of his type the most. He also stayed in only the best hotels, all of which were reserved solely for the highest Communist officials or the foreigners. The shops within these hotels displayed luxury goods which only he—but not the Chinese people—was permitted to purchase, and the prices charged him were absurdly low. At the end of his visit he usually was given expensive and carefully chosen gifts, so that he would leave with a warm feeling of regard for his hosts.

We were hosts to three categories of foreign guests: those who came from the Soviet Union and the Socialist bloc, from the neutralist nations and from the "imperialist" countries. The act we put on for each was basically the same, but the attitude we were to show to each was different. With our "elder brothers" from the Soviet Union, for example, we could be relatively relaxed and informal. Because of the fraternal relationship, these guests expected to be shown only a favorable picture of the regime, and in fact they *intended* to see nothing else.

With the neutralists, we were to be as friendly as possible. Usually, the neutralists were idealists who *wanted* to believe our comforting fabrications, and they therefore were easy to deceive. Even Prime Minister Jawaharlal Nehru of India and President

Sukarno of Indonesia were apparently impressed by the staged productions they were shown.

The "imperialists," however, were apt to be more skeptical. We were to treat them with polite dignity, avoiding any touch of the old servility. We national capitalists were always apprehensive about receiving them, because the cadres then watched us with even greater care. The "imperialists" would try hard to discover something of the true nature of Communism, and more pains, therefore, had to be taken to keep it hidden from them.

An example I remember of the pains taken to create a good impression on foreigners concerned the wives of two visiting African officials. The Chans were instructed to have the two ladies to tea. In preparation for the event, Charlie's wife was told to buy a special doll for her three-year-old daughter. The doll was to be painted black, and the child was to be taught to think of it as something special. At mealtimes, therefore, Charlie's wife would ask the child to bring the doll, and we would all make a big fuss over it. My role was always to kiss the doll and ask the little girl, "Don't you wish you had a nice 'black auntie' like this?"

The child seemed to enjoy the attention she got with her new possession, and she appeared to like the doll well enough. One day, then, she was told that as a special treat some "black aunties" would visit her. Charlie's wife was told to buy a few chocolates. When the African ladies arrived, the little girl was to rush up to them and give each of them a kiss. The sweets were to be her reward.

Charlie's daughter did as she was told—much to our relief—but she was too shy to make the gesture seem really spontaneous. Nevertheless, it was remarkably successful. The two ladies were so touched that they had tears in their eyes. Once again we were surprised at the Communist skill at creating a desired impression.

What always surprised me even more, however, was the Communist custom of pretending to approve and support precisely what they really abhorred and suppressed. Family life was an example. Marriage Reform, which was inaugurated early in the regime supposedly to correct the abuses of arranged marriages and the dowry system, was implemented deliberately so as to break up as many families as possible. Moreover, the tactic of forcing family members to betray and denounce each other in the campaigns was effective in destroying family ties. Nevertheless, for foreigners, an elaborate show was always staged to create the impression that, under Communism, family living was highly regarded and vastly improved.

J.P. was especially good at putting on this show. A visitor would find J.P.'s wife contentedly knitting a sweater for her husband. Through the French windows, a neatly uniformed nurse wheeled a baby across the lawn while two dogs frisked about merrily. On a wall, a crucifix discreetly suggested freedom of worship. The bookshelves showed Shakespeare as well as Marx, and in another room, J.P.'s daughter practiced the piano; all of this implied cultural liberty. When J.P. entered he good-naturedly submitted to being measured by his wife for the sweater. His conversation was about the garden; one would think that he had nothing more to worry him than the correct fertilizer for the peonies. I remember the awed comment of the wife of a French visitor who witnessed this touching tableau. "I have never seen a more contented family," she said.

Invariably, J.P. would be asked how a great capitalist like him could be so contented and unworried under a system that was opposed to capitalism. J.P. would purse his lips and consider the question gravely: "I *was* worried at first," he would confess finally. "When the Communists liberated Shanghai, we were apprehensive, if not for our lives, at least for our property. We were also not quite sure we could rely on the Communists' promise to protect national capitalists." At this point, he would look his guest in the eye and his voice would ring with sincerity. "But the Communists *have* kept their promise. We have come to realize that the Chinese Communists never deceive people—"

The Communists made equal effort to deceive people about religion. Shanghai, in the old society, for example, had had hundreds of Buddhist temples. Now, less than ten were permitted to remain open. Moreover, anyone who exhibited religious tendencies was apt to be grouped with the "backward elements." Almost all the monks had been forced to return to civilian life. The few who remained were completely cowed showpiece monks. They were State employees who occupied State-operated temples; they even had their own trade union and, like everyone else, were made to attend group meetings to learn Party policy.

When the Tibetan Dalai Lama's visit was expected, however, the famous Yu Fe and Bubbling Well Temples, which had housed government offices for a long time and whose "temple" activities were confined to an ill-kept corner in each structure, were suddenly refurbished. The government offices moved out and more than US$250,000 was spent on redecoration in order to give the Dalai Lama the erroneous impression that the Communists encouraged religion. Thereafter, almost every foreign guest in Shanghai sooner or later found himself visiting these temples and listening to the monks' practiced speeches about the religious renaissance under the Communist Party.

The authorities apparently had the most difficulty with the showpiece workers. In the factories specially equipped and operated to illustrate socialism's industrial triumphs, the workers were carefully picked and trained; they almost always made the proper responses and gave the planned impression that they were working hard and enthusiastically for the regime. Shanghai, however, had a model village called Shao Yang Terrace in which the private life of the workers in the New China was demonstrated. The workers hated it so much that only a small percentage volunteered to live there, and the rest had to be "persuaded" to do so. The people lived in the village like animals in a zoo, under the constant scrutiny of visitors and officials. They had to be always clean and neat and dressed in their best clothes. They had to put on that peculiar act, a mixture of prudery, industriousness and childlike simplicity, which the Communists expect from the working class. Worst of all, they *and* their children had to be letter perfect in making the cadre-prepared stock answers to questions from visitors.

I know from my employees at the mills how much the workers dreaded going to Shao Yang Terrace. Whenever I accompanied a group of visiting foreigners through the village, I was always filled with sympathy for the inhabitants. The one small example of decent housing which the authorities did give to the workers was paid for by the workers with their last tiny bit of privacy and self-respect. I had the feeling that some of the more sharp-eyed observers were horrified by the inhabitants and perceived that the village was not intended for the workers as much as it was meant to create another illusion about the regime.

My own most worrisome experiences with creating illusions about the regime came from foreigners who attempted ruses to get under-the-surface glimpses of life in Communist China. The ruses seldom if ever worked, although the foreigner was always made to think they did. Once, I joined the Chans when they were entertaining an English businessman who planned to write about his experiences in Communist China. He suddenly turned to me and said, "Mr. Loh, would you mind accompanying me to the next room? I want to have a few words in private with you."

I immediately glanced at the "interpreter" who had been writing down the conversation. She nodded slightly, which meant that I had to go with the guest.

As soon as we were behind the closed doors of the other room, he said to me, "Whatever we say will be between just the two of us. Now, tell me frankly, are you really a capitalist? Or are you just a Party member pretending to be a capitalist in order to win over visitors?"

His naïveté exasperated me. Couldn't he see that the time of our private talk was being noted and would be reported by several people? Couldn't he guess that I would have to report this conversation, and that I was in the dangerous position of having no one to confirm it for me? If, after he returned to England, he wrote some fictitious version of our talk, I would be held answerable. Even if he disguised the name, time and place of the talk, it could be traced to me, simply because every contact he made while in Communist China was recorded.

Moreover, his question was hardly intelligent. If I were really a disguised Party member, I certainly would not betray the Party by telling him so. After I convinced him that I was a real capitalist, however, he asked an even more naïve question. "Since we are both capitalists and not Communists," he said, "tell me honestly whether you really favor the regime or are only made to pretend you do?"

If I had told him that I was forced to pretend I favored the regime, and if back in England he wrote that I was anti-Communist, what did he think would happen to me? I said passionately that I loved the Communist Party and the regime more than my life. He replied that he was disappointed in me, but I was concerned only with getting back to where the cadres could record my conversation. Moreover, for the next two weeks I had to endure interrogation by suddenly suspicious entertainment officials on what had "really transpired" between the Englishman and me.

The suspicion could not have come at a worse time. I did not realize it then, but my efforts in the regime's behalf were already bringing me favorably to the attention of Party officials. I probably was even under consideration for positions of greater prestige. In any case, the authorities now exposed me to another long and severe test.

The test was made through a campaign which was begun in early 1955 and became known as the "Elimination of Counter-Revolutionaries." It must not be confused with the 1951–2 "*Suppression* of Counter-Revolutionaries" which had disposed of the ex-Nationalists. The new campaign was directed against the intelligentsia. The 1951–2 "Thought Reform" had suppressed the intellectuals who had had no definite political convictions, but generally had passed over those who had consistently supported Communist principles. The authorities apparently realized that these leftist intellectuals would have seen enough of Communist practices by now to have become disillusioned with the regime. Thus another possible source of political opposition was to be eliminated.

The "elimination" began with an all-out propaganda attack on a well-known writer named Hu Feng. He had been pro-Marxist since the 1930's and had been one of the early members of a Communist front organization called the Left Wing Writers Group. The authorities, however, wanted writers to serve only the workers, peasants and soldiers. To this end, writers were subjected to such strict control that they either gave up in despair and merely turned out uninspired propaganda or they made the effort to retain their individuality. Those of the latter group were generally the older and long-established writers, and they always were in more or less open conflict with the authorities.

Hu Feng was an outspoken member of this group. He believed, for example, that political indoctrination for writers could be profitably abolished and that certain literary magazines should be exempt from Party control. Worse, he apparently led a group of like-minded writers and attempted through concerted action to persuade the authorities to his viewpoint. Party policies, however, were to be implemented—never questioned—and even the hint of united opposition to them was sure to bring swift retaliation.

Thus people at group meetings throughout the country suddenly found themselves denouncing Hu Feng and his clique. Next we found ourselves examining his ideas and looking for any similarities between them and our own. Finally, we were engaged in a full-scale campaign to uncover any "counter-revolutionary" thinking among the fellow members of our particular discussion groups.

The Elimination of Counter-Revolutionaries was not as brutal as Thought Reform had been, but it followed a similar procedure. Everyone classed as an intellectual prepared an autobiography that began at the age of eight and concentrated on the ideas he had had during his lifetime. Each paper, then, was studied by the other members of the author's group who searched for evidence of past unacceptable ideas. Generally, the cadres allowed most of the autobiographies of a group to be passed with only token criticism and warnings, but they chose from each group one or two "heavy points" who received concentrated attention. A heavy point endured pressure from his fellow group members to confess the "real truth" of his past thinking. The suffering of this unfortunate was intended as an object lesson for his companions, who would thus be discouraged from harboring unacceptable ideas. In my discussion group, to my dismay, I found that I was made the heavy point.

No matter what I wrote in my autobiography, my companions rejected it. And with each rejection, the scorn, insults and threats they heaped on me grew worse. During the day in my office at the mills, I faced much the same from the workers. No one who has never lived day and night as the focal point of such vilification and hatred can understand the effect it has. I could think of nothing but the paper I was having to write and rewrite endlessly. I was long past caring what I confessed to; I only wanted desperately to discover what the Communists expected of me.

At the same time I did not expect to be accused and punished as a counter-revolutionary. In my case, no real evidence of unacceptable thinking existed; moreover, I had given every indication that I supported the regime and endorsed Party policies. I remembered the case of my friend Professor Long who, during Thought Reform, had broken under pressure and had confessed to crimes of which the authorities later exonerated him; nevertheless, because he had collapsed he had been regarded as being "unable to stand up to the test of political purity." Thus I guessed that I was merely being tested, and my only real fear was that, through some unwitting mistake, I might fail to pass.

During this time of mounting tension, I was still allowed an occasional night off from my group meeting struggle to put on my act for visiting foreigners. This was when the Englishman had taken me off alone to ask me his ridiculous questions. I was fighting desperately to survive in Communist China, and he was "disappointed" in me because I would not tell him that I disapproved of Communism. How I hated him.

Although my own survival was not directly connected with the outcome of the Elimination of Counter-Revolutionaries Campaign, other intellectuals were not so fortunate. Mr. Ming, an old schoolmate of mine, for example, told me about a colleague of his. After Thought Reform, Ming had been given a low-grade university teaching job. He lived with other teachers in university quarters; his were No. 12. One night at 2 A.M., he was awakened by pounding on his door. He opened it to find two plainclothes policemen and six uniformed security police armed with automatic weapons, which were leveled at him. One of the police said, "Don't move, you counter-revolutionary."

Ming was grabbed roughly and handcuffs were put on him. While a rope was being tied around his neck, a college security officer appeared and said, "Not *him*. It's number 21." Ming was released, and the police left to arrest the man in No. 21, who was never heard of again. Ming suffered a nervous collapse and for several days was unable to speak coherently.

Meanwhile, the wife of the man in No. 21 stayed on in the quarters with their two children, one an infant and the other a three-year-old girl. One night two weeks later, the wife's amah came to Ming highly agitated. She asked him to come at once because she could not wake her mistress. Ming, of course, did not dare go near the family of an acknowledged counter-revolutionary, but he helped the amah telephone the authorities. Within half an hour the security police arrived at No. 21, and later Ming learned from the amah what happened.

The wife was lying on the bed unconscious, an empty Lysol bottle on the floor beside her. She had the baby in her arms, and the three-year-old girl was clutching her hand screaming for her. The police cadre studied the scene, standing with his fists on his hips and his legs apart. Finally, he spat on the floor. "You stupid intellectuals think you can fool *us*," he said. "I know you're putting on an act. And I warn you. You'll be sorry if you don't stop this nonsense immediately—"

The woman, of course, was not putting on an act, and she died. The cadre had made a mistake for which he probably was reprimanded.

168

Nevertheless, if I had been the cadre, I might well have taken the same approach. This was because Party members and people who worked directly for the government had to be concerned with the problem of "right deviation" or "left deviation." If the woman had been feigning suicide, and if the cadre had given her help or even sympathy, he could have been accused of leniency to a counter-revolutionary's wife who, according to the Communists, was equally unacceptable. The principle was that leniency to the people's enemies was cruelty to the people. The cadre's leniency therefore would have been interpreted as bourgeois sentimentality. He would have made the mistake of "rightist deviation"—a serious error in *principle*—and his punishment would have been severe—possibly as severe as if he had been a counter-revolutionary himself.

"Left deviation," however, came from being merely overzealous or harsh "for the good of the people"; this would be only a *technical* error for which the penalty, if any, would be light. By assuming that the woman was feigning suicide, therefore, the cadre was exposing himself only to the possibility of "left deviation"; in fact, he had no choice, because any other assumption, based on human compassion, could have endangered him with the fatal "right deviation." This is one of the means whereby Communists are dehumanized and given the peculiar robotlike quality that almost always identifies them.

This situation also explained the anxiety I endured during the struggle against me in the Elimination of Counter-Revolutionaries Campaign. If the cadre who controlled my discussion group made the mistake of "left deviation" and overzealously forced my companions to exert too much pressure on me, I might well become another Professor Long.

As the weeks passed, however, I slowly perceived that the period of my stay in the United States interested the cadre the most. Finally, I got on the right track. What was wanted from me mostly was confirmation of the weird picture Communists have of America. I had only to remember the anti-American propaganda and invent personal experiences that made the usual misconceptions seem accurate. Thus I wrote fictional stories of having witnessed horrible scenes in which American police suppressed workers and minority racial groups. I described incidents in which I had suffered unspeakable humiliation. I listed the names and guessed-at addresses of every American I had known, and when the list was not considered long enough I added to it a score of fictitious names and addresses. In every case, these Americans, according to my account, had denounced the Communist Party and had persecuted me because I would not accept their viewpoint. Anyone who read my autobiography would think that I had barely managed to escape from America. I found that the worse I made my picture of the United States, the lighter I could make my own errors in thinking. Ultimately, I needed to say merely that, because of my bourgeois background, some of my own feelings and attitudes had been similar to the American imperialists', and only now did I realize that I had harbored such evil thoughts.

After eight weeks of being struggled against, my autobiography, now 70 pages long, was suddenly accepted as "relatively thorough." The ordeal was over. Later, I figured that the authorities must have checked with Frank Chou and Yung Won-yuan, the two underground Party members at Wisconsin University; both would have reported that in the U.S. I had not been pro-Nationalist and had not engaged in anti-Communist activity. This may have been the final confirmation needed to end my case.

I felt now that I had successfully passed a test. An easing of the attitude toward me was noticeable. The workers and cadres at the mill were as unpleasant as ever, but I found that I no longer had much to do in my office and was not required to go there often. Instead, my time was taken up in long conferences with Entertainment Committee officials. I also attended innumerable meetings with J.P. and Charlie in the Federation of Industry and Commerce, the front organization which was much concerned with the problems of the transition to socialism. Finally, my participation in political affairs as an "elected" representative to the Shanghai People's Congress was increased. I was at last moving toward a higher political status within the regime.

Nevertheless, after the Elimination campaign, the atmosphere in Communist China was once more altered drastically. The whole intellectual stratum of society, including even the pro-Marxist-Leninist intellectuals, was reduced to a beaten, helpless minority too terrified to express original ideas any longer and capable only of parroting Party policy. A few, however—probably no more than a few hundred—had come through the ordeal like me, sufficiently crushed and remolded so as to be considered potentially acceptable to the regime. This meant that they could expect to receive positions of increasing prestige. They would never be really trusted, of course—they would lose their positions the first time they showed personal initiative or individuality, and would be suppressed at the slightest indication of disaffection—but at least they could now hope to survive.

Of this small group, the majority of those who were, like me, Western-educated, were older men. They had returned from abroad in time to establish themselves solidly with the Communists before the new regime controlled the mainland. The few who were about my age either had made up their minds to throw their lot once and for all with the regime and were working toward the hope of being accepted as Party members—or like me were planning escape. The handful who might be planning escape stood out in sharp relief for the simple reason that they had no family ties which the authorities could use as a hold. Thus, at this point, my most important problem was to alleviate the automatic suspicion I aroused by not having a wife and children.

The opera singer Mai Mee offered the only solution I could think of. I made a conscious effort to put Li-li out of my mind, and I began an act which I worked out as carefully as I did the performances for the foreign visitors. I let it be known that I was hopelessly infatuated with Mai Mee. "Isn't it just my luck," I would say with a calculated mixture of sadness and bitterness, "to fall in love with a married woman?" Occasionally, when I was with Communist officials, I would act despondent enough so that I would be asked about my troubles. I would let them drag out of me the confession of my unrequited love and I would ask for advice. I had to be careful not to offend the puritanism of the Communists; if I had suggested that I actually coveted another man's wife, I would be considered to have degenerate ideas. My hopeless love was regarded as bourgeois sentimentality. I was advised to "forget such nonsense and devote my energy to the people." Nevertheless, the Communists considered sentimentality one of the weaknesses expected of people like me, and my pretense therefore was more effective with them than it would have been with more normal human beings.

The normal relationship between all human beings in China was further altered by the Elimination campaign. Although the campaign turned out to be against only one segment of society, the terror was spread throughout the entire population. It must be understood that the pressure from the authorities came in a kind of rhythm. Suppression was inflicted, released slightly, and then applied again. Each time the weight descended on us, our apprehension was greater and fear sank deeper. People now were increasingly frightened of each other, and we were so wary of even our closest friends and relatives that free discussion was almost impossible.

I remember the evening when this was brought home to me. I was with the Chans, relaxing in their living room—J.P., Charlie, their wives and me. The children were in bed, and the servants had retired. J.P. happened to mention something about military conscription, and Charlie suddenly said, "What a pity I am over thirty years old, and thus do not have a chance to be conscripted as I would wish. I regret that I miss this opportunity to serve my country and my people."

For a moment, we were silent as we adjusted to the shock of hearing "group-meeting talk" in a private living room.

Charlie's wife then said quietly, "You are in your house with your family, Charlie. You needn't speak like that to us."

But she was wrong, and we all knew it. I think that each of us was picturing in his mind what would happen if one of us were found unacceptable to the regime. If we were then to save ourselves we would have to denounce him and use our knowledge of him, acquired from years of close friendship, to betray him. Instinctively each of us in that group realized that the others represented the source of his greatest danger. For months, although we outwardly seemed unchanged, our conversation together had been the most inconsequential "small talk" interspersed with such "safe" ideas as Charlie had automatically expressed. I know also that when Charlie made his comment each of us experienced a new depth of despair, but we were afraid even to show our anguish. Instead, we returned to the meaningless chatter.

The same night that Charlie made his comment, I began to keep a diary. A lesson I had learned thoroughly from the Elimination campaign was that what we could say with impunity today might be regarded as a capital offense a year later. Many who had been suppressed in the campaign had been heroes not long before. Thus, in my diary, I noted down what I had said during the day in public and in private, and I worked at making all my utterances "correct" and model.

I also worked harder at making Mai Mee seem my reason for not marrying. When she returned on a tour to Shanghai that summer, I immediately booked a seat for every one of her performances. I deepened my air of despondency and tried to look like a man who loved hopelessly from afar. The Communists who saw my act did not bother to hide their impatience with me, but at least this indicated that my deception was working.

In fact, the only trouble was that it worked too well. Mai Mee had been in Shanghai a week when the story of my silent suffering for love of her reached *her* ears.

Until then, our relationship had been the same as before. After the performances, I would visit her in her rooms at the theater for an hour of pleasant conversation. We offered each other easy companionship and a welcome temporary escape from the difficulties of our separate and completely different lives. Moreover, she had been following my advice on how to avoid trouble with the Communists, and her position in the regime was more secure; this knowledge added an intriguing conspiratorial spice to the indescribable delight of being able to relax together and to act for a while like normal human beings.

One night when I arrived at her rooms, however, I found that the atmosphere was subtly changed. Mai Mee was less talkative than usual, and I caught her several times studying me with sidelong glances. "Would it interest you to know," she said, when she handed me a cup of tea, "that I have decided to get a divorce?"

I almost dropped the cup. If she did get a divorce, my excuse for not seeking a wife would be gone. In order to confirm my act of hopeless love, I would then have to woo Mai Mee. If she accepted, she would immediately become a hostage for my behavior, and I therefore would have to give up any hope for escape. "I don't know what to say," I stammered.

"Then I'll say it for you," she said. She sank down on a cushion and looked up at me mischievously. "I think we ought to marry—"

In my defense, let me say that I was genuinely tempted. Despite my unchanged feelings about Li-li, I had thought many times that Mai Mee would make a perfect wife for me; in fact, by being married to her, we both could achieve more security in Communist China than either of us could otherwise expect. Moreover, I think I really did want her, and living with a girl of such wit and charm promised endless delight. At the same time, I could not face the horror of devoting the rest of my life to the degrading deceptions which the Communists demanded. By now, I was almost obsessed with the idea of escape, and in fact only the hope of it enabled me to get through each day. Thus, at this moment, although my resolve was weakened the most, it did not break. I therefore could not marry Mai Mee and, worse, I could not let her know that I had no such intention.

I took her hand, and stammered something about how fond of her I was. She took my confused utterances to mean that I was too honorable to speak fully of love to her as long as she already had a husband. I felt that I was the worst scoundrel who ever lived; my only rationalization was that decent people do not survive in Communist China, and I would have to be a scoundrel if I was ever again to have the chance to live like a decent human being.

In my subsequent meetings with Mai Mee, I found a means of temporarily putting off the subject of marriage. She had the idea that because of my education, background, and business experience I would make an ideal manager for her and her opera company. Actually, the job would have been ideal, and unquestionably we could have done well together. I pretended, however, that if we married I would want her to give up her career, knowing that she would never agree to it. Obviously, however, she was confident that she could bring me around to her viewpoint once she had a divorce, and meanwhile therefore she tactfully dropped the subject.

As a result of our increased intimacy, we no longer bothered to meet discreetly only in her rooms. I took her to two small dinners at the Chans' house and once to a restaurant. Gossip about us immediately spread. I was worried that the Communists might think of me as a "degenerate" type for going out with a married woman, but she herself was already saying publicly that she intended to divorce her husband. Fortunately, the Communists I knew accepted this as adequate. In effect, I had confirmed the act I had previously put on, and they believed that at last I might settle down to marry. Thus, for the time being, the suspicions about me were lulled.

This was in mid-1955. Although we did not fully realize it, the Communists were preparing to intensify their drive to introduce socialism. In fact, the Elimination of Counter-Revolutionaries had been a preliminary move intended to stifle in advance the criticism they could otherwise have expected of the harsh measures they planned.

The authorities turned their attention first to the peasants. During the 1950 Land Reform, millions of landlords had been liquidated and their holdings distributed among the grateful peasants. For a short time this had resulted in increased production, but the government taxes had been as bad as, or worse than, the previous rents. Only the most efficient farmers or the owners of the best lands could attain economic security. The others

176

tended to sell their holdings to those better off, and a new "rich peasant" class had risen.

To make matters worse, the authorities had been pushing the peasants toward cooperativization. In key areas throughout the country, the farmers first had been badgered into organizing "mutual aid teams" in which the fields were tilled jointly but private ownership of the crops, land and tools was retained. From the "mutual aid teams" the farmers had been made to join "voluntarily" the "elementary agricultural producers' cooperatives." In these, each peasant's land was donated to the cooperative but he retained title to it and received dividends like a shareholder in a corporation. His main income, however, was calculated on the number of "work days" he contributed, the value varying according to the type of work. Finally, the authorities managed to inaugurate a few "advanced" agricultural cooperatives, similar to the Soviet collective farms, in which the peasants turned over all their land to the cooperative and depended solely on their "workday" wages for their livelihood.

The success of these cooperative-type ventures depended on the farmers' willingness to work as hard "for the people" as for themselves. Self-interest, however, had been traditionally the motivation of the Chinese peasants, and all of them resented the coercion that the cadres had used. The result was that production in the cooperatives was so low that their usefulness was doubted by many senior Communist officials. A few provincial officials even allowed wide-scale dissolution of cooperatives in their areas.

By 1955, the failure of the cooperatives together with the rise of a new "rich peasant" class had played havoc with the agrarian economy and the Communists were compelled to adopt drastic measures. Mao Tse-tung himself spent several months touring rural areas studying the problem. His conclusion was that more, not less, cooperativization should be encouraged. He foresaw "throughout the countryside, a new upsurge in agricultural co-operativization." The nation braced itself for another bloody campaign. Within a few months, more than 90 percent of China's agrarian population had "voluntarily" joined cooperatives of either the "elementary" or the "advanced" types.

We urban dwellers received only the backlash of this grue-some campaign. Some overzealous official, for example, appar-ently became carried away with the propaganda and decided that all hands were needed on the land. Thus everyone who could be spared in the city was given the fare to migrate to the countryside. Two of my younger servants were caught up in this movement. They returned after several weeks with stories of appalling chaos. The thousands of urban dwellers had been called to the land with no real plan or purpose. They had no place to go, almost nothing to eat, and little if anything to do. Often, a law-and-order problem was created by the rapid influx. Funds for solving the problem by giving the people fares to return to the cities were not readily available and the situation became steadily worse. Meanwhile the demoralized farmers were killing off the livestock and eating all the meat they could get. They were hiding food supplies and even using their best clothes for daily wear; this was because they now realized that soon all their possessions would be taken from them by the State.

Despite the incredible inefficiency and waste, however, the Communists achieved their aim. By the end of 1955 the peasants were landless, helpless, docile and completely dependent on the whim of the authorities.

The authorities, therefore, could turn their attention away from the peasants and concentrate on another group. One night in early December, I received a confidential telephone call from the Secretary-General of the Federation of Industry and Commerce. I was informed that I must attend a meeting to be held at the Sino-Soviet Friendship Hall at a specified time and that both the call and the meeting were to be considered confidential.

When I arrived at the hall, I found that about eighty of Shanghai's top businessmen had been ordered to attend. I immediately found J.P. and Charlie, but neither of them seemed to know what the meeting was for. Just when everyone was becoming apprehensive, the main door to the hall opened and Chen Yi, who now was the country's Vice-Premier, appeared. He held open the door and Mao Tse-tung entered.

The Communist Chairman is tall for a Chinese; he is a heavy, soft-looking man who appears younger than his pictures usually suggest. He is very slow. He walks with his toes pointed out; he takes short steps and swings his arms more than seems necessary for his ponderous gait. His face is animated. He smiles often, and his expression is usually friendly and mild. He gives the impression of being a kindly, simple, honest peasant. A cigarette is almost always held between his pudgy fingers, and his teeth are stained black from chain-smoking.

We all stiffened with surprise, and I heard a gasp from the assembled businessmen. We could hardly believe that we were really seeing the world-famous figure. Chen Yi introduced us individually to Chairman Mao. We were too nervous and confused to do more than murmur an automatic greeting.

Mao then eased himself into the center chair at the speakers' table, from which the other tables were arranged like the rungs of a ladder. We found our places, and sat down bewildered. No one touched the cigarettes which were on all the tables.

"Why don't you smoke?" Mao asked us calmly. "It won't hurt you. Churchill has smoked throughout his long life and he is in good health. In fact, the only man I know who doesn't smoke but has lived long is Chiang Kai-shek."

179

We all laughed at this. I could feel the tension dissipating. Unquestionably, Mao was making a good impression on us.

Mao began by praising the great contribution the "national capitalist friends" had made in the past. "Now I have come from Peking to seek your advice," he went on. Many businessmen, he said, had been requesting that the socialist transformation of private enterprise should be hastened, "lest the national bourgeoisie lag behind in the progress toward socialism."

"I don't think I can agree with that," he informed us, "but I am not well informed on the subject. I want to listen to your opinions. I have brought only my two ears to this meeting, and if you expect to hear more from me, you will be disappointed—"

In a formal address before a large gathering, Mao speaks poorly, but his slow drawl is remarkably effective in a small, casual group. An elaborate tea had been served to us and by the time we had finished, most of us had our wits about us again. Mao urged us to "speak freely" and he sounded as if he meant it.

J.P., as the leading national capitalist, spoke first. He paid the leader some graceful compliments. "We feel," he said then, "that the Party should seriously consider accelerating the transformation of private enterprise to socialism." He mentioned the major problems of the transformation but said that, at the present pace, more than 20 years would be required to change all the existing private firms into Joint State-Private enterprises. "This is much too slow," he said.

Thereafter leading representatives of all the different types of business spoke in much the same vein. They all said that socialism should be introduced with the least possible delay, and some suggested that the transformation of private enterprise could be made in as little as five years.

Mao listened attentively for two hours. When the speeches were over he thanked us and said he would give serious thought to our opinions. He still felt, however, that before deciding to accelerate the pace of transformation he would have to consider carefully the best interests of the "national capitalist friends."

After he was gone, the businessmen were skeptical. Most of them had been counting on the original understanding that 25 years would be allowed for the transformation. They realized now that they would be "self-supporting laborers" much sooner. The consensus was that this unhappy event would take place within six years.

Only a few weeks after Mao's friendly talk with us, however, the authorities announced that in Shanghai the transformation was to be accomplished within the next *six days*.

CHAPTER 8

Ah, you should smile that you
Have passed successfully through all these ups and downs.

— SU TUNG-PO

THE ANNOUNCEMENT that the "peaceful transformation from capitalism to socialism" was to be made within six days stunned the Shanghai businessmen. I never thought of myself as a businessman, however, and my reaction was that the situation offered a heaven-sent opportunity to bring myself dramatically to the attention of the authorities.

By this time, early 1956, Charlie Chan was the chairman and I was the deputy chairman of the "Working Committee of Young Businessmen." The "young businessmen" numbered about 18,000 and were affiliated with a Communist front organization, the "Democratic Youth Association of Shanghai." The "progressive" young businessmen, therefore, became the activists in the campaign to socialize the country's nominally private enterprise. As the leaders of this group, Charlie and I worked out a system of "shock-attack teams" which were to facilitate the transformation. Our team became the model which was duplicated by the hundreds in Shanghai during the next few days and by the thousands throughout the rest of the country.

Shanghai, however, contained half of all the business firms in China, and thus our Shock-Attack Teams had the most to do. We worked closely with the Federation of Industry and Commerce. We notified the businessmen of the special immediate meetings. We helped the cadres explain the campaign, especially to the less well-educated businessmen. We put pressure on the few who were reluctant to give up their enterprises. We aided the businessmen in making out their applications for the Joint State-Private status.

And, most of all, we cooperated with the propaganda cadres and the press to publicize the campaign. Announcements and speeches had to be made, news released and slogans written, placards printed and pictures taken. We helped the Federation of Industry and Commerce to create competition between the separate trade groups to achieve 100 percent application first. As soon as all the applications from one of the guilds were in, we staged an elaborate parade of the members. We had banners, bands, drums, gongs, firecrackers and slogan-shouters. Crowds were collected to cheer. Cooperating with trade unions, student associations and women's organizations, we placed "encouragement stations" along the route of march. As the paraders approached, the encouragers would shout such slogans as "Salute the patriotic national capitalists who are marching bravely toward socialism," or "Welcome our national capitalist friends to join our socialist family." Pretty girls would give flowers and refreshments to the marchers. The parade would be led by men carrying stacks of large red envelopes which contained the applications. The envelopes would be delivered, with appropriate speeches and ceremony, to the head of the Federation of Industry and Commerce. Thereupon the parade would proceed to the various government and Party headquarters to "report the good news." The hitherto despised businessmen had suddenly become the country's heroes and received high praise for having taken "the road to socialism."

Charlie and I received high praise for our role in the campaign; during that week we were featured almost daily in every paper in the country. Nevertheless, I had never worked so hard; I did not once get more than four hours of sleep at night.

Moreover, my activity on the model Shock-Attack Team was only a part of the effort. As a leading member of the Shanghai Federation of Industry and Commerce, I was put in charge, for the campaign, of the section that included the city's eight flour-milling companies and more than 100 rice-processing plants. This meant that I was responsible for seeing that applications from these firms were sent in according to the timetable. It also meant that I had the honor of handing over the big red envelope of these applications to the Federation Chairman, and thus received the acclaim for the owners who had "accepted socialist remolding."

On the sixth day of this remolding we reached the climax of the "high tide of socialist transformation." Private enterprise in China no longer existed; all commerce and industry became functions of the State. The occasion was celebrated with wild jubilation. The city's streets were jammed with shouting, chanting, singing, dancing throngs led by activists carrying banners and placards. The din made by bands, gongs, drums and firecrackers went on around the clock.

The formal ceremony took place in the Sino-Soviet Friendship Hall. J.P. handed the mayor an enormous red envelope symbolizing all the applications made by Shanghai businessmen for the Joint State-Private status. The mayor announced that Shanghai was "entering socialism." In between the speeches, cheering and slogan-shouting, delegations representing different classes such as workers, peasants, students, etc., burst into the hall to congratulate their "national capitalist friends." They paraded in the aisles with bands, banners and placards. The scene reminded me of the Presidential nomination conventions in the U.S.

The next day, a huge rally was held in the former race course, which was now the "People's Square." Here the people were made to demonstrate their joy informally. They danced the Communist-approved folk dances and sang patriotic songs. The authorities encouraged elaborate dancing parties to be held throughout the city for the next fortnight.

I still had no time, however, to celebrate "entering socialism." The Chans, as the country's leading capitalists, were in effect the spokesmen for their class. During this period, they were required to make innumerable speeches and press statements. By now I had learned well the distinctive Communist language, and I acquired the job of writing most of both the Chans' speeches and articles. Although I was only a ghost-writer, I knew that my efforts did not escape the notice of the authorities. Thus, by being self-effacing about this writing, I could strengthen the impression that I was a sincere supporter of the regime who understood Communist theory and policy thoroughly. Under J.P.'s name, I wrote two articles for the *People's Daily* which were reprinted in papers throughout the world. I also wrote for J.P. several speeches that were tape-recorded and given international broadcast.

This material and all the Chinese Communist propaganda at the time emphasized the "miracle" of businessmen happily surrendering their enterprises. The inference was that they clamored for socialism because its benefits had been proven to them

186

by the patient, kindly, generous, always truthful, meticulously honest and infinitely wise Communists. People in the Communist bloc and the more naïve in the neutralist nations accepted this explanation without question. I have gathered that the Westerners, however, have been confused ever since by the picture of businessmen begging to be beggared.

It is true that the Chinese businessmen did exhibit wild enthusiasm, but they acted out of fear. Each had been made to understand that his future depended on his contribution during the "high tide of socialist transformation." Once he had given up his enterprise, he knew that his sole means of livelihood would depend on the whim of the Communists. In short, he was struggling with almost hysterical intensity simply for survival.

Moreover, he knew he would not survive at all if he refused to apply for Joint State-Private status. Of the 165,000 firms in Shanghai, I knew of only one whose owner did not make the application. He was an elderly man whose enterprise was a medium-size paper mill. I spoke to him and attempted, for his own good, to make him change his mind. He was too panic-stricken, however, to face the future without the possession of the enterprise which, throughout his life, had been his sole means of security. He quickly lost his possession, of course; immediately after the campaign the government cut off his source of raw materials and refused to place further orders with him. The bank refused him loans. Within two months, he was bankrupt. He was sued by his employees' Trade Union and by the Tax Bureau. He was arrested and sentenced to the work gangs of labor reform.

Most of the businessmen, however, had been remolded during the "softening-up" period of the previous year and a half. In this period, the owners of pilot projects for Joint State-Private Enterprise had enjoyed every possible advantage. The others had suffered continual persecution and harassment; many, therefore, tried to escape their troubles by asking the government to put their firms into the joint status, but they had always been refused. Thus, by the time of the campaign, they were more than willing to do anything the authorities demanded.

A final inducement for businessmen to apply for the Joint State-Private status concerned the nature of the campaign itself. All of us had expected that "crossing the barrier to socialism" would entail the brutality and horror of Five-Anti. The regime's reputation abroad, however, had never fully recovered from the excesses of that campaign, and this time, therefore, the authorities took the trouble to create an impression of joy. When we found that in the campaign we were to be heroes instead of victims, we were almost dizzy with relief. Thus some of our joy was genuine, although none of it came from "entering socialism" as the propaganda claimed.

Moreover the joy was short-lived. As soon as the campaign was over we ceased being regarded as heroes. We waited apprehensively to learn how we were to be victimized.

All private enterprise was expropriated by the government under the so-called "Redemption-Purchase Policy." The term was pure Communist double-talk; the property of the capitalists was neither purchased nor redeemed. Nevertheless, the capitalists did receive token compensation. An elaborate inventory was taken of the assets of every firm. The cadres who directed the inventory program made the assessments at an average of about one-fifth of the real value. Each owner, then, learned that he would be credited with 5 percent per year of the assessed value of the property he had so patriotically turned over "to the people." Moreover, this annual "fixed interest" of 5 percent would be paid for only seven years. Finally, he and his executive capitalist-class employees would receive from the government the same salaries they had been drawing previously.

The details of this arrangement were worked out over a six-month period. As usual, the pretense was maintained that the capitalists themselves, through their mass-organization meetings, had suggested the arrangement which the government finally had magnanimously accepted. Immediately upon this acceptance, the capitalists found themselves beseeching the authorities to shorten the seven-year period of payments and to lessen the amounts credited to them. "Do not hold us back," we would plead. "Allow us to forge ahead into socialism. Give us the chance to rid ourselves of evil exploitation and become self-supporting laborers—"

Once in reply to such requests, I heard Director Liu of the United Front Works Department of the Party's Shanghai Committee say that while he welcomed "the attitude of capitalist friends who wish to wipe out the last vestige of exploitation," Peking could not accept the offer for fear that "our friend Mr. Nehru in India would not approve of it." This was meant as a joke, of course, but it indicated that what little compensation the businessmen did receive was given only for the purpose of deceiving foreigners.

The foreigners were further deceived by the use of the wholly inaccurate term "Joint State-Private" status. The propaganda abroad implied that the assessments were made in order that the government could give just compensation for only a *share* of each enterprise and that, therefore, the original owner and the State had become equal partners in running the firm. In China, however, the businessmen were made to understand clearly that henceforth they had no rights whatsoever in their firms and that what they received was not meant to be "compensation"; the

189

payments were intended solely to ease their "climb over the socialist barrier."

Nevertheless, the small businessmen quickly found that what they received would not enable them to make the climb at all. Eighty percent of the Shanghai firms were assessed at JMP2,000 (about US$800) or less. Usually this type of "capitalist" owned a small shop, a part of which also served as living quarters for himself and his family. Customarily, most of his living expenses were paid "out of the till," and for bookkeeping purposes he credited himself with a nominal amount—about JMP20 a month, for example—as salary. In the evaluation of such firms, the owner's personal possessions, down to his pots and pans and the baby's crib, were not only included but were taken away from him when the State assumed control of his enterprise.

The owner, therefore, was impoverished by his "contribution" to socialist construction. To ease his climb over the socialist barrier, the 5 percent per year of the assessed value of his meager holdings would hardly pay for his cigarettes. If he were made to continue running his shop as a State employee, he was paid the JMP20 a month which he had previously shown as his salary. Out of this pittance, however, he would now have to pay rent and buy food. Thus he and his family faced starvation. If he tried to get a job, he found that he was classed as a capitalist, which meant that he was denied the benefits that gave the workers some semblance of security. Thus the position of about 80 percent of Shanghai's businessmen was nearly hopeless, and a new wave of suicides began.

This time, however, the authorities acted quickly to stop the suicides. The propaganda abroad was proving unexpectedly successful in convincing foreigners, even Westerners, that the transformation was being achieved peacefully and that the capitalists were delighted with socialism. The deception could not be maintained for long if the mass suicides among businessmen began again. Thus the younger and more vigorous of the small businessmen were given employment by being taken from their families and sent to the border wastelands to work on "socialist reconstruction," which, like the "Honor Roll" for workers, was a euphemism for the slave labor of labor reform. Financial assistance, however, was given to the older men and to those who were much respected in their neighborhoods. The assistance came from a "mutual fund" which the authorities created by reducing to 4½ percent the annual 5 percent payments to the ex-owners of the more solvent firms.

The payments to these ex-owners were reduced even further because only a small part of each was paid in cash. The balance was given in non-negotiable government bonds. It was well understood that when these bonds became due, both the principal and accrued interest were to be reinvested in more bonds. Thus the owner could not count on the use of these funds. Ninety percent of J.P.'s annual 4½ percent credit from the government was paid in bonds, but his holdings had been so vast that even the small balance left him was more money than he could possibly spend.

His three flour mills which I managed were assessed at JMP4 million, although their real value was at least JMP18 million. The assessment was further reduced by JMP600,000 which was the "adjusted" amount I had confessed to embezzling during Five-Anti. These mills, therefore, were treated slightly more harshly than the average in the "peaceful transformation to socialism." A firm with a real value of $500,000, for example, was apt to be assessed at around $150,000. From this, roughly $50,000 would be deducted for the levy from Five-Anti. Of the remaining $100,000, the 4½ percent paid annually for seven years would total $31,500. An average of three-quarters of this amount, however, was rendered in the non-negotiable—and, in effect, non-redeemable—government bonds. Thus, the owner really received for his half-million-dollar property only $7,875; a capitalist rarely was given as much as 1 percent of his property's real value.

It is important to understand, however, that the capitalists were no longer really concerned over ownership rights in or compensation for their properties. Ever since Five-Anti, the fact that capitalists had any rights at all was merely a pretense maintained by the Communists. The real worry of every capitalist was the job he would be given by his new employer, the State.

The small businessmen fared ill under the new order, but the big capitalists found that they were not too badly off. J.P., for example, received only a tiny fraction of the income he previously had derived from his holdings, but the amount was still large. In addition, the State paid him the same salaries he had drawn as the chairman of several boards of directors. The only important difference was that the *nominal* authority he held within his industrial complex was sharply reduced. Before, he had been nominally the director and had only been "advised" by the various Party officials who really ran his enterprises; now, however, a State Representative was appointed by the government for each of his factories, plants and mills to "represent the people's interests." The State Representatives, of course, had complete authority over the enterprises, and J.P. was expected to uphold the fiction that he merely represented "private interests" in the joint status.

The capitalist managers who had worked for the big industrialists found that their position was similar; they received the same salaries as before, but their status was sharply reduced.

Only a few hundred even retained the title of manager and held nominal authority with the State Representative. The majority became merely deputy-managers or department heads and were assigned insignificant duties in the enterprises that previously they had had the nominal status of directing. An acquaintance of mine named Mr. Hui was typical. He had graduated from the Massachusetts Institute of Technology as an industrial chemist and in Shanghai he had managed a large paper plant. Under the new order, he retained the same salary but he became only a deputy-manager in charge of looking after the mosquito nets in the workers' dormitory and of supervising sanitation in the plant's mess hall.

Finally, a small number of ex-managers were given an insignificant clerkship, without even the dignity of a lesser title, in the establishments that previously they had nominally managed. By this time, only capitalists who had proven "progressive" and had learned to cooperate effectively with the authorities had survived, but the Communists never trusted anyone and inevitably a few capitalists made mistakes which either aroused the authorities' suspicions or incurred their displeasure. These unfortunates were made to be shunned by their former friends and associates, and although they would continue temporarily to receive their previous salaries, they knew that they were on the downgrade and had no future.

To my horror, despite the favorable impression I had made during the "high tide" of the transformation campaign, I feared that I might be classed with these few rejected capitalists. This was because of an incident that occurred shortly after the campaign, when the evaluation program was under way.

An assessment committee was set up in each firm. In my mills, the 15-member Committee consisted of the Party Secretary, the Chairman of the Trade Union, various representatives from the workers, technicians and supervisors, and myself. We appointed 20 inventory teams who fanned out through the mills. They submitted lists with estimated values of every item in the establishment, down to broken rat traps and a torn cushion from a rest room chair. We on the Committee studied the evaluations. If anyone questioned the value given for an item, the head of the inventory team concerned took another look at it, and on the basis of his reconsidered estimate we Committee members reached a decision. The Party Secretary, of course, made all the decisions; I quickly realized that the whole laborious process was another typical Communist pretense. The authorities probably had decided in advance the figure at which the property would be officially evaluated; if so, the Party Secretary's duty was to see that this final figure was not exceeded. In any case, the Party Secretary questioned the inventory teams' already absurdly low figures only when he wanted the evaluations reduced even further. I pretended to give serious consideration to the figures, and then I made the appropriate comments of approval.

Nevertheless, my relationship with the Party Secretary and Trade Union Chairman had subtly changed. Officially, I had "crossed the barrier to socialism." I was a "remolded capitalist." Previously, as an unregenerate capitalist, I had been treated with all the loathing and antagonism that the Communists directed at the class; I was assumed automatically guilty of all the "crimes" they associated with the class no matter how innocent I really was or how "progressive" and cooperative I had been. Now, however, my sins apparently were forgiven. I received no respect, but at least I was spared insults and abuse. The trouble was that my new role was unfamiliar. I was not quite sure what was expected of me. This made me apprehensive, and during the inventory at the mills I tried to remain even more alert than usual.

Thus, one day, when I came across an inventory item that seemed to have been treated outside the normal pattern, I spent a sleepless night thinking about it. I finally decided that I was meant to question it.

The item was an electric motor. It was old, and we did not use it, but according to our chief electrician it was in perfect working order. Only two weeks previously, a government buyer had offered to purchase it for JMP50,000. Our electrician had reported to our Party Secretary, however, that the motor was worth JMP70,000. The Party Secretary, therefore, had instructed me to reject the offer. The buyer then had offered us JMP60,000. Thereupon the Party Secretary had decided we should sell the motor. "We don't need it," he had said to me. "The offer is below its real value, but we can consider the difference a contribution from us to socialist reconstruction."

The transaction, however, was postponed because of the government order which "froze" all assets during the evaluation of the mills. I now found that the motor was assessed at *JMP 3,000!* At first I thought the figure was a mistake; an amount of JMP30,000—less than half the real value—would not have surprised me, but one-twentieth seemed overdoing it.

Discreet inquiry, however, revealed that both the assessment team and the Party Secretary had placed the value at JMP3,000. I therefore concluded that I was to put on an act which would furnish the Communists with one of the frills they often use. Because, only two weeks before, an official had established the value of the motor at JMP60,000, and because the Party Secretary himself had admitted its true worth to me in front of witnesses, I could expect that I was meant to reject the assessment on this one item. After a vigorous stand during which I would quote the official pronouncements on "fair dealing to our national capitalist friends," the Communist members of the assessment Committee would back down, compromise on the assessment of the motor and prove that they had indeed made every effort to deal justly with me. In my thinking, the Communists would feel that if I never once objected to an assessment, someone might suspect that I was under some kind of coercion.

The moment I questioned the item, both the Party Secretary and the Trade Union Chairman reacted with surprise and indignation. When I nevertheless persisted, the Party Secretary suggested that we ask the opinion of the Chief Electrician, the man who had evaluated the motor at JMP70,000 two weeks before. I agreed. I believed that now the argument would begin to turn in my favor.

Instead, however, the electrician's assessment now was JMP-3,000. Moreover, he implied that this was an inflated amount, proving that the regime was being overly lenient with capitalists. Even the metal in the motor was worth more than JMP3,000 as scrap. Thus I knew that the electrician was lying; he knew I knew it, and we both knew that the Party Secretary knew it as well, but as always the pretense was scrupulously maintained.

The electrician, of course, had been coached by the Party Secretary; the moment I understood this, I should have realized that I had blundered. Instead, I considered that I knew Party policy better than the Party Secretary. I thought that the situation was similar to my conflict with the Labor Bureau arbitrators over the transport workers' demands. Moreover, once started on a course like this, the best procedure usually was to stick it out and hope for success. I knew enough to avoid proving that the others were liars, but I made my arguments calmly logical. I even pointed out that only a few months before, Tax Bureau cadres had evaluated the motor at JMP325,000. This really infuriated the cadre.

Two days later, however, J.P. telephoned and asked me curtly to see him immediately. When I entered his office, he said, frowning, "You've always been progressive, Bob. Why are you being so stubborn about that damned motor?"

He had never spoken to me this way, and I was shocked. I stammered in reply that because the assessment of the motor had been so absurdly low, I thought that the authorities would want me to question it.

J.P. made an impatient gesture. "You of all people should know Party policy better than that," he said. "Just remember that *all* the assessments are fair and just. Besides, the property is mine. I don't care what happens to it. So why should you risk your future for it?"

I broke into a cold sweat. I understood now that I had misjudged the situation about the motor. I had made a mistake that might prove seriously damaging to J.P. and could jeopardize my whole future. Unless I was able to correct it, I might start on the downgrade that could end in the oblivion of labor reform.

Downgrading was one of the frightening aspects of life under the Communist regime. Survival required a constant upward struggle. Promotion was given to those who implemented Party policy the most vigorously, who served the regime unquestioningly and with the most self-sacrifice. Because of my efforts, I was achieving comparatively high status, but a static position was almost impossible. Unless I kept pushing upward, the direction of my progress would be irrevocably reversed. I would descend faster than I had gone up, and nothing could save me.

Thus, if my mistake about the motor was to be held against me, the first step of the downgrade would be an assignment to some insignificant position in the mills. I would immediately be avoided by my friends and denounced by other "progressive" capitalists who would rightly fear being contaminated by me. I would lose all prestige in the Federation of Industry and Commerce and in the young businessmen's group of the Democratic Youth Association. These were the front organizations through which the Communists controlled people like me; far from supporting me, my fellow members would be the first to revile, accuse and finally expel me, once I had fallen out of favor with the Communists. My one misjudgment, therefore, could mean the loss of all hope for a chance to escape.

I spent most of the night fighting panic and trying to figure a way out of my predicament. I realized that, in my new role, the Communists were not going to attack me directly as before; they had sent their warning through J.P. I also understood that the Communists were no longer bothering to cover their depradations with finesse; they would evaluate the capitalists' property as they found convenient, and they were making only a crude pretense to the contrary. In my case, I decided that I could compensate for their inadequate pretense only by making my own even more convincing. To begin with, I concluded that, as a remolded capitalist, they would expect me to be as cooperative as always but that they would not want me to act as cringingly subservient as before.

The next day at the office, therefore, I faced the Committee with as much dignity as I could muster. I stated that I had made a mistake about evaluating the motor and that I accepted the assessment of JMP3,000. Instead of apologizing for my mistake, however, I searched for explanations of how I could have made it. My conclusion was that I had been too far removed from the assessment operation and thus had developed a "lofty bureaucratic attitude." To correct this deficiency, I suggested that I volunteer for duty with the evaluation teams which were working around the clock. The suggestion was accepted and for the next three nights I scrambled through a dusty warehouse until the early hours of morning.

When the assessment was finished, the head of the Food Bureau—which now had supervisory authority over my mills—conducted a discussion meeting in our dining hall. During the

198

meeting, he said formally to me, "Mr. Manager, as a capitalist, have you any complaint against the workers and cadres for the way the assessment was carried out? Did they exhibit the principle of 'fair play'? Have they maliciously underevaluated any of the assets of this firm?"

"Indeed not, Comrade Bureau Director," I jumped up to say. "The men here displayed an excellent spirit of 'fair play.' We capitalists are thoroughly satisfied that the assessment has been made in a just, and even lenient, fashion." I added the customary words of praise for and gratitude to the Party and Chairman Mao.

When I sat down, the mills' Party Secretary stood up, and to my surprise addressed me. "Mr. Manager, the statement you just made," he said, "did it come from the bottom of your heart?" I realized that he was rubbing my face in the mistake I had made about the motor. He was also putting into the record protection for himself, just in case any future official inquiry uncovered the motor's ridiculous assessment.

"Comrade Party Secretary, how can you ask such a question?" I said. My voice throbbed with emotion. "For years, we capitalists have had the benefit of education and remolding under the leadership of the Communist Party and Chairman Mao. We have learned thoroughly that we must always reveal only what is in our hearts. I assure you, therefore, that my statement was utterly sincere—"

I saw the Food Bureau Director and the Party Secretary exchange a look, but I could not tell what it meant and nothing more was said to me.

For the next two weeks I suffered the agony of suspense to learn my fate. J.P. and other capitalists I knew were told promptly what their positions would be under the new order; I was the only one kept waiting.

Finally, I was called to the office of the Food Bureau Director. He informed me that I was to be retained at the flour mills as "manager representing the private interests." This was the best possible assignment I could hope for, and my relief was so great that I had to fight down hysteria.

Nevertheless, the Director was far from friendly. Obviously my mistake about the motor had made the authorities doubt me again, and the whole affair had been considered carefully. The fact that I had atoned for the mistake in a proper manner, plus the fact that my contribution during the campaign had been not only outstanding but also widely publicized, finally caused me to be judged "pure" enough for a prestige position in the regime's Joint State-Private enterprise. I had had a narrow escape. I could not afford another mistake, and I would have to watch my step even more carefully in the future.

My future was now in the hands of Comrade Yang, who came into the mills as the State Representative. The most pleasant aspect of his arrival concerned the mills' former Party Secretary and the Trade Union Chairman. These were the two who, before I had "crossed the socialist barrier," had been so diligent in their duty to humiliate and demoralize me. They had become accustomed to complete authority over "management," and had developed superb arrogance in their position. Now, however, "management" was not a decadent capitalist but a high Communist official. Within a few days, the two former despots were humiliated, demoted and transferred.

Comrade Yang, the new despot, was a sullen, heavy-jowled bear of a man. He was an ex-peasant who had become a lieutenant general in the Army and had fought in Korea, but he could barely read and write. I sensed at once that he was prepared to hate me. I think he considered me a despicable effete capitalist and expected that I would use my education and experience in the mills to show up his ignorance and incompetence. I know that he anticipated a struggle in achieving complete dominance over me.

Winning him over, therefore, was not particularly difficult. He and I shared the same office, and in fact sat on opposite sides of the same desk. From the beginning, I made a pretense of looking elaborately busy but at the same time being careful to do nothing. Thus we created the illusion that I knew the Communists wanted: the representatives of public and private interests working in happy harmony. Comrade Yang, however, made every decision, no matter how trivial the problem. Whenever I had to pretend participation in the decisions, I flattered him indirectly by acting as though he were far more clever than I. Before long, I could see him discovering that instead of the difficulty he had expected from me, I was actually helping him maintain his position. He began to treat me in a gruff avuncular fashion, and I had no trouble with Comrade Yang.

Oddly enough, the workers had more trouble than I because of the socialist transformation. In their Trade Union group meetings, for example, they found themselves volunteering to give up that decadent capitalist practice of the annual bonus which amounted to about a month's salary and traditionally was considered part of their wages. They also surrendered a number of other privileges and comforts which the new owners of the mills found inconvenient to grant them. The workers obviously could not understand why they received *less* after the evils of exploitation had been removed. Along with the State Representative, therefore, a group of other State-appointed cadres came into the organization. Their main job was to "supervise personnel," and the workers thus found that the control over them was very much tightened.

Finally, the transformation of our mills resulted in a vastly expanded administrative operation. Because of the wheat short-age, the mills could operate no more than a few days a month and the workers were idle most of the time. Nevertheless, our previous supervisory staff of 86 was increased to 174 and the number of departments from six to sixteen. Moreover, the new management demoted the previous supervisors, foremen and de-partment heads, replacing them with young Party members. In every case, these new men were entirely without experience and, as usual, had only the qualification of political purity.

The results could have been foretold, but they amazed even me. The paper work, bureaucratic duplication, the backbiting and struggle to evade responsibility, the waste and inefficiency reached truly fantastic proportions.

Happily, I could remain apart from the endless paper work and aloof from the intrigues at the mills. The only really awk-ward moments I endured came every payday. The government gave me the same wages I had received before, in order to "ease my adjustment to socialism" and to show outsiders that in Communist China the living standard of ex-capitalists was not reduced. Comrade Yang, however, was paid at the standard rate which had been fixed for State-operated enterprises and which was as little as a third of the wages paid by private enterprise. Our money was brought to us only when we were in the office together. Comrade Yang's small bundle of bills was placed be-fore him with an air of sad regret. My comparatively large stack of notes was then laboriously counted out for me by the ac-countant. Thereupon Comrade Yang invariably made the same comment: "Manager Loh, this salary is not like your old salary at all, is it? Now you receive what you *deserve* for your services to the people."

This was sarcasm meant to humiliate me. He and I were cooperating to maintain the illusion, as his remark seemed to suggest, that progressive national capitalists like me could use their abilities to aid the course of "socialism." At the same time, both of us knew that I was really doing nothing about running the mills. In fact, more than half the correspondence between the Food Bureau and the mills was marked "confidential" so that I could not even learn much about what was going on. Thus, his remark was also intended to make me wonder if I was really earning my much higher salary, and to make me worry that I might not get it much longer.

If I did earn my higher salary, it was not in the mills but in outside political activities. I was still helping to deceive visiting foreigners, but my main contributions now were in the Federation of Industry and Commerce and in my position as a representative to the Shanghai People's Congress. On the whole, under the new order, I found that I was better off than before. Soon, I was being appointed to committees of higher prestige. I was even sent several times to Peking to represent the progressive young businessmen in top-level meetings.

Finally, my newly discovered ability as a ghost-writer for the Chans gave me another means of proving my usefulness to the regime. My efforts received favorable comment from some senior officials, and the Chans called me their brain trust.

Even Charlie's wife used me in this capacity. She was a dainty little creature, beautiful but not very bright. Nevertheless, her position required her to participate actively in various women's organizations. One day she approached me, worried because a reporter had spoken to her about a trip she was preparing to make to Peking as a delegate to the All-China Meeting for Progressive Women of Commerce and Industry. The papers wanted her to write a letter to her husband, giving her impressions of the experience, and permitting the letter to be published. Charlie's wife had no idea what to say. I wrote the letter for her even before she went on the trip.

It was a simple chore. At this time, one had only to praise "socialism," and no matter how extravagant the praise it was always accepted. In the first paragraph of the letter, therefore, I described the train journey to Peking and mentioned that the girl had seen two tractors. "Although this is only a small number," I had her say, "it is the first light of the dawn of socialist agricultural mechanization."

The second paragraph described the meetings she "attended." This also was easy, because all the meetings were stultifyingly the same. Because I did not know who would make the speeches, I had her praise the words of the "leader." Accenting the limited role of women in the past, I wrote for her: "I used to be like a canary in a cage, but with the coming of the enlightened leadership of the Communist Party and Chairman Mao we women are given a chance to discuss affairs of State with our country's leaders." And for a feminine touch, I added, "After the leader gave a statistical analysis of the process of the industrial transformation to socialism, I was moved to tears."

The last paragraph concentrated on her gratitude to the Communist Party and Chairman Mao and ended with the comment: "I intend henceforth to strengthen instead of to weaken my husband's determination to accept and work for the transformation to socialism."

The letter contained every cliché that I had heard the Communists use, but it was published widely throughout the country. No one ever bothered to send Charlie a copy of the letter, and he had heard nothing about the matter. Thus he was astonished to read the letter from his wife to him in the paper.

"Under the leadership of the Communist Party, everything is supposed to be ahead, and how right they are," Charlie commented. "The Party is even ahead of a husband in getting a letter from his wife. In fact, the Party *instead* of her husband gets her letters!"

CHAPTER 9

If one word does not suffice,
A thousand are wasted.

—CHINESE PROVERB

DESPITE THE hysteria of the "high tide of socialist transformation," the businessmen knew they had been robbed. They had been powerless to resist, and they were grateful to have escaped with the loss of only their property. They had long known that eventually their property would be expropriated, but they had been taught through fear to hide what they really felt about the Communists' banditry.

Nevertheless, they were amazed at how successfully they had been depicted abroad as having joyfully donated their possessions to the State. They viewed the deception with mixed feelings, because it had an important bearing on their own fate as well as on the regime's international strategy.

The strategy, of course, was designed to bring about the ultimate worldwide triumph of Communism. The people in the

Western democracies, however, had been growing increasingly powerful and increasingly less impressed with both Communist theory and practice. The Chinese Communists, therefore, had turned their attention to the people of the so-called backward countries of Latin America, Africa and free Asia. The intention was to turn these huge masses against the Western democracies and eventually to align these areas with the Communist bloc.

In the struggle for these masses, the Communists had several advantages. Since World War II, the people of the backward countries had been in open rebellion against either Western colonial rulers or local feudalistic regimes. Sympathy for the aspirations of these impoverished people came from the Western democracies, but the Western governments tended to support the conservative elements who were attempting to suppress the revolutions. Moreover, aggressive Western commercial interests still practiced in these areas a form of economic exploitation. Finally, the racial bigotry of some Westerners convinced many in the backward countries that democratic ideals had little value.

The Communists, in fact, had only one disadvantage. The backward areas were still so politically undeveloped that the inflamed masses could not organize effective revolutions without the support and leadership of the middle classes. The bourgeoisie, however, identified themselves with the same class in the Western democracies, and instinctively accepted democratic idealism. They distrusted Communism, if only because Marx had declared their class an enemy and because in Soviet Russia the class had been brutally liquidated. If left to themselves, they ultimately would have aligned their new or reformed countries with the West.

The Communists would have permitted this to happen if they really believed their own dogma that "socialist revolution is not for export," and that human social development follows an immutable pattern that human will cannot alter. The circumstances in China, however, had been the same as those in the backward countries; the bourgeoisie had been dissatisfied with the Nationalist regime but as long as they supported it, the Communists had no chance for victory. Nevertheless, Mao Tse-tung, "re-interpreting" Marxist-Leninist theories, succeeded in his bid for political control by using a trick which nullified the strength of the Chinese bourgeoisie. Once he and his Party were in power, the bourgeoisie discovered that the Communists had been guilty of calculated treachery, but by then it was too late to resist or even complain. The Chinese bourgeoisie now saw the same trick being used in the regime's international strategy.

Mao's trick was to create a seeming difference between the bourgeoisie of the Western democracies and the same class in the backward areas. The powerful Western capitalists, he said, dominated and exploited the "weak" capitalists of the "semicolonial, semi-independent countries." The Western "monopoly" capitalists were "imperialists" while the others were national capitalists —or "national bourgeoisie," as he officially designated them. The imperialists were the deadly enemies of mankind, and because Russia's capitalists had been imperialists, the Soviets had been right in liquidating them.

Conversely, the national capitalists could be saved. They were wrongfully exploiting their employees and therefore required "re-education," but they were also "progressive" because they were anticolonial and antifeudalistic and because they themselves needed to be "liberated" from the imperialists. Thus they were not enemies, but allies. Once this idea had been successfully planted in the backward countries, the bourgeoisie would lose their fear of Communism and could begin to accept help for their revolutions from their "friends" in the Communist bloc. Communist propaganda, then, needed only to keep pointing up examples of undemocratic practices of the democracies, and the bourgeoisie could be expected to turn increasingly against the West.

The national capitalists in the backward areas, however, could not be turned from the West merely by propaganda and Mao's theories. They needed proof of the Communists' friendship. This was the one reason why in China every possible subterfuge was being used to make outsiders think that we Chinese "national capitalist friends" were happy to be liberated from imperialists, that we welcomed Communist Party leadership, and that our economic and social status had improved under a Communist regime. In short, we were permitted to survive only for the purpose of this deception.

Moreover, our survival of the "socialist barrier" was only the first step of the deception. The bourgeoisie in the backward areas were not merely to be turned *from* democracy, they were to be turned *toward* Communist socialism. In the next step, therefore, we Chinese bourgeois were to demonstrate that even capitalists could achieve "political enlightenment." Thus, as soon as the Peking Communists had accomplished the miracle of turning private enterprise peacefully into socialism, they began on the even more astonishing miracle of turning capitalists into Marxists. They used "thought reform," which was administered in special schools to the entire national capitalist class. The Federation of Industry and Commerce was made to sponsor the schools, but they were typical of the ones that, ever since, have caused so much consternation over the apparent ability of the Chinese Communists to "brainwash" whole segments of the population.

For propaganda abroad, the announced purpose of the thought-reform schools for businessmen was to help us understand our position in the new order. After the transformation, the Communists said, our socio-economic status had changed so drastically that our thinking tended to "lag behind." Special training, therefore, was necessary in order to make "our ideology catch up to our status."

The real, but unannounced, purpose of the schools was to deceive foreigners into thinking that capitalists, or anyone else, would come to accept and believe voluntarily in Marxist theories if given the chance to study and understand them.

Naturally, none of this deception could be maintained with us. Officially, we were given to understand that, because of our altered status, we needed a systematic course of thought reform in addition to the regular thought remolding that we received in the discussion group meetings of our mass organizations.

Moreover, we learned later that, apart from the deception of foreigners, our thought-reform schools had another unannounced real purpose that concerned only us. Our schools were begun in April 1956; this was only a few weeks after the high tide of the transformation, but it was several months before the capitalists finally learned what their position would be in the new order. The authorities already knew that the capitalists would be given token compensation for their property and would temporarily be allowed to draw the same salaries as before, but that their status would be greatly reduced. Thus the schools also were intended to condition the capitalists to accept their demotions in the manner desired by the Party officials.

The Party officials drew up the lists of the "students" who would attend the schools. I was included in the first batch, which was made up of a thousand of Shanghai's leading capitalists. We had our thoughts reformed in a four-month course which consisted of morning and afternoon sessions, six days a week. In the beginning, the plan was to give examinations at the end of the course, but the students were so terrified at the thought of what failure might mean that they were rendered incapable of learning anything. Thus, the examinations were dropped. In fact, the cadres rarely sat in on our discussions. Obviously the authorities intended the ordeal to be as painless as possible. Foreigners were brought in frequently to visit us, and the atmosphere was not meant to be strained.

Actually, the atmosphere was pleasantly relaxed. The hours were not long, and we were not required to go to our offices, although we drew full salary during the course. The surroundings were comfortable, even luxurious; the headquarters for Shanghai's "Ideological Institute for Businessmen," as our thought-reform school was officially called, were in the magnificent former Bankers Union Building. We also attended lectures and were shown films in some of the city's best theaters. Diversity in the form of frequent "field trips" to museums, factories, model agricultural institutions, etc., was provided. Upon graduation, an elaborate celebration was staged; we were given diplomas and were entertained and congratulated by high officials.

I was especially congratulated. The course had been easy for me because I had begun my study of Marxist theories six years before and had kept up with the shifting application of the theories to Party policy. Thus, I knew what questions to avoid asking because they might embarrass the lecturers. Equally, I knew what responses from me would indicate to the authorities that I was cooperating loyally with the program. I was made chairman of my 15-member discussion group during the course, and whenever possible I steered the talk away from the loopholes that are apparent in Marxist-Leninist logic to any rational educated person. In short, I made myself a stooge in this tragicomedy that was being staged for foreigners. For this, I was treated as a brilliant student, and I knew I could expect some reward.

My reward, however, exceeded all my expectations. I "graduated" in early July 1956. Two weeks later, J.P. called me to his house, and in an awed voice told me that I had been appointed to the lecturing staff of the Ideological Institute for Businessmen.

The status of this post meant a great leap upward for me. Only 14 men were on the lecturing staff; of these, 12 were the city's top Communist officials. They included the mayor (who also held the even more important title of First Secretary of the Shanghai Communist Party), two deputy mayors, the chiefs of the Propaganda Bureau and the United Front Works Department and some of the country's most famous professors of Marxism. I was regarded as "reliable," and I was familiar with Marxist-Leninist theory; these were necessary qualifications, but the main reason for my appointment was to help maintain the fiction that the businessmen were indoctrinating themselves in a kind of voluntary group brainwashing. Moreover, the authorities hoped that a capitalist might be more convincing than a Communist in teaching Communism to capitalists. Nevertheless, I was now in exalted company whose influence, if carefully nurtured, could soon put me into a position from which escape might be possible. I began to have hope. Thus I threw myself energetically into the job of brainwashing my fellow capitalists.

The brainwashing course was divided into three sections. Each section contained several lectures. After each lecture, to ensure that the "students" understood every point raised, a number of discussion-group meetings were held. The points were further underscored with field trips, audiovisual aids, and informal talks from veterans of the Long March, exploited workers, etc.

The first section of the lectures was called "Love of Mother Country." It began with a comparison between the old society and the new regime. We were told that, previously, because we loved our country, we had been distressed by our country's social evils. Now, under Communist Party leadership, these evils had been eliminated, and thus our patriotism must be expressed in love for the Communist Party. This new love, however, was not enough. Foreign imperialists were desperately trying to bring back the social evils. To ensure our protection, the Chinese Communist Party had to unite with other "fraternal" parties outside. Hence, by the end of the lectures, our love of the mother country was equated with love for International Communism.

The next section was called "The History of Social Development." The lectures dealt with the familiar Communist idea that as a human society increases its material production, it progresses upward through stages called primitive communist, slave, feudal, capitalist, socialist, and finally Communist. Each stage represents a new social order which begins by coping more efficiently than the last with the increased production of goods and ends when further increases make a higher social order necessary. To Communists, this view of society's development is a law that cannot be altered by any act of human will. In the lectures, the idea that socialism and Communism "are on the side of history" was stressed.

The final section—the longest and most important—covered Marxist theories of political economy. We were taught that "reactionary" meant anything that hindered material production, and "progressive" referred to that which encouraged it. After feudalism, capitalism at first was progressive because it coped more efficiently with higher production and stimulated further increases.

In the Communist view, however, this stimulant comes from the capitalists' uncontrollable greed. A capitalist's wealth is accumulated by paying his workers less than the value of what they produce for him. With profits from this "exploitation," he expands his industrial holdings. Production and profits thus are increased but so is the number of exploited workers. Simultaneously, the capitalist class becomes smaller. Moreover, the capitalists raise their profits even higher by pushing wages always lower. The ever-fewer rich become richer and the ever-increasing poor become poorer. Finally, the masses are living near the subsistence level and no one can buy the goods produced. The depression cycle starts. This hinders the progress of production, making capitalism reactionary. The depressions come with increasing frequency, each more severe than the last. In the end, the workers rise, seize the means of production, and a new progressive social order begins.

During the lectures on this subject, the national capitalist students were pressed continually to admit that they had exploited their employees and that capitalism's inherent defects rendered its downfall inevitable.

My own lecture—one of those in the third section—was called "The Inevitable Downfall of Imperialism, the Highest Stage of Capitalism." I used America as a typical example. Many Communists took the aproach that America's vast material achievements were mere imperialist lies and that Russia, if not China, had outstripped the U.S. long ago. No one believed this, and I therefore admitted that the American monopoly capitalists lived in fabulous luxury. Nevertheless, I twisted the facts by insisting that the masses were correspondingly impoverished and were growing ripe for an uprising that would destroy their exploiters. This conformed to the Marxist theory of what *should* be happening in America, and thus was acceptable to the authorities. At first I could not determine what stories to illustrate this theory about America would be acceptable, but finally I evolved a foolproof system. I merely considered the evils that were only too apparent in the Communist regime and invented anecdotes that credited these evils to American society.

My heartrending story meant to illustrate the inhumanity of American society was especially effective, and the authorities made me retell it constantly. In New York, according to my fiction, I had known of a poor unemployed workman who was spurned in all his desperate attempts to find a job. Finally, out of extreme bitterness, when he and his family were starving, he wrote a letter to *The New York Times*, saying that at a given hour two days later he was going to jump off the Empire State Building. The news item was picked up by the advertising director of the Coca-Cola Company. The starving worker was approached by the director, who offered to give the man's family $25,000 if he would publicize Coca-Cola with his suicide. The next day, the streets were jammed with people who had come to see the worker jump from the high building. As the worker stood on the ledge, a man came to him with a microphone and asked him what he would like more than anything in the world before he died. The worker replied that he would like a bottle of Coca-Cola. The drink was brought to him, and when he had finished it, he jumped.

I think I am safe in saying that not one of the students, nor even the more intelligent Communists, believed this story. Nevertheless, everyone solemnly agreed that it illustrated superbly the picture of America authorized by the Party. In fact, I am also safe in saying that every student who attended the whole course graduated *less* convinced about Communism than when he began. The more educated businessmen, on their own, had read much on Marxist-Leninist theory and had natural doubts about its logic. The course confirmed their doubts but because, like me, they understood the real purpose of the Institute, they maintained the customary pretense and gave the lecturers no trouble with awkward questions.

The smaller and less well-educated businessmen, conversely,

were a source of constant trouble. To many of them, because of the power achieved by the Communist Party, Communism seemed a kind of magic which they sincerely wanted to understand. Frequently, they had shrewd minds and reduced even the top experts to evading the issues with propaganda clichés.

In the first series, few students dared ask the unanswerable question why it was not possible to love the mother country without loving the Communist Party. Instead, they adhered to the safer subject of internationalism. In class after class, the pattern of student questions was as follows: The U.S.S.R., representing internationalism, lent money to China but charged interest; the U.S.A., representing imperialism, had sponsored U.N.R.R.A. which sent gratis large quantities of food and medicines to China. Moreover, the U.S.S.R. had taken the machinery from Manchuria after World War II; the U.S.A. had brought machinery to China and had sent technicians to teach Chinese how to operate it. And again, the Russians were occupying Port Arthur and Dairen, but the U.S.A. leased no Chinese territory. Why, then, was Russia's "internationalism" so completely good, and America's "imperialism" so completely bad? What was the difference between the two? Had not China benefited more from America's so-called imperialism?

The second series—concerning the inexorable law of the materialistic development of society—provided even more difficult questions for the lecturers. If the pattern of progression was unalterable, the students asked, why had it altered so drastically? Mongolia, for example, had been in the early feudal stage, but in defiance of the law had jumped straight into socialism, skipping the intermediate stages. If its production rate made socialism inevitable for Mongolia, why had not the U.S.A. become socialist long ago? In fact, why were the very countries which, according to the "law," should be the most advanced into Marxist socialism, the very ones furthest from it? Was it not true that, today, the only Communist countries were those which had been occupied by the Red Army? In short, could it be denied that Marxist socialism, far from being a natural inevitable development, occurred only when it was imposed by force?

In the last series, the businessmen felt on surer ground, and their questions became the most searching. Despite pressure, they steadfastly refused to admit they had exploited their employees. They pointed out that in State-owned enterprises, workers' wages were far less than in private industry; by taking a much larger profit on the workers' production, the State's exploitation of labor was much worse. Thus, as long as the Communists refused to admit they were guilty of exploitation, the capitalists would do the same.

Moreover, the businessmen would not accept that "contradictions" within capitalism made the system's doom inevitable. Using official Communist figures, they showed that in the U.S., for example, capitalists had been growing richer at a miraculous rate, but that American workers, instead of becoming correspondingly poorer, were enjoying greatly increased purchasing power. Also, the depression cycle in the West, instead of growing in frequency and severity, was doing just the opposite. "Perhaps," the students suggested frequently, "the American workers were resisting socialism so that they would not have to suffer the reduced living standard that always seemed to occur wherever Marxist socialism was introduced."

Such blunt questions and comments occurred only while the students were innocently trying to discover some meaning in Communist theories. As they slowly perceived that the theories did not even make enough sense to cover up what was nothing more than primitive power politics, they questioned the lecturers more cautiously. Nevertheless, the intent behind their questions was unmistakable. "Is it true," one student might ask, "that al-most every American worker can afford a motorcar?" And an-other might want to know, "Is it true that a Russian worker must spend half a month's salary for a pair of leather shoes?" The pattern never varied; we lecturers were always asked to explain some good aspect of the West or some deficiency within the Communist bloc.

These were the ideological results of "brainwashing." The au-thorities knew perfectly well that no one who took the thought-reform courses given to various groups within the population was ideologically persuaded. In fact, every person who was given one of the courses found that upon graduation he was automati-cally demoted within his profession or, in a few rare cases, re-tained his same position. Soon after graduation, for example, we businessmen were reduced in official status from nominal owners and executives to nominal assistant managers and department heads. If the authorities really believed that their "brainwashing" worked, as they so carefully maintained, we should have become more useful to the regime, and we would have been at least nom-inally promoted. Nevertheless, after our thought reform, the authorities considered us even less reliable and despite enormous additional problems of inefficiency and waste, preferred to re-place us with inexperienced cadres.

As a result of the thought-reform course, any respect the busi-nessmen might have had for Marxist-Leninist theory was de-stroyed, but they did learn thoroughly to speak and act in the approved manner. This apparently was all the regime expected. Moreover, we had plenty of evidence that the frequent foreign visitors to the school were always deceived. A person who had never lived under a Communist regime invariably seemed to be-lieve that anyone who spoke like a Marxist must be a Communist. I remember the awed comment of a famous French statesman to members of his party: "I have actually seen with my own eyes," he said, "businessmen teaching Communism to businessmen!"

During this period, I kept up my reduced nominal status as a businessman by making occasional token visits to the mills where I would pretend to help Comrade Yang. Most of my time now, however, was spent on polishing my lecture and in conversing with my fellow staff lecturers on ways of improving the whole course. My experiences as a teacher at Shanghai University and my more recently acquired knowledge of businessmen enabled me to make occasional useful suggestions. The result was that the high Party officials with whom I now associated began to treat me almost as an equal. In my new self-confidence, escape seemed much more possible, and I began to consider actual plans.

In early September 1956, I happened upon a means that would test the strength of my position and at the same time provide a clue to the elements that might or might not be useful in an escape plan. I had an acquaintance named Pao who for five years had been applying for an official exit permit. He really lived in Hong Kong where his father was an important businessman, but in 1951 he had come to Shanghai with his family to dispose of some of his father's mainland property. When Pao had tried to return, however, the permission was refused. Since then he had lived in Shanghai on the money from the sale of his father's property, but he had nothing to do except nag the local authorities for an exit permit. He would occasionally call on the Chans or me when worry or frustration depressed him, but we could give him only sympathy.

One night, however, he came to my house in a state bordering on hysteria. Earlier that day, he told me, he had made another of his innumerable applications for an exit permit. On previous applications, he had been merely informed that the permit was refused, but this time the police had rejected it angrily. "Get out and don't come back," the policeman had shouted. "Find a job and forget about trying to leave." This was bad enough, but then the policeman had added, "You have escaped arrest so far only because your father is an important overseas Chinese, but don't think his influence can protect you forever."

Pao now was terrified. He said he could not stand living here any longer and he begged me to help him get out. My first impulse was to avoid involving myself in the matter for fear of risking my own position, but Pao was in a pitiful state and I feared he might do something desperate or foolish. I calmed him therefore by saying that I would help him if I could. I took him out to the garden where no servant could overhear us, and I made him tell me everything he knew about his situation.

Three aspects of his situation seemed worth thinking about. The first concerned the fact that the policeman had referred to Pao's father as an "overseas Chinese." Strictly speaking, as the term was used, the father was not an "overseas Chinese"; he did own, however, a large factory in Indonesia which was run by Pao's elder brother. It suddenly occurred to me that the authorities might be impressed as much—or even more—by the position of Pao's elder brother. I had always known that the Communists took special interest in the overseas Chinese. I had thought that this was because the overseas Chinese were a source of much-needed foreign exchange. Now, for the first time, it struck me that the authorities might view the overseas Chinese as even more useful in the deception of foreigners about national capitalists.

Another aspect of Pao's situation was that he always made his applications through the "census police." These were the watch-dogs stationed in every neighborhood to check and report on the activities of the residents. No one was permitted to leave the city or to stay away from his house more than 24 hours without an acceptable reason and the knowledge of his local census police. These police tended to be officious at best and to be especially uncooperative with national capitalists like us. Having earned the antagonism of his census police, Pao's only hope now was to make his future application as high as possible over the policeman's head.

For this purpose, as a final aspect of Pao's situation, I learned that his father-in-law in Peking was a friend of Li Chi-shen, a Deputy Chairman of the Standing Committee of the National People's Congress; this was merely a figurehead position but it should carry sufficient influence to get a letter directly into the hands of Premier Chou En-lai.

The plan which began forming in my head even while I talked to Pao required him to give up requesting an exit permit for Hong Kong and instead to apply at the very top for a *passport* to Indonesia. It was the all-or-nothing approach, and I thought that the sheer audacity of the application might momentarily overwhelm the authorities.

That very night, I helped Pao write a cryptic letter to his elder brother in Indonesia. The letter, although its meaning was disguised for the censors, instructed the brother to go at once to the Chinese Embassy in Djakarta. The brother was to say that he was ill with a serious ulcer and was incapable of running the factory properly without Pao's help. He was to request the Embassy to send Peking a recommendation for Pao's passport. I counted on the fact that the Embassy would give Peking background information on the elder brother's influential position.

For the next two weeks, I spent my spare time composing two letters for Pao. One was for Premier Chou En-lai and the other for the Deputy Foreign Minister in charge of passports. The gist of the two letters was the same. The request was stated, enough background was given so that the influence and status of Pao's family would be understood, and then I had Pao say, in effect,

"I sincerely believe that a man like me can do much for my country and my people by helping to run my factory in Indonesia. In addition, my five years here under the enlightened leadership of the Communist Party and Chairman Mao will enable me to acquaint the people there with the splendid socialist achievements in the New China." Finally, I had the letters end on a note which I thought might earn the most response. "The fact that I have been unable to return to Indonesia although I am badly needed by my family is causing a misunderstanding. My relatives and their acquaintances are getting the false impression that I have been detained here by the government. I am worried that people there may become apprehensive about the government's policy toward the overseas Chinese—"

It happened, at this time, that I had to go to Peking with a report from the thought-reform school. I therefore took Pao's letters with me. I delivered them and a suit-length of fine English woolen to his father-in-law. The next morning the old man gave the letters and the cloth to Li Chi-shen, who saw to it that the letters reached the proper persons that afternoon.

I returned to Shanghai a week later. The next evening, Pao came to my house, and I saw at once that he had had good news. He had received the passport for himself and his family that afternoon and had already made the travel reservations for a week hence. He was jubilant and pathetically grateful. He told me gleefully that he had just come from his census police, to whom he had reported his travel plans. He had shown the policeman his passport as the authorization for his trip. The policeman had snatched the passport from his hand and had thrown it on the floor. "Then leave," the official had said, "we're well rid of you—"

My miraculously speedy success with Pao taught me two important lessons. One was that I should deal only with top officials

—never with underlings. The other was that the authorities must be even more concerned about the overseas Chinese than I had imagined. With this in mind, I began to work out an escape plan of my own. Pao was going to Hong Kong, ostensibly en route to Djakarta, and after much hesitation I decided to risk asking for his help.

The night before he left, I had him to my house for a farewell dinner. He was too excited to eat. To me, the knowledge that someone I actually knew was able to leave this place forever was an indescribable delight. Merely the idea that escape was possible made me almost as excited as Pao, but I forced myself to be calm in order to do what I had carefully planned.

While we were having tea, Pao thanked me for the thousandth time for my help and added, "Do you realize that you have given me the rest of my life?"

The servant had left the room. I leaned across the table. "Good," I said in a low voice. "Now will you give me the rest of *my* life?"

Pao's eyes widened. "You, *too?*" he whispered. "But I thought you were one of *them.*"

I suppose by "them" poor innocent Pao meant the real Communists, whoever they were. I would guess that most, if not all, the Communists I knew would escape if they could. Perhaps this is what made escape so difficult; so many people thought so much about it that every possible angle to it was known by the police. For years, whenever I was depressed my favorite daydream was to imagine myself swimming to freedom. A few hardy fishermen had managed it, but for me the idea was absurd. I could barely swim at all, and besides, the constant patrols along the rocky coast near Kowloon used dogs that were trained to ferret out escapees and pull them down. Moreover, I would not even be able to reach Canton; no one could travel anywhere in the country without an officially accepted purpose, and any reason I might submit for going to Canton would invite immediate suspicion of the authorities. My whereabouts every moment of the day and night was checked and known. Thus if I tried some trick to get to Canton without the knowledge of the census police I would be reported missing within a matter of hours and would be run down long before I could even reach the coast. Nevertheless, swimming had been the only way out I could think of—until now.

For Pao, the situation was different; he had been a resident of Hong Kong and had been attempting to get back to where he legally belonged. He had not realized how complete was the hold over us who were legal residents of the mainland. When he understood that I desperately wanted to escape and that my only hope for it was to achieve a position of such importance in the regime that the authorities might sometime momentarily relax their vigilance over me, he was visibly shaken. I could see that he was considering some of his Shanghai friends in a new light. Nevertheless, he eagerly agreed to help me.

I took pencil and paper and wrote out for him a short letter which I made him memorize. After two hours, when I was sure that he had every character firmly in his mind, I burned the paper carefully. When he reached Hong Kong he was to dictate the letter to my brother who, on a signal from me, would send me the letter, exactly as I had dictated it, through the open mail. The signal to my brother was to be the words, "My cousin is feeling well these days." I would include the phrase in a letter to Pao, who would pass it on to my brother.

This was the first time I had risked telling anyone my feelings about escape, and the moment I had done it I felt vulnerable and exposed. Pao and his family left Shanghai around noon the next day, and they were to arrive in Hong Kong three days later. If all went well and my brother received my message, Pao was to telegraph me ARRIVED OKAY. I figured I would get his telegram on the fourth day after his departure. Meanwhile, I suffered badly from anxiety; I expected any moment to find the security police at my door.

On the fourth day, I was kept at the thought-reform school by a staff meeting until late in the afternoon. I was almost incapable of concentrating and as soon as the meeting was over I hurried home to see if the telegram had arrived. As I entered my living room, a woman stood up. It was Mai Mee; "I have been waiting for you for two hours," she said, pouting.

My mind was still on the telegram, and thus I was confused by Mai Mee's unexpected arrival. I stammered something about not knowing that her troupe was in Shanghai.

She led me to the sofa. "I'm not with the troupe," she said. "I've come to settle the business details for next spring's tour." She was still holding my hand, and now she knelt on the sofa beside me. She looked most appealing. "Bob," she said, "I want you to arrange the details for me."

"But I know nothing about them," I said.

Mai Mee dropped my hand and took a cigarette from the coffee table. "They're not complicated. I can tell you what you need to know." She tapped the cigarette daintily on her crimson thumbnail. "Once you see how easy the business is, I know you'll like it." I lit her cigarette, and she smiled at me through a smoke cloud. "The point is," she said, "that you understand this government, and I don't. You're becoming really influential. Even in Peking I hear about you. You can get us many advantages. We'll make a fortune."

I frowned. What Mai Mee did not realize was that when I was merely a mills manager, the job of being her business director would have been intriguing even though it would have meant a step downward. Now, however, my lecturer's post at the Institute was infinitely higher and gave me much prestige. I would be foolish to give up the post to join her troupe even if I somehow managed to get permission to make the change. If I so much as hinted that I wanted to make the change, the authorities would be displeased, and I would lose the influence she was counting on—

"Dear Bob, don't you understand?" she continued. "There's nothing to hinder us any longer. I've got my divorce."

I was stunned, but I was saved the necessity of replying because the servant entered just then with tea. As she put the tray on the coffee table, I saw a telegram next to my cup. I forgot everything else. I forced myself to reach for it and to open it casually. ARRIVED OKAY—PAO, it read. My heart was pounding, but I managed to throw the telegram back onto the tray with seeming indifference. The first step of my escape plan had been taken successfully, and now I could not turn back. I was started down a road that would lead to freedom or to some dimly imagined horror. I was filled with both excitement and fear. Finally, I remembered Mai Mee. "What—did you say?" I asked vaguely.

Mai Mee stared at me wide-eyed for a moment and then suddenly threw her cigarette across the room. "You've changed," she said. "I suppose you've become such an important personage that I mean nothing to you any more—"

"That's not true," I protested.

Mai Mee stood up. "Bob, tell me. Are you going to join me with the troupe or not?" she said.

"We must not be hasty," I said, also standing up. "I must think about it carefully."

Mai Mee picked up her purse. "Don't bother thinking about it; you've answered my question," she said. She seemed to grow inches taller as she looked me up and down. "I thought you were different, but I was wrong," she said finally. "You're the same as the others." Without another word and without looking back, she walked to the door. Her dignity was magnificent, but she slammed the door with a crash that shook the house.

I sank back to the sofa. I did not know whether to laugh or to feel crushed and terrified. I understood now that Mai Mee's interest in me had been based on the usefulness to her of my influence. My vanity, I suppose, was wounded, but I had realized long ago that the regime deliberately isolated each individual, forcing him therefore to fight for his survival selfishly—if weakly —alone. I could hardly blame Mai Mee for an attitude that was shared by me and the rest of our countrymen. I was upset, however, at the thought that she might feel vindictive. No one's position was so secure that he could not be endangered by another person's active antagonism. I spent the rest of the evening composing a letter to her. I apologized for having seemed preoccupied and indifferent; I swore that I was quite otherwise. I pleaded worry and overwork. I appealed to her sympathy, and I flattered her. But I received no reply to my letter.

This was in October 1956. Mai Mee may have felt, as did I, that this was a time for extreme caution. Events in Europe were causing much excitement and confusion within China.

The excitement had begun on June 28, 1956, when workers in Poznan, Poland, revolted against the Communist rulers. The uprising was crushed with 44 officially listed as killed, hundreds more wounded, and a thousand people arrested. The importance of this event was in the fact that it belied one of the basic tenets of Communist theory. If workers were the rulers in a socialist society, against whom could they revolt? At the Institute this question was raised repeatedly by the students, and the official answers were never satisfactory.

228

Then, in October 1956, Wladyslaw Gomulka was given the leadership of Poland's Communist Party. In a dramatic speech that was printed fully in China, he promised "socialism with freedom." He also insisted that a socialist regime ought to be truthful and not deceive the people with false statistics. The Chinese who, since the "liberation," had seen increasingly higher food production figures but always lower food rations, greeted this pronouncement with much approbation; one heard the matter being discussed everywhere.

Even more interesting to the Chinese, however, was Gomulka's statement that Polish land under collectives produced much less than the privately owned farms, and the State-operated agricultural units much less than the collectives—in fact, State-operated units yielded 37 percent less than private farms. This confirmed what everyone suspected was happening in China's farm program; it indicated strongly that Communist "socialism," far from being "progressive" as the Communists claimed, was actually "reactionary."

Finally, the most consternation was caused by Gomulka's remarks concerning Poland's relations with Soviet Russia. He claimed that Poland was forced heavily into debt by Russia's unfair policy of buying cheaply from Poland but selling high. In other words, the Russian Communists were guilty of "imperialist exploitation."

Just when speculation about the Polish situation was at its height we received the electrifying news of the Hungarian revolt. The Hungarians had been chafing under oppressive Communist rule and had demanded the recall of the more moderate Imre Nagy, who was made Premier again on October 23, 1956. Discontent still continued, however, and when on the same day security police opened fire on a Budapest crowd, a wave of violent riots began. Russian troops were called in to suppress them, but revolutionary councils sprang up throughout the country. A full-scale revolt of the masses against a Communist regime was on.

The excitement this news engendered in the Chinese people cannot be overstated. For the first time, newspapers were read avidly. Previously, we had been forced to read them because the official press items were used as discussion topics in our regular mass organization meetings. Now, however, absenteeism soared while workers waited in block-long queues for a chance to buy a paper.

The news of Hungary, of course, was played down and some-times we had to read between the lines to know what was hap-pening. Nevertheless, we felt that the situation in the satellite countries was serious enough so that our own leaders would be warned. They would *have* to be frightened by the picture of what could happen in China if they oppressed the masses too severely.

Our leaders were frightened. We had no proof of it, but we could *feel* it. During the last week in October 1956, for example, I made one of my regular token visits to my office in the mills. Comrade Yang was away, and a young cadre was in his place. That morning, a short circuit had damaged a motor, and the cadre was investigating to see if negligence had been the cause. While I was there, he questioned one of the assistant electricians, and he became abusive. Suddenly the worker leaned on the table and thrust his face near the cadre's. "Watch your tongue, com-rade," the worker said. "You Communists are getting too arro-gant. China can have a Hungarian Revolution too—and don't you forget it!"

The cadre stared openmouthed at the worker towering over him and seemed to shrink within his loose uniform. Finally, the questioning was resumed as though the interruption had not occurred. Nevertheless, the cadre was now most polite, and afterward the worker left the room with a definite swagger.

In other factories, some of the workers actually rioted against the cadres, and in Shanghai at least a few small-scale strikes took place. University students held demonstrations to protest Communist oppression. Anti-Communist slogans and posters began to appear on public walls. In the villages near Hangchow, hungry peasants suddenly attacked and killed the local cadres and then broke open the granaries. These examples of unrest, however, do not amply indicate the spirit which suddenly animated the whole nation. One could feel new life flowing back into the beaten-down people, and it was indescribably exhilarating.

Equally indescribable was the changed attitude of the Communist officials. They were confused as well as frightened, and their arrogance was gone. They tried to placate everyone, especially the workers whom always they seemed to fear the most.

The matter of workers' loans was typical. Previously any worker needing a loan was required to go through red tape that took months. More than half the applications were refused altogether, and those who did receive advances usually were given half, or less, of what they had asked for. After the Hungarian revolt, however, the policy changed. Cadres called personally on all those whose applications had been rejected and asked if the money was still needed. If the man had asked for JMP20 previously, he was now promptly given JMP40.

Even the national capitalists were treated with something that amounted to respect. The Ideological Institute provided a dramatic example of the changed attitude. During that last week of October 1956, the regular course at the Institute could not be given. The students demanded that the discussion should be limited to the Hungarian situation. The debates included such subjects as whether or not the International Communist Front was collapsing and whether or not inherent defects in Marxist logic might not mean the inevitable failure of Communism. For the first time, I saw and heard the students shouting with anger and derision at the Communist lecturers.

Oddly enough, during this exciting period I was apprehensive. My escape plan was now in operation, and I could think of little else. Success depended upon keeping the authorities convinced of my reliability. When the authorities were lenient, or when they themselves were confused, however, my seeming loyal support of Party policy did not show to any advantage. It is important to remember also that normally the Communists exercised strict control over our behavior. When, as now, they failed to exercise the control completely, we were in danger of doing something that later would be regarded as "unacceptable." Thus, although I felt keenly the excitement, I tried to stay in the background and to express no opinion on the Hungarian revolt.

In China, the climax of the revolt came on October 28, 1956. The news that day was that the Russians had agreed to withdraw their troops. This implied that Hungary would have its freedom, and that the insurrection was successful. On November first, however, we suddenly heard that Hungary had tried to withdraw from the Warsaw Pact and that the Russians with 200,000 troops and 2,500 tanks and armored vehicles were moving against the Hungarian "counter-revolutionaries." We realized that the Russian promise had been merely an act of treachery designed to lull the Hungarian uprising until the Soviet troops could get into position. We felt almost sickened by despair and by revulsion for what we knew would happen to the Hungarian freedom fighters.

The moment that the Russian action in Hungary was defined and understood, the Communists in China tightened up. The change was as definite as the snap of a whip. We had had a glimpse of what would happen if the regime lifted even lightly and momentarily its oppression of the Chinese people, and now we could expect the lid to be clamped down even tighter.

Meanwhile, on October 29, 1956, Israel had invaded Egypt. France and Britain bombed Egypt two days later and landed troops on November 5. In our discussion groups, the subject of Hungary was dropped completely, and we found ourselves beating on the tables in fury over the imperialist aggression. What we were really saying with genuine emotion was, "Why don't the French, British and Americans go to the aid of the Hungarians?" Nevertheless, the Communists were again back in control of our behavior. At the Institute the "free" discussions were no longer permitted. Cadres sat in with each group and recorded the comments made by each member. The penetrating questions from the students ceased; even the most naïve and uneducated businessman quickly learned to say only what the authorities wanted him to say.

We could feel the dull apathy of despair seep through the country again.

CHAPTER 10

Hoping for salvation, the northerners defied death;
Yet how many people are shedding tears this night?
—LU YU

THE SOVIET attack on Hungary in November 1956 destroyed Russian prestige in the satellite countries and disillusioned many people in the neutralist nations. International Communism nearly collapsed. The Peking officials came to its rescue by reaffirming Sino-Soviet unity. They proclaimed loudly to the rest of the world that the 650 million Chinese stood solidly behind their "Soviet elder brothers," and to prove it they hastily dispatched five important delegations to the U.S.S.R. The delegates were well-known figures from among the top government officials, trade union chiefs, the intellectuals and even the ex-national capitalists.

Thus, in early December 1956, I suddenly received instructions to make arrangements through the International Tourist Bureau for a sight-seeing tour of the Soviet Union. J.P. told me that I was one of the country's 12 leading businessmen chosen to help demonstrate Chinese enthusiasm for Russia. In order to make the businessmen's enthusiasm seem spontaneous and thus more genuine, we were to go as "tourists"; in fact, we were the first "tourists" ever to travel from Communist China. To confirm our tourist status, we were obligated to pay one-third of the trip's expenses; the balance was divided between the Chinese and Russian governments. To help make us *look* like a tourist group, the wives of three of the businessmen accompanied us. Finally, two Communist officials from the Tourist Bureau also joined us, ostensibly to learn something of the problems Chinese tourists would face.

In reality, of course, we were completely under the authority of the two officials. Comrade Ho was in charge of us. He was a guerrilla-fighter veteran who attempted with loudmouthed bluster to disguise his appalling ignorance. Nevertheless, he and his equally uncouth assistant were the only members of our delegation whose admiration for the Russians was unqualified and genuine.

Contrary to official pronouncement, the mass of Chinese detested the Russians. Thus the indoctrination we received for the tour was administered with special care. The training began on December 10, 1956, when we left Shanghai for Peking. From that day on, we were given the luxurious accommodations normally reserved only for foreign dignitaries and top Communist officials. These comforts were not intended for our pleasure; they were meant to familiarize us with the living standard that the authorities were trying to make outsiders believe was widespread in China.

To enable us to speak intelligently to the Russians about their contributions to China's industrial progress, we visited various installations that had been built with Soviet assistance. And finally, of course, we listened to a series of lectures from high officials in Peking.

Background information on the Russians themselves was given to us by the President of the Tourist Bureau. He described them as emotional and demonstrative. We were not to be shocked if Russian men hugged and kissed us. If the women did the same, we were to respond with brotherly affection only; further intimacy with them was prohibited.

We were warned about Russian drinking habits. Unlike the decadent imperialists, we were assured, the Russians took alcohol only as an antidote to the cold weather, but at banquets they were apt to carry on dinner table conversation through the medium of toasts; we were to drink the toasts with water.

The language problem was solved by teaching us three Russian phrases. One meant, "Do you mind if I smoke?" which we were *always* to ask before lighting a cigarette in the presence of ladies. Another meant, "Where is the toilet?" which we were *never* to ask in the presence of the opposite sex. The third phrase was, "I do not eat mutton." Most Chinese find this meat unpalatable.

We were instructed to appear well dressed at all times. Each of us was issued a magnificent fur hat, and we were permitted to buy excellent fur-lined coats at a reasonable price. The "capitalists" of our group had to be outfitted with Communist-style uniforms for use on formal occasions. Conversely, the two Communists who accompanied us had always worn the uniform and thus were supplied with lounge suits for informal wear.

The political aspect of our indoctrination was handled by Premier Chou En-lai himself at an informal tea party. He told us that he was leading a government delegation that also would be visiting Russia soon, and he implied that our "tourist" trip was no less important than his own. He said that the objective of both delegations was to help dispel the "misunderstandings" that had followed the Russian action in quelling the "Hungarian revolt." While in the U.S.S.R., our every word and action were to be directed toward strengthening Sino-Soviet relations. If we met people from the satellite countries—the "fraternal nations of Eastern Europe," he called them—we were to take special pains to make our unswerving support of the U.S.S.R. clear to them. Chou closed with the friendly advice that if we found anything to confuse us in the Soviet Union, we were to put our questions to our own authorities and not to bother the Russians with them.

In addition to these instructions, we learned from Comrade Ho that when we returned from our trip, we would have the duty of helping to spread "friendly understanding among the Chinese people toward the Russians." Comrade Ho was also responsible for the one final aspect of our preparations for the tour: our group had to be organized in the manner which the Communists consider proper.

The group therefore was divided into two "discussion" sections, one led by Ho and the other by his assistant. Every member of the group would write out a daily report on everything he had seen, heard and done. Every evening the discussion sections would hold meetings at which the reports would be considered in detail. The idea was to ensure the utmost efficiency in achieving the tour's objectives.

We were also divided into functional committees. For example, a committee of four was assigned the task of gleaning from all the daily individual reports a comprehensive daily report for the whole group. One of the committee writers would concentrate on the instances of Russian friendliness, another on evidence of the high living standard in the U.S.S.R., another on details of Soviet industrial achievements and the last one on agricultural matters. In addition, the reporting committee would write any speeches which the leaders of our delegation might be required to make. I was given this assignment.

Another committee was assigned to deal with the interpreters. This task required such political purity that only Comrade Ho and his assistant could take responsibility for it. The rest of us knew more about Marxism and the Party Line than they did, but we could not be *trusted* to do the job. One of the wives could speak Russian, but she would not be allowed to use her knowledge except in an emergency.

Finally, each member of our delegation was assigned a specific task. A woman with a good voice, for instance, taught us two popular songs, "Moscow-Peking" and "The East Is Red"; when the Russians entertained us with little shows and reciprocation from us was required, she would lead us in group-singing these songs. Another member was responsible for seeing that we were all properly dressed on every occasion. I had a kind of protocol function; at banquets I was to signal when we should sit down, when we should depart, and I was to frown at anyone using bad table manners.

By December 23, 1956, our delegation was able to perform its functions with machinelike precision. We were each permitted to buy 100 rubles (about $25), which was considered adequate for any personal expenses we might have. Our passports then were issued to us and at noon that day we boarded the International Express, which makes the trip from Peking to Moscow in eight days and nights.

The accommodations were luxurious and the food was good. Chinese dishes were served, and the train was run by a Chinese crew as far as Manchouli, the last stop before the border. We were excited about reaching the border, but outside we could see nothing except an endless flat expanse of snow. About ten minutes beyond Manchouli the train stopped for 30 seconds.

A hundred yards or so further on we passed a snow-covered mound. On the slope, mud had been daubed on the snow to read LONG LIVE SINO-SOVIET FRIENDSHIP in both Chinese and Russian writing, and we knew that the previous stop had been at the border. Our officials now lectured us on this fine example of "the border of eternal friendship" where no garrison—not even a solitary guard—was needed. Each member of our delegation busily took down notes from this lecture to incorporate in our daily reports.

A few minutes later, we reached the little border station of Otpur where the houses and the dress of the people were miraculously changed to the Russian style. We had a four-hour stop-over while the cars of our train were lifted by huge cranes and put on different wheels for the wider-guage Russian railways. The weather was extremely cold—the temperature in fact was 40° below zero F. We huddled shivering in the bleak station, impatient to get back to the well-heated train. When we boarded the train again we settled down to a long, monotonous journey. The scenery was unvarying—flat snow-covered plains occasionally broken by clumps of black trees or a shabby village—but we were kept occupied. We had a large amount of material on Russia to read and discuss at our long daily meetings. We memorized additional useful phrases in Russian and practiced singing our two songs.

We were also permitted to converse with the other passengers as long as we did it under the watchful eyes of our two supervisors and noted down the details of our talks in our daily reports. Among the passengers were a number of other Chinese; some of them were students on their way to Russian universities and some were technical workers going for industrial training in Russia or East Germany. They had been well indoctrinated politically, and they had been given a whole month of training in Western customs and manners. Their behavior, however, was apt to be crude, and most of them were in a pitiful state of confusion because of the train's unfamiliar facilities.

The Russian passengers were of three easily recognizable types. One included average citizens, most of whom rode the train for only short distances. They were always shabbily dressed and never very clean. They all had that timid, anxious, subservient air peculiar to those who live under totalitarian regimes.

Another type, high Russian officials, could be recognized instantly by their arrogance, although they also tended to dress shabbily. I talked to one man who was a member of the Supreme Soviet, and I began to get a picture of the Russian privileged class. He possessed a permanent pass that entitled him to travel free about the country even when not on government business. He obviously had plenty of leisure which he regarded as his right and which he enjoyed as uninhibitedly as any aristocrat.

The final type were Russian technical experts returning from assignments in China. They could be recognized because they were the best dressed. Some of them knew a little Chinese or English and therefore were easier to talk to. What surprised me about them was their obviously genuine fondness for China and the Chinese. In China, they were universally detested; they were paid many times more than a Chinese doing the same job received, and they were granted many privileges that set them apart. To us, they were no different from the Western "imperialists" who had humiliated us during the previous regime. The Russians, however, seemed completely oblivious to being disliked in China and spoke glowingly of their Chinese friends. Not one of them was glad to be returning home. Most of all, they were childishly delighted with the clothes, watches, pens, cameras and other such Western-manufactured articles which they and the privileged few were still able to obtain in China.

One day a Russian woman—she was a schoolteacher, we learned—approached our group and exclaimed ecstatically over the boots worn by the three ladies in our party. She was incredulous at how little they cost. She asked us if we could obtain a pair for her, and was ready to count out the rubles for them at once. We were not permitted to accept money from the Russians, but we took her name and address and promised to have the boots sent to her as a gift. The woman responded with extravagant expressions of gratitude; she even hugged and kissed each of us, just as we had been told in our indoctrination course.

Comrade Ho was delighted with the success of this gesture toward Sino-Soviet friendship; if possible, he became even more self-confident. As we entered the dining car that evening, he stopped by the table of an attractive Russian girl and patted her on the head. He meant only to be friendly, but she looked up at him, screamed, and cringed away from him, obviously in terror. A crowd collected and there was much loud talking in both languages. From the girl's account, the Russians apparently thought that Comrade Ho had tried to molest her in some unpleasant way. The woman in our party who could speak Russian finally succeeded in calming everyone down and in making suitable apologies. Nevertheless, the Russian girl tended to shrink away from Comrade Ho whenever he passed near her.

In our discussion meeting that night, one of our group suggested that Comrade Ho had made an incorrect gesture toward the Russian girl and that we should discuss the matter for the purpose of ensuring that a similar mistake was not made again. Comrade Ho's heavy face grew actually black with fury, and he began shouting at us. He said that we stupid bourgeoisie did not comprehend the proper relations between people. He insisted that he and the Russian girl had had perfect comradely socialist understanding and sympathy, but that we others with our bourgeois misconceptions had created unnecessary confusion. We immediately agreed, and the man who had dared criticize Comrade Ho stammered in his haste to castigate himself. Moreover, in the official report for the group that day, Comrade Ho was commended for his people-to-people diplomacy and the rest of us criticized ourselves for having caused a misunderstanding; we pledged ourselves to renewed vigilance against bourgeois ideas.

The official report for the next day also required slight modification. We arrived at Novo Sibirsk where, for the first time since Otpur, we had a several-hour stopover. While exploring the large station I came across Comrade Ho, who was close to another fit of temper. He was stopping people and asking in Russian, "Do you mind if I smoke?" I realized immediately that he had mixed up one of the three Russian phrases we had been taught in Peking, and that what he wanted to say was, "Where is the toilet?" The people he questioned would look at him strangely and then hurry away. He could not imagine himself wrong, and apparently he assumed that the people could not hear him. Thus, he had begun to grab people by the arm and to shout his question in their faces.

Some kind of awkward situation was sure to arise any moment. I therefore asked the proper question of a passer-by, and had the washroom pointed out to me. I then went to Comrade Ho and offered to show him where it was.

The washroom we entered was a shock to both of us. I have never before or since seen such filth. The stench was overpowering. To make the place even worse, a man was being violently sick. Ho and I left immediately.

A moment later, however, the man who had been vomiting came up to us. We perceived now that he was quite drunk. He had at least a week's stubble of beard, he was very dirty and his clothes were almost in rags. He took the cloth of my coat and rubbed it between his hands, making odd grunting sounds of pleasure. He even rubbed the cloth against his cheek. Ho and I were so embarrassed that momentarily we could do nothing. Just then, however, a plainclothes policeman appeared and pulled the drunken man away from us. He shouted for two uniformed policemen who ran to us and grabbed the drunk roughly by the arms. As the prisoner was being propelled away, he made little animal-like whimpering sounds. He stumbled, and as he was being dragged along his trousers slipped down. The whole scene was unspeakably depressing.

Nevertheless, the plainclothesman turned back to us and dismissed the incident with a shrug and an apologetic grin. He beckoned us to follow him toward the other end of the station. On the way, I had my first chance to view Russians in a crowd rather than as individuals. The general impression of shabbiness and uncleanliness was even more pronounced. Presumably, these people were passengers waiting for trains. Most of them carried their belongings in untidy bundles, and they waited in a kind of dull apathy, lolling against the walls or sprawled on the floor. They created an atmosphere of slovenly disorder and indifference. What shocked me—and, I am sure, Comrade Ho as well—was the fact that the authorities allowed such an atmosphere to exist. In China, under the new regime, the poverty and disorder were equally bad, but would never be permitted to show, particularly in a place where foreigners might catch a glimpse of them.

Nevertheless, the policeman, far from being embarrassed by these people, drew our attention to them. He twisted his face into an exaggerated expression of disgust, and dismissed the people with a deprecating gesture of his hand. He led us into another waiting room and now, all smiles, indicated that this was the place for important people like us.

Comrade Ho was thoughtful for a long time. Finally he suggested that we did not need to tell the others or to put down in our reports what we had seen and heard in the station. He explained that the Soviet Union, after 40 years of Communist socialism, had reached civilization's highest stage. He and I, he said, were too naïve and ignorant to understand all the benefits offered in such an advanced country. Thus we could easily make mistakes in interpreting what we saw. Rather than damage the socialist cause by such mistakes, therefore, we should not comment on any matter about which we had doubts.

Naturally, I did not contradict Comrade Ho. I suggested instead that, in our report, we describe the heavy-industry installations for which Novo Sibirsk was justly famous. Moreover, as an illustration of the benefits of Communist internationalism, we should point out that 1,500 Chinese comrade workers and technicians were at this very moment living in Novo Sibirsk receiving training from their generous Soviet "elder brothers." Comrade Ho considered my words with pursed lips, and finally intimated that the suggestion had some merit. Nevertheless, for the rest of the trip to Moscow he was subdued.

He brightened, however, at the elaborate welcome staged for us at the Moscow station. We arrived in the morning of December 31, 1956. We were greeted with a blaze of flash bulbs. Motion picture cameras recorded our arrival on film. A crowd carried banners and placards and shouted slogans of friendly greeting. Important officials made speeches. For simple "tourists," we certainly were being received royally.

We now met for the first time the two Russian interpreters who would be assigned to our party for the rest of our tour. The older of the two was an ex-army officer who had served in Manchuria, where he had learned Mandarin. The other was a young man from Moscow's language university. His knowledge of

Chinese was too academic to be really useful, but he could speak English fairly well. Thus he and I were able to converse. Our talking in English made Comrade Ho nervous, but did not really worry him. He could be sure than an interpreter assigned to us by the Soviet government would be politically "pure" and would instantly report any comment of mine that was out of line.

Outside the Moscow station, a line of chauffeur-driven Ziss and the smaller Moscva motorcars awaited us. We delegates were assigned two passengers to a car. According to the young interpreter this indicated our status. Visitors of top importance were given individual cars and those with rank less than ours rode in buses. We were driven to the Metropole Hotel, which was reserved for visitors who were not government officials. We delegates were assigned two to a suite of rooms. Each suite contained a drawing room, study, bedroom and bathroom and was furnished with heavy old-fashioned opulence. The place was well heated, and plenty of hot water was available. I was frankly delighted with the luxury and the red-carpet treatment we were receiving and I wondered if foreign visitors to China felt the same. I also wondered if the contrast was as great in Russia as it was in China between what the foreign visitors enjoyed and what the masses endured.

The hotel's manager gave us a welcoming tea in a private dining room and invited us to a New Year's Eve dinner party that would begin at 11 that evening. Meanwhile, when the tea was over, our two-to-a-car delegation was whisked off to see the highlights of the city's points of interest. I was interested most in the people we saw. Wherever we stopped, large crowds gathered around us. Invariably, they expressed extravagant admiration for our clothes and cameras. The Moscow people looked less threadbare than the Russians we had seen in the smaller cities.

Nevertheless, their clothes were made from coarse, harsh, cheap materials of a uniform nondescript shade and were cut in unattractive old-fashioned styles. The drab sameness of the people made their enthusiasm for our outfits understandable. At the same time, the people also seemed genuinely delighted to see Chinese. Because the Russians were so unpopular in China, I still found our popularity in Russia hard to believe. Nevertheless, the affection of the people who stopped to talk to us was obviously spontaneous and sincere. It was also tiring.

We were grateful, therefore, that our hosts permitted us a chance to nap before the late evening celebration. At 10 P.M., however, Comrade Ho gathered us for a special meeting at which we were given a final briefing before our first big banquet. He outlined once again the general behavior expected of us, and then asked those of us entrusted with the separate details of deportment to address the group. Thus I demonstrated again the proper use of the knife and fork, and I admonished the delegates to avoid sucking soup noisily and to keep their mouths shut when chewing. Only Comrade Ho and his assistant needed such instructions, but of course I pretended to address only the group. A last check was made concerning our dress, and we filed down to the main ballroom.

The place was gaily decorated, crowded and noisy. Nevertheless, as we entered, the band burst into the song "Moscow-Peking." The other diners rose, raised their glasses to us in a toast, and shouted friendly greetings. We were astonished by the reception, but also flattered and even a little touched. We were taken to a large banquet table beside the dance floor. The table was decorated with the Russian and Chinese flags. Our two interpreters and their wives rose to greet us.

Comrade Ho, as head of our committee to deal with the interpreters, was seated between their wives. The two Russian women toasted him with their glasses and Comrade Ho, catching on, did the same to them. Then, beaming at the two ladies, he asked in Russian, "Where is the toilet?"

I realized with horror that he still was mixed up about the meaning of this phrase and the one for "Do you mind if I smoke?" I certainly did not intend to incur his dangerous wrath by pointing out his error, and the other delegates obviously felt the same. The Russian ladies looked at him bewildered, and Comrade Ho, still beaming, repeated his question.

I leaned across the table and whispered in English to the younger interpreter that Comrade Ho was asking permission to smoke. The interpreter understood the situation at once and told Comrade Ho in Chinese that the ladies had granted him the permission. The interpreter then evidently explained the matter in Russian to the women. The women began to giggle, but were stopped by stern looks from their husbands.

This incident seems funny to me now, but at the time it was quite otherwise, and everyone in our delegation was worried about it. Obviously no one—not even the Russian interpreters—dared explain the blunder to Comrade Ho. Nevertheless, if he ever learned about it, we knew he would be furious, and we knew equally that someone else would be blamed for it. Whoever took the blame might well face catastrophe.

We also feared catastrophe from the possible effects of alcohol on Comrade Ho. He seemed to treat vodka with contempt as though defying the puny stuff to have an effect on him. Each drink had the effect of making his gestures more exaggerated and his voice even louder. Fortunately, however, his increasing boisterousness was drowned in the crescendo of noise that marked the Russian exuberance.

In fact, the gaiety of the party that night was almost irresistible, and in spite of ourselves our anxieties were suppressed. A

248

parade of well-wishers came to our table to toast and chat with us. We were frequently invited to join other parties for a drink or two and an exchange of pleasantries. The Russian women were especially friendly, and we always had plenty of dancing partners.

I was curious about what stratum of Moscow society could afford a party like this one. I learned that the guests paid 120 rubles ($30) each as a cover charge which included supper. The top officials and foreign diplomats were partying at the Kremlin. I assumed, therefore, that the Russians celebrating at the Metropole were lesser-but-still-high officials—or perhaps mainly the children of high officials.

The guests also included next-to-the-top diplomatic officers. I saw, for example, a beautiful Indian girl in a lovely sari, and I could not resist asking her to dance. We got on well together; I think both of us found considerable relief in being able to converse easily in English. She told me, however, that she was fluent in Russian and had been Prime Minister Nehru's interpreter when Khrushchev and Bulganin visited India the previous year. I mentioned this fact to Comrade Ho and the older interpreter when I returned to my table and I asked if they did not think the girl was beautiful. The two men frowned. "I think she is revolting!" Comrade Ho said to me. From this I understood that I was not to seek friends among the "neutrals" and that I was being warned to watch my step. I was disappointed, but for the rest of the evening I concentrated on our "Soviet elder brothers and sisters."

The evening lasted until 6 A.M. We had four hours' rest and then met for our regular discussion. Comrade Ho looked ill and obviously was suffering from a hangover. He was the only one who had drunk too much, but now he admonished us sternly

249

about drinking, and we all pledged ourselves to be more careful in the future.

Oddly enough, what seemed to disturb Comrade Ho the most was the jazz music we had listened to for the entire evening. In the New China, jazz was labeled "yellow" music; it was regarded as one of the worst aspects of capitalist depravity and was forbidden. Thus, why was it permitted in the more advanced socialist stage of the Soviet Union? Comrade Ho's slow brain chewed painfully on this stony idea until we suggested tactfully that the lyrics rather than the music made jazz degenerate; this was safe, because we could be sure that Comrade Ho would never be able to understand the Russian words to the music he heard. When we also suggested that our Soviet elder brothers had reached such a high socialist level that they no longer needed to fear contamination from any bourgeois influence, Comrade Ho was visibly relieved, and these conclusions were incorporated into our official report.

Our report also had much to say about the rich food served to us by our generous hosts, the Russian people. The fact that most of the fruit had come from China was also noted. What was not noted, or even discussed, was the fact that such fruit was unobtainable in China. I was beginning to see why the Russians liked the Chinese but why the affection was not returned. One reason of course was that at the time, the Chinese were the only people in the world who were showing the Russians anything but suspicion, anger or hatred; we conversely tended to resent being made to show them an affection we did not feel. Probably a more important reason, however, was the fact that most of what little luxury food and what few consumer goods were available to the Russians came from China. The source of these gratifying luxuries was apparent, but the Russians paid for them with steel, precision instruments and heavy industrial equipment which went unnoticed by the average Chinese. The Chinese masses were aware only that everything they produced which might help alleviate the drabness of their existence was taken away by the Russians.

Such aspects of Sino-Soviet relations were not considered by our group. Instead, in our report that day we reached the "unanimous conclusion" that the party had been a great success because it had revealed to us how deep was the fraternal love between the Russian and the Chinese peoples.

The next six days were devoted to concentrated sight-seeing in Moscow. We were always accompanied by *Pravda* and Tass reporters and photographers. While we were being interviewed in Moscow's famous subway, the fact that I had been in New York became known. I was immediately asked to compare the New York and Moscow subway systems. Obviously, the journalists had learned that this was a safe question, and I gave the answer I knew was expected. I said that the Moscow subway, as befitting a social order devoted to the people's welfare, was the last word in beauty and cleanliness. In New York, where the profit motive was paramount, the people had to ride in squalid discomfort. I did not say that the New York system provided efficient transportation, a claim that could hardly be made about the Moscow subway. Nevertheless, my picture and comments appeared widely in the Russian newspapers and later in the Chinese press as well.

The impression about Russia that struck us most forcibly was the fantastic prices of what few consumer goods were obtainable. All of us in our group had wanted to buy a few small souvenirs and a present or two for friends at home, but we could find nothing that was not prohibitively expensive. To us, this was a minor disappointment, but the shortage of consumer goods must have meant real hardship to the Russians. We were told that the average Russian worker earned the equivalent of $150 to $200 a month. His food alone, however, took half this amount; his other basic living expenses were such that he barely managed to get by, and wives generally were forced to take jobs as well if a family was to be supported. Nevertheless, a man's suit, for example, cost as much as a whole month's salary. A woman's nylon blouse or a pair of leather shoes cost about half as much. Worse, the quality of such items was the lowest possible. Among the businessmen in our group were two textile manufacturers; they wanted to see Russian textile factories, but their requests were always met with evasion, and we were not shown even one. Moreover, the few showpiece consumer goods factories we did see were far behind comparable units in China.

Conversely, Russian heavy industry was impressive. We visited, for example, the country's outstanding motorcar factory and saw the production of trucks identical to those which in China were called "Liberation" brand. To our surprise, the factory's chief engineer could speak Chinese; we learned that he had spent four years in the automobile factory at Changchun in Manchuria. This proved that the Russians were indeed sending their top engineers to China.

Also, the fact that the trucks produced in both countries were identical proved that the Russian and Chinese industrial systems were being tied irrevocably together. Politics aside, therefore, the Chinese were becoming increasingly dependent upon the Russians and could not pursue an independent course even if they wanted to. We businessmen in the delegation had been vaguely aware of this situation, but it was brought home to us during our Moscsow sight-seeing and I knew that they were as depressed about it as I was.

We were even more depressed at the realization of what the Russian concentration on heavy industry at the expense of consumer goods would mean to China's future. Here in Russia, after 40 years of planned economic growth, light industry could not meet the very modest demands of the people; imports even from "backward" China were prized. Because China was following Russia's lead in industrial development, we too could expect to have fewer and fewer of the goods that seem to make life worth living.

To the Communists, of course, powerful heavy industry is necessary for their military security at home and abroad, but I am convinced that they dare not allow more consumer goods production. Primarily, their excuse for seizing absolute power is their claim that a high living standard for the masses cannot be achieved without their "leadership." If the masses received even a taste of civilized comforts, however, they would begin to expect and demand more with increasing impatience. But comforts cannot be enjoyed without some leisure, and leisure is meaningless without the liberty to use it as one chooses. In short, any real rise in the living standard for the masses would be impossible without political freedom and thus would threaten Communist power. We Chinese businessmen were familiar with the low living standard of the masses in our own country, but what we saw in Russia shocked us.

Comrade Ho saw what we were shown, but he looked at it differently. He *believed* that he was seeing the world's highest living standard, and he refused to accept any evidence to the contrary. When, for example, he was told the price of a Russian overcoat, he marveled at how cheap it was. If I had told him that an American worker could buy an infinitely better coat for one-half the price, he would simply accuse me of spreading imperialist lies.

At the same time, Comrade Ho was quite unmoved by the one example of real magnificence we were shown in Moscow: the

Russian ballet at the Bolshoi Theater. We saw it twice, and the performances were the best I have seen anywhere. I was told that 500 craftsmen were needed to stage the productions, and I can believe it. Nevertheless, Comrade Ho fidgeted through the performances, visibly embarrassed by them. I think he was even a little shocked. Like most Chinese Communists, he tended to associate abstract beauty with "decadent bourgeois idealism" and was subconsciously afraid of its power to make materialism seem cheap.

He was much intrigued, however, by the fact that, at the ballet, our delegation was given the "royal box" which in the old days had been reserved for the Czar. The rest of us were also pleased, but our pleasure at being treated like royalty was diminished by the fact that during the intermissions we could not afford to buy the cheapest refreshments offered, not even the tempting fruit from China. This did not bother Comrade Ho, who had learned to expect nothing and thus to be mawkishly grateful for anything he did receive.

He was also impressed by an odd custom of the Russian women who attended the Bolshoi Theater performances. Each carried a bag containing a pair of shoes and a pair of nylon or silk hose. Arriving at the theater, the women changed their shoes and hose in the ladies' lounge and changed back again after the performance. We Chinese "capitalists" found this pathetic, especially because the shoes which the women were protecting so carefully were of such pitiful quality. Comrade Ho, however, looked upon the custom as an example of clever thrift that proved again the superiority of the Russian social order; in fact, this idea was a "unanimous conclusion" given in our delegation's report concerning the ballet.

To me personally, at the ballet, an ironic incident occurred. The Russians had a way of devoting the intermission periods to serious exercise; they would form lines, four or five abreast, and stride briskly around the lounge as though bent on getting a thorough leg-stretch. Like most Chinese, I am inclined to eschew physical effort whenever possible, but at the theater I could not avoid it without obstructing the rapid flow of traffic. Thus, on one occasion when I entered the lines, I found myself cantering next to a Chinese who, to my chagrin, turned out to be the ex-Dean of Shanghai University. He was the one whom the authorities had sent to replace my friend Dr. Yui during the fearsome days of Thought Reform; he was also the one who had reorganized the university along "progressive" lines and, in fact, had been responsible for forcing me to resign. Since then, naturally, we had not spoken, and now we would have avoided each other except for the difficulty of getting out of the line once it had begun to move at full speed. He made some lofty comments expressing polite surprise that the authorities would send someone like me to Moscow. He told me that he was with a special delegation of 25 Chinese university presidents and deans. He also said smugly that he was being put up at the Metropole Hotel and, when he learned that I was there too, he said that he could understand why he had not run into me before. "They have put me in the part that has two-room suites," he said.

I nodded and replied, "I suppose that is separate from the three-room suites where I am staying."

The dean actually stumbled; his face showed incredulous surprise, but he recovered quickly and tried again. He talked about the magnificent ballet performance and mentioned that his seat was in the first row of the orchestra; he expressed the hope that I could see the show adequately from where I sat.

"I can see it fine," I said. "We're in the so-called 'royal box.'"

I had been unable to resist putting a barb into an old enemy, but I was sorry immediately afterward. I understood clearly his confusion and consternation. He had tried so hard and so long to think and believe as the Communists demanded. They had demanded that he hate the bourgeois intellectuals and "capitalists," and yet they were giving me—an example of both groups—more status than they gave him. His attitude toward me changed immediately. He became humble and apologetic. He hoped that we could meet again in Shanghai and "talk over old times." He was really the same as I, except that he had more sincerity; he was still trying to find in the regime's ideology something that could command his genuine loyalty. He embarrassed me.

The most embarrassing aspect of our Russian visit concerned the subject of Stalin, whose fall from grace had occurred only the year before. I believe now that while we were in the U.S.S.R. the Russians were still confused about his status. Obviously, Mao Tse-tung had not accepted Stalin's "demotion" to the extent that Khrushchev advocated. To the Chinese Communists, therefore, Stalin was still one of the great revolutionary leaders and not to express interest in him would be an affront. Nevertheless, the Russians invariably grew silent and quickly changed the subject whenever Stalin's name was mentioned, but the awkward situation arose time and again. Stalin's pictures were removed from the art galleries and public buildings, but his statues were frequently seen. The rumor in China had been that his body had been removed from the Lenin Mausoleum in the Red Square and sent to his native Georgia. If this were true, we thought, Stalin's demotion would be official and final. Thus when we were invited to visit the famous Lenin tomb, we were especially interested because it would give us the chance to learn the truth.

In the tomb, no one was permitted to speak, and the hush had a deeply sacred quality. Two bright beams of light were focused dramatically on the faces of the bodies in the two glass cases. We mounted stairs to get a close look at the reclining figures.

Stalin was there, all right, lying in state next to Lenin. The two bodies were amazingly—even gruesomely—lifelike. Lenin wore a plain Communist-style outfit, but Stalin was dressed in a marshal's uniform. I was surprised that Stalin looked so much older than Lenin.

Mounting the steps to the glass coffins, one of our party gasped. A guard immediately stepped forward and touched his shoulder in warning. In the discussion meeting that night, we criticized our companion for his gasp, but for once Comrade Ho insisted upon lenience. "It is understandable that one can be carried away in the presence of the great Lenin and Stalin," he said. I had the feeling that his reaction and ours to any situation would always be the opposite.

Nevertheless, only the next day his reaction was the same as ours to a ceremony at which Premier Chou En-lai was given an honorary law degree by Moscow University. The university's impressive auditorium was full for the occasion. Khrushchev and Chou En-lai appeared from the rear and walked down the aisle to the stage. They were followed by Molotov, Malenkov, Kaganovich and others who have since disappeared from the public eye. The university's president introduced Chou, praising him as "our most faithful friend." After receiving the degree, Chou made an excellent speech in Chinese. In effect, he said, "My capabilities are inadequate for this great honor, but I am glad to have it, for I shall use it as a whip to drive myself harder in the cause of the international proletariat." At this, Khrushchev stood up and started the applause, which swelled into a mighty ovation. Despite my cynicism concerning the policies of the Soviet and Chinese governments, I experienced a thrill of pride, and every other Chinese there felt the same. The honored treatment we were receiving from the Russians was not only lavish, it was obviously sincere as well, and we would be inhuman not to feel flattered.

At the ceremony for Chou En-lai, I met a Chinese girl who was studying at Moscow University. She said that many Russian girls would like to marry Chinese boys. Such marriages had been prohibited, but the ban had been lifted a month before, and now the first Sino-Soviet student wedding was to take place the next week. The Russian girls knew that technicians returning from China brought rich goods unobtainable in the U.S.S.R. They also were aware that most of what little luxury food was available in the U.S.S.R. came from China. They assumed therefore that by marrying a Chinese they would move into a better life. They would, of course, be bitterly disappointed.

Comrade Ho faced a whole series of disappointments during our tour of the Soviet industrial cities, and we spent most of our discussion meetings helping him to rationalize much of what we saw. We made the tour, for example, in a special railway carriage that would be attached to regular trains making scheduled runs. Invariably, the other cars on the train were dilapidated and filthy. Even Comrade Ho could see that they were in worse condition than Chinese trains. Nevertheless, as we had begun to learn, the Russians always assumed that everything they had was the biggest and best in the world. Thus, when they expected us to admire even their trains, Comrade Ho was forced to pretend that the Russian railways were superior to the Chinese. Ho could lie easily enough in defense of Communism, but this was a lie to Communists about achievements under Communism in the U.S.S.R. versus China, and it stuck in his throat. We convinced him that the better Soviet railway equipment always just happened to be in some other part of the country.

We had more difficulty in explaining away to him some of the seamier aspects of life in the workers' paradise. At our mealtimes on the train, the dining car would be cleared of other passengers, and the whole car would be given to our small group. Comrade Ho once suggested to the steward that this would not be necessary, and in fact we would welcome the chance to eat with our Soviet friends. The steward, however, insisted that we would be much better off by ourselves. "The people," he explained, "are noisy and ill-mannered, and they're apt to get troublesomely drunk."

We could blame a "tactless" steward for such a remark, but the truth was we saw examples of drunkenness constantly wherever we went. We had always been told that under imperialism, capitalists drank too much because they were degenerate and that the workers sometimes drank excessively as a temporary escape from misery. In China, known alcoholics and drug addicts had been ruthlessly disposed of in the early days of the Communist regime, and now anyone who appeared intoxicated in public would be quickly in serious trouble. Thus, the seeming laxity of our Soviet elder brothers in dealing with alcoholism disturbed Comrade Ho. I helped him a little by suggesting that the drunks we saw must be veterans who had suffered terribly during World War II and used liquor to forget.

We met a veteran in the plane we took to Stalingrad. He was a Russian general who approached us for a friendly chat. Comrade Ho, as an ex-guerrilla fighter, was much flattered to receive attention from such a high-ranking officer. He wanted to talk about the general's experiences in the glorious Red Army; the general, however, wanted to talk about his experiences with women. He told us that he greatly admired Chinese women who, he said, were passionate and had fine slim figures. Comrade Ho looked embarrassed and murmured politely that Russian women also had good figures.

When this comment had been translated, however, the gen-

259

eral shrugged. "They're all right when they're young," he replied. "Even my wife had a good figure when I married her, but now she's as big as a beer barrel—and just as easy to get into." He burst into laughter and reached over to slap Ho's knee.

Comrade Ho tittered politely—until the general's words had been translated. In Russian, perhaps, the remark was subtle, but in Chinese it was graphically crude. We bourgeois were a little shocked—no Chinese would ever talk this way about his wife— but Comrade Ho was shocked to the core of his puritan Communist soul. A Hero of the Soviet Union was automatically a hero of his, and he apparently felt that he had been betrayed. Later we tried to tell him that the general had regarded him as a friend and an equal and was merely trying to make a joke, but Ho was depressed for the rest of the flight.

I was depressed as well. The incident made me realize for the first time that no one joked in China any more. I had heard nothing funny since the new regime began, and we had forgotten how to react to humor.

We were not embarrassed by anything humorous in Stalingrad, and Comrade Ho cheered up. We were shown films of the terrible fighting and destruction in the city during World War II. The fact that the number of war widows, orphans, and cripples in Stalingrad was huge enabled us to express genuine sympathy for the people in our reports. We could also report truthfully that the inhabitants had been impressively successful in rebuilding the city.

The Stalingrad factories we visited were a special delight to Comrade Ho because several of their top engineers could speak Chinese. This meant that the engineers had been in China to direct the building of duplicate installations. Thus we had further "proof" of the advantages of Communist internationalism and of socialist progress.

I was beginning to have difficulty, however, in showing un-flagging enthusiasm for Russian factories; to me, they all looked much alike and seldom were as impressive as the ones I had seen in America. The parking lot of Stalingrad's huge tractor works, for example, contained only four motorcars. The factory, we were told repeatedly, belonged to "the people," but I learned that the cars belonged to the Party Secretary, the Trade Union Chairman and the two chief engineers. I remembered that in the U.S., a factory with 30,000 employees might be owned by cap-italists but its parking lot would contain many thousands of cars belonging to the workers. Needless to say, I did not bring up such an odious truth in our discussion meetings.

Our discussion meetings in Sochi, the Black Sea resort, were difficult because we found less suitable material for our reports. True, the place was beautiful and the palatial villas built during the Czarist days were magnificent. We were able to write several ecstatic paragraphs in our reports about how all this luxury was intended for the workers. The fact was only too obvious, how-ever, that such a small number of workers could ever have a chance for a Sochi vacation that the resort could mean little to the proletariat. Moreover, although plenty of the Soviet elite and foreign dignitaries were in evidence, vacationing workers were not.

For example, we were taken through one of the showpiece hospitals in the city. It compared favorably with the hospitals that can be found in any American city, but—we were assured—this one was solely for the benefit of the laboring class. In the effort to obtain some human interest material for our reports, Comrade Ho asked one of the patients what kind of worker he was. We expected to hear that the patient was a farmer, a machin-ist, an electrician or, perhaps, a steelworker. The interpreter addressed the question to the patient and the two of them had a long animated conversation. Finally, the interpreter told us that the patient was "just an ordinary worker."

In our discussion group meeting that night, however, the Russian-speaking Chinese woman told us that the interpreter had been wrong. The patient had replied that he was the Party Secretary of a large district; he had been offended at being called a worker and furthermore had insisted that he was important enough so that the authorities would not put him in a hospital for mere workers. Comrade Ho was infuriated at the girl; he said that her Russian must have been faulty and that she had misunderstood the conversation. For our reports, we noted down the translation given to us by the official interpreter.

We were not able to interpret so simply the social life we saw in Sochi. At our luxurious hotel, for instance, the guest whose table was next to ours in the dining room was an army general. He drank heavily, and each evening he was accompanied by a different girl; all his girls were exceptionally attractive. The way he carried on with them, even at the table, indicated that they could not possibly have been his daughters. Comrade Ho, I think, was still disturbed by the conversation he had had with the general on the plane to Stalingrad and now he seemed morbidly anxious to find an explanation for this new general's behavior. We finally decided that the general was a widower and that during the war he had been a great hero, thereby earning a host of "admirers."

We soon perceived, however, that a rather large number of these attractive women were available to accompany the top Party officials, famous scientists and literary figures, and the high-ranking military officers who were the other guests in the hotel. Also, we could see that some of the women had different escorts every night, although they were always embarrassingly affectionate. Nothing about the girls suggested that they were model workers rewarded with a Sochi vacation for their contribution to the country's industrial progress. In fact, Comrade Ho and the three ladies in our delegation were shocked by them. I had heard rumors that prostitutes existed in Russia and, as nearly as I could tell, these in Sochi operated like the "call girls" in America.

In China, however, such "degenerate elements" had long since been eliminated. We therefore could not admit officially that such "elements" existed in the more advanced "socialist society" of the Soviet Union. Thus we referred to the women simply as "admirers" of the Soviet notables, but Comrade Ho was visibly depressed.

Unfortunately, an incident occurred in Sochi that at first uplifted Ho's spirits but then depressed him even more. One day we were given a cruise of several hours along the palm-studded Black Sea coast. The ship accommodated about one hundred passengers, almost all of whom spent the cruise listening to jazz records. We had already learned that most Russians were astonishingly enthusiastic about American jazz; we heard it everywhere. On the ship, some of the records included the New Orleans type of jazz which I remembered well from my visit to that city eight years before. I was singing under my breath one of my favorites among these songs when I suddenly realized that I had a fascinated audience. It included our younger interpreter and several of the Russian passengers. When they found that I knew a little about jazz, that I had actually seen and heard some of the famous American bands and that I had even met several of the famous jazz musicians, my prestige with them soared. Within a few minutes almost all the passengers were gathered around the interpreter and me and I was plied with innumerable questions. They did not have the lyrics to many of the songs that they liked particularly. In most cases, I did not know the words, but I knew at least the general idea. This was adequate, however, and many of the Russians took notes on what I was able to tell them.

I was aware that Comrade Ho was glowing with this successful example of Sino-Soviet people-to-people rapport. Because the discussion was carried on in English and Russian, he did not know the subject of it, and I planned to tell him that we had talked of "cultural" matters.

As we were leaving the ship, however, Ho asked the interpreter what we had talked about. The young Russian said happily, "Mr. Loh has been giving us the words to all the American jazz songs." Ho's face fell. I know that in his mind he had been framing an enthusiastic report, the whole basis for which was now knocked out. In previous reports, we had already rationalized the Russian liking for jazz by explaining that only the salacious American words made it "yellow."

I was able to get the Russian-speaking Chinese girl aside and brief her on the situation. In the group discussion meeting that evening, we both insisted that the interpreter had given Ho a wrong impression. True, I had given the Russians on the ship the words to some American jazz songs, but it was to illustrate how degenerate the songs were. Mostly, I said, we had discussed "music as a means of increasing understanding between the peoples of the socialist nations."

Comrade Ho accepted our comment without argument but I think it was mostly because of another aspect of Soviet society which became apparent during the cruise. The majority of the other passengers had been boys and girls in their late teens or early twenties and we had learned that they were children of important officials. From the beginning of our tour, we had noticed that young people like these always formed a sizable part of the crowd enjoying the hectic night life. We now began to realize that the children of the Soviet elite formed what appeared to be a separate class with leisure, wealth and privilege which they themselves had not earned. This was extremely difficult to explain in our reports, because it contradicted one of the basic principles of Marxism. We finally came to the tentative conclusion that these youngsters were exceptionally brilliant or gifted and were encouraged and rewarded for their *potential* contribution to society.

In Kiev, which we visited next, however, we found little evidence to support this theory. One night in the hotel ballroom, for example, the younger members of our delegation were invited to the table of two young couples whose guests we were for the entire evening. We learned that they were the children of local officials. We tried to find out from them what work they themselves did or what careers they planned, but they treated the matter as a joke and we never got a sensible answer from them. Nevertheless, they entertained us with casual extravagance; the food and drink they paid for for all of us that evening would have supported the average Russian worker for a month. One of the young men even had a motorcar of his own.

Moreover, we had evidence that did not speak highly of the intelligence of this set of privileged youngsters. It happened that in Kiev the Western film stars Yves Montand and Simone Signoret were staying at the same hotel in which we were lodged; in fact, I had a pleasant chat with M. Montand one evening. Whenever he left the hotel or returned to it, he would be set upon by hundreds of wildly emotional teen-agers, mostly girls, who often had waited in the street for hours merely to get a glimpse of him. The shrieking crowd had to be held back by police, but the girls struggled to get near enough to touch him and beseech him for his autograph. I had seen a little of this sort of adolescent hysteria in America, but I never imagined it in

Russia. Comrade Ho had difficulty in hiding his disgust, and I know that he was deeply shocked.

Ho's worst shock of the whole tour, however, occurred during our visit to a showpiece collective farm called "Red Ukraine." The collective included a thousand households and was supposed to be highly mechanized. The Russians were extremely proud of it and Comrade Ho was much impressed with it. I had difficulty pretending enthusiasm, however, because even the little farm mechanization I had seen in America was infinitely more advanced.

The climax of our visit was a "real Ukrainian farm dinner" served in a small building which apparently was used as a private dining hall for officials. Outside the building, hundreds of farm workers gathered and serenaded us for three hours, much of the time standing in a cold drizzle. After the dinner, we had a chance to question the chairman of the collective.

The chairman spoke to us with surprising frankness. He said that in the Soviet Union agriculture lagged behind industry and that the collective farms had not met their goals during the previous Five-Year Plan. He complained that the returns paid by the government for the farm's produce were inadequate. This fact, together with high taxes and obligatory contributions, left the farm workers inadequately compensated for their labor. He blamed the situation on mismanagement, particularly in relation to distribution and transportation, under Stalin and Malenkov.

What we were expected to find here for our reports was evidence of glorious Soviet agricultural achievements that would help to justify Peking's agricultural policies. Thus the comments of the "Red Ukraine's" chairman were hardly helpful.

Comrade Ho asked him if he expected improvement under the leadership of Premier Khrushchev. "We have been promised some relief," the chairman replied. He did not sound very hopeful, but the words themselves were at least useful.

Almost in desperation, Ho fell back on theory which, among Communists, is never subject to public conflict of opinion. "How will the Soviet Union make the socialism-to-Communism transformation in which collective ownership will become State ownership?" he asked.

We waited for the expected formulas and slogans—any one of us could have made the reply, correct in every word. Instead, however, the chairman looked blank. "I have no idea," he said. "We never think of it."

If the chairman had slapped him across the face, Comrade Ho could not have been more shocked and hurt. We knew that the chairman was not being indifferent to ideology. He was an important official and must have been politically "pure." He had meant simply that he was concerned with "first things first" and that the press of his daily problems prevented him from giving attention to abstract planning for the distant future. Nevertheless, his translated words, which in our position we were obligated to quote exactly, gave a really bad impression, especially when preceded by his comments on the inadequate state of agricultural production under collectivization. For the first time, I actually felt sorry for Comrade Ho. His shoulders slumped and he looked very tired.

Back in Moscow we had a chance to relax for a week before beginning the long train journey home. We now were "old hands" in Russia and new delegations from China were the center of extravagant attention. We were relieved to some extent from the necessity of taking constant notes, and our group discussion meetings were shorter. In order to have a slight feeling of privacy occasionally, I tried to take a daily walk by myself.

During these walks I could collect my thoughts and sort out all my impressions of Russia and the Russians.

I was convinced that the Russian people were friendly, kindly, peace-loving and sincerely fond of the Chinese. Politically, they were controlled by the Communists just as completely as were we Chinese. The Russian officials, however, were not so rigidly doctrinaire as our authorities, and they did not exercise their control as harshly. The result was that the Russian people had lapsed into many social habits which, if seen in a non-Communist country, would be regarded by the Chinese Communists as evidence of "ideological backwardness" or even "reactionaryism." These were the aspects of Soviet society that disturbed men like Comrade Ho. Nevertheless, Comrade Ho soon convinced himself that what at first had seemed like indiscipline and political indifference among the Russian masses was in fact proof of the advanced state of the Soviet social order.

I imagine, however, that even Ho was dismayed by the living standard achieved for the Russian masses after nearly four decades of Communist "socialism." He would never admit it, perhaps not even to himself, but I know that the propaganda we had received about the Soviet Union had led us to expect far more than what we saw.

Nevertheless, the propaganda did not exaggerate the amount of industrial aid China was receiving from the Soviet Union. We had plenty of proof that the very best Russian heavy equipment and their top engineers were being sent to China. I no longer saw anything of generosity in the gesture, however, because the fact was now apparent that the two countries were being welded into one inseparable economic—and therefore political and military—unit. Almost half of mankind was dominated by a political order which was maintained solely by force. This meant that the fate of perhaps all mankind was in the hands of the few who controlled the force. From what I knew personally of these few autocrats, the mere thought of the future could be depressing.

But the one aspect of Russia that depressed me most of all concerned the naïveté of the people after four decades of Communist control. There now lived an entire generation of Russians who had never made a real decision for themselves and who knew only what the authorities wanted them to know. They lived very near to poverty and yet they really believed that they had the most of the best in the world. In their ignorance, they could easily be made to feel with all sincerity that they had the duty to bring their "advantages" to the rest of mankind. The thought that eventually a child of mine would grow up to be one of these dangerous innocents was almost unbearable.

One day, while walking alone in Moscow, I came across a crowd and idly stopped to see what had taken the people's interest. They were looking at a motorcar parked by the curb. At first I thought it was some fabulously expensive custom-built limousine, but then I saw that it was a new 1957 Ford.

I had not seen any new American car styles for eight years, and the changes since the last Ford I saw were phenomenal. How sleek and racy it was. How bright and comfortable it looked. There was gaiety and even wit in the color and design. It was beautiful. It symbolized a different world where people could find joy in living, where progress was as automatic as breathing and not the hysterical unkept promises of dictators. I looked at the others studying this mechanical symbol of a world from which they were carefully shielded. Their faces were blank, and no one spoke. I think they were seeing and not believing. I had often watched Ho's face as his shackled mind went through the process of twisting fact to conform to a preconceived principle, and these expressions were similar. But for me, the weight of all

269

the pretense and hypocrisy I lived with settled down again on my shoulders and I felt the familiar despair.

Only a few steps further, I realized suddenly that I was across the street from the American Embassy. Obviously, the car belonged to some minor Embassy official who had parked it in the street outside.

And now I found that my heart was pounding furiously. I had only to walk across the street, step through the open gateway in the iron fencing in front of the building, and I would be in that other world. My mind raced with what I would say to the American officials. I could throw myself on their mercy, ask them for political sanctuary. But what if they could not take me in, if they would have to turn me back to the Russians? I shuddered, but I put the thought out of my mind.

I know that I was just about to take the one step that would send me irrevocably toward the Embassy. At that moment, however, common sense intervened. The thought occurred to me that all fifteen members of our group wanted to escape. The same was true of thousands of visitors from the satellite countries. Undoubtedly, many more thousands of Russians would escape to America if they could. Thus if the American officials in Moscow were able to accept such refugees, long lines of people would be waiting outside the Embassy day and night.

Still trembling, I turned sadly away. Nevertheless, I determined to put my own escape plan into operation the moment I arrived back in Shanghai.

CHAPTER 11

When I hear your voice
The ten thousand sounds of the world are hushed.

DURING THE eight-day journey from Moscow, our delegation worked on two important reports. One was a comprehensive summary of our tour. This report was long, but we had no difficulty with it. In effect, Comrade Ho decided what should be mentioned; the rest of us merely went through the customary pretense in which we seemingly, of our own volition, reached his conclusions.

Unanimous agreement on the other report, however, was not easy. The Tourist Bureau officials had asked us to submit our criticisms of the way the tour had been handled. Theoretically, Comrade Ho and his assistant, being Tourist Bureau officials themselves, were not to participate in the preparation of this report.

The one important criticism we could make was the Bureau's

271

mistake in sending abroad a pair of louts like Comrade Ho and his assistant. We had had to cover up their blunders, apologize for their bad manners, and even provide their ideological explanations for much of what we had seen in the U.S.S.R. Their behavior and the embarrassment it had caused us—three of our group insisted—should be described in our report.

The idea was foolhardy. It enraged Comrade Ho to the extent that he accused our three companions of the serious crime of "reactionary behavior." Unquestionably, he was required to write his own reports on us. He was a Party member, and in any conflict between him and us, only his word would carry weight. If he chose to be vindictive, therefore, our three companions would be in real trouble.

Ironically, our three companions were the most "progressive" of our group. They believed in the regime and were motivated by a sincere desire to be helpful. The rest of us were motivated by self-preservation. We felt no obligation to give the regime the benefit of our constructive criticism, and we certainly would not endanger ourselves to do it. Conversely, we had nothing to lose but much to gain by telling the authorities what they wanted to hear, which in this case was that our tour had been an unqualified success.

Comrade Ho's threats quickly brought our three companions to our viewpoint. Nevertheless, the report on which we reached "unanimous agreement" did contain criticisms. We said, for example, that the Bureau officials had been wrong in thinking that the Russians would permit us to bring in only two rolls of film for each of our cameras. We also pointed out that because laundry was very expensive in Russia and because tipping was still customary there, the 100 rubles to which we had been limited were insufficient. We did not add to these trivial complaints, however, any mention of the difficulties which Comrade Ho and his assistant had caused us. On the contrary, we went out of our way in the report to compliment these two on their "untiring devotion to duty" and on "the invaluable help and guidance" they had given us.

The inclusion of this falsehood disgusted our three dissenting companions. They seemed to feel it was practically an act of sabotage. Typical of the idealists, they still did not realize that the authorities were not concerned with discovering truth, but with maintaining an illusion. In support of the illusion, we were required to act as though we believed that all Communists were wise and noble, that under Communist leadership we lived in a free and democratic society with the world's highest living standard, and that all people labeled "imperialist," "counter-revolutionary" or "reactionary" were our enemies. Facts which could be twisted to give verisimilitude to these fables were accepted; those which could not were rejected.

After eight years of pretending to believe the untruths, my act was becoming automatic and habitual. I probably could have gone on for the rest of my life living the same pretense, although I doubt if I ever would have grown to confuse the facts and fictions of a Communist society. Within only another decade, however, a new generation of Chinese would become adult, knowing nothing beyond what the authorities wanted them to know. From early childhood, they would have learned to survive by never questioning Party policy and by rejecting facts which did not support the officially established illusions. In effect, therefore, they would really *believe* the illusions and would not have to act out a deliberate pretense. The authorities then would not have to concentrate on enforcing a rigid behavior pattern, and could afford to be less meticulous about maintaining outward appearances.

This is what I had learned, to my horror, in the U.S.S.R. Also, it explained why our three idealistic companions who had not learned it would have incurred official antagonism, not approbation, if they had insisted upon including "unacceptable" truths in our report.

Moreover, they had what should have been proof of the regime's indifference to truth shortly after we returned. The untruths we had so carefully established in all our reports were rejected by the authorities and calmly replaced by a different set of fabrications. After crossing the border, our delegation took a side trip into Manchuria to visit some of the Chinese copies of the Russian factories we had seen. This trip was cut short, however, and we were hurriedly brought back to Peking because the authorities were impatient to begin exploiting the propaganda value of the material in our reports. We were given luxurious accommodations in the Hsing Chao Hotel where, for the next two days and nights, Central People's Broadcasting Station cadres worked with us to prepare a special program.

Our material, obviously, disappointed the cadres. Before the tour, we had been instructed to gather evidence on Russian friendliness to the Chinese. Plenty of such evidence had been available, and we had recorded it. This, together with ideologically correct explanations of what we had seen of Soviet social life, made up the bulk of our reports.

The cadres, however, wanted evidence of Chinese friendliness toward the Russians and of the Soviet high living standard. We had almost nothing on those subjects simply because the Chinese were not really friendly toward the Russians and the Soviet living standard had been shockingly low. The cadres seemed to feel that we were deliberately suppressing the true facts about the Soviet Union or, at the least, that we had done our job inadequately. Originally the plan had been to interview us on the air, but now apparently we could not be trusted to this extent. The cadres wrote their own version of our tour. "Do you mind if we put it *this* way?" they asked us, and then the program they had devised was read out to us.

According to their account, we had begun our tour with secret prejudice toward the Russians and serious doubts about Soviet society. The doubts and prejudices were precisely the ones felt by most Chinese. Inside the U.S.S.R., however, we had found that the Russians were wonderfully wise, dignified and, as befitting sympathetic elder brothers, always patient and understanding with us. Slowly our prejudice gave way to respect, then admiration, and finally love. At the same time, our eyes had been opened by the peace and harmony in which the people lived under the gentle guidance of the Communist Party. Also, despite the fact that we capitalists were used to comfortable living, we had been constantly amazed by the luxuries available to the Russian masses. We had returned from our tour not merely impressed with Russia and the Russians, but actually in awe of them.

Comrade Ho scowled as he tried to reconcile the official version of our tour with his own real impressions. As the three idealistic delegates listened to the cadres, their faces showed, first, astonishment, then embarrassment and finally bitterness. The rest of us, being less naïve, showed no surprise whatever. We immediately accepted the cadres' version of our tour and praised them for having caught the "true essence of our experience."

We knew we were safe in authorizing the deception. Only the Russians could expose it, and they would hardly deny the picture of themselves that they had been trying to project for 40 years. My reaction was that the Peking authorities must have become worried about the anti-Russian feeling in China and were beginning a serious campaign to counteract it.

Only the next day, I discovered why the authorities considered the campaign necessary. While we had been working with the broadcasting cadres, J.P. had arrived at the Hsing Chao Hotel to attend a conference of our mass organization, the Federation of Industry and Commerce. The moment I was free, he took me to one of the meetings, and I gave a short talk on my recent tour.

I made my comments conform to the version of the tour now officially established by the broadcasting cadres. To my surprise, however, the audience was coldly unresponsive. As soon as I finished, listeners began to ask questions. To my chagrin, the queries were sarcastic and indicated that no one had believed me. The whole atmosphere of the meeting was unfamiliar. The people were not exactly speaking out openly against the U.S.S.R., but the intensity of their anti-Russian feeling was unmistakable. During the Hungarian uprising in November 1956, the Chinese had expressed freely their dislike of the Russians, but the authorities had clamped down as soon as the Soviet attack on Hungary began. By the time I had left on my tour in late December 1956, no one would have dared to talk as the Federation delegates now were doing.

This suggested that within the last two months a new policy of leniency had been inaugurated. An unexpected change in Party policy always had the effect of undermining my self-confidence, and now I was confused and frightened. J.P. must have sensed my feelings; he casually invited me for a chat in his rooms after the meeting.

As soon as we were alone, I asked him why my talk had had such a negative reaction. From his cautious reply I gathered that the Peking authorities were faced with a dilemma as a result of their attempt to make the rest of the world believe that the Chinese wholeheartedly supported the Russians. The deception would be exposed if force had to be used to suppress anti-Russian feeling; in fact, the authorities dared not officially admit the existence of such feeling. Apparently, many Chinese could not resist taking advantage of the situation; they made their feelings clear even if they did not openly denounce the Soviet Union and Peking's policy. J.P. did not think that the matter was important, but it worried the officials, and he thought it afforded me a good opportunity to raise my status even higher. "The anti-Soviet feeling is balanced by equally strong pro-America sentiment," he said to me. "You're now familiar with both countries. You should be able to give some lectures that will really win the Party's gratitude."

My fears vanished, and my self-confidence returned. In my mind, I began immediately to revise my lecture for the thought-reform school. If I indicated to the authorities that I supported them now when almost everyone else was expressing thinly veiled antagonism to the Party's policy, my position should be secure enough so that my escape must be assured.

"However, I asked you here to give you a warning," J.P. continued. "Some high officials are mentioning your name favorably these days, but they also have begun to ask why you don't settle down and raise a family."

I should have known that this problem would grow increasingly serious the higher my position became. J.P. did not have to tell me that the authorities would always distrust me until they had hostages who could constantly guarantee my behavior. With Mai Mee's help, I had postponed the problem, but I realized now that since I was no longer associated with her, some other such arrangement would be necessary for my escape plan. "It *is* time I got married," I said to J.P. I hoped to make him change the subject. "I'll think about it seriously."

"I've been thinking about it for you, and I may have the answer," J.P. said. With that, he handed me a newspaper. I saw

277

that it was a four-day-old copy of the *People's Daily*, folded open to a picture on a back page. The picture made me catch my breath. It was Li-li. I read the caption avidly. It said that she was in Peking attending a week-long conference of some women's group. She was referred to as a "reformed counter-revolutionary's wife." I looked up at J.P. in surprise and confusion.

"When you came to work for me, I made you promise to give her up," he said, "but now I take it back."

"I don't understand," I stammered. "Why?"

"Apparently no other woman will ever intrigue you to the extent she does and now her position has changed," he said. "She's a widow and she has reformed. I am told she is much respected."

I knew immediately what he meant. The Communists never neglected anyone who could be useful to them. Thousands of wives of "counter-revolutionaries" were living a hand-to-mouth existence and were contributing nothing to the regime. A few of them, willing to cooperate with the authorities, were designated "reformed" and served to demonstrate to the others what behavior would help overcome the "counter-revolutionary" stigma. Such "reformed" people were given much publicity and often achieved high status.

Nevertheless, the idea that Li-li had achieved any status at all and that J.P. was actually speaking about her with complete respect was so unexpected that I could not believe it. "Do you mean that you would accept Li-li as my wife?" I asked.

"My dear Bob, we never had anything personal against the girl. We were concerned only with your future," J.P. said. "And now, frankly, I think you would have a better future if you married her."

I stared at him in silence as his words sank in. Emotions I had

278

long forgotten had returned and I was shaken by the intensity of them. I felt that my whole life was changing drastically, and I was powerless to prevent it. I was both frightened and excited.

J.P. stood up. "I should tell you," he said, "that she is staying at the Chien Mien Hotel." At the door, he put his hand on my shoulder. "My advice is that you look her up without delay," he said.

He was telling me, I realized, that he considered the problem of my bachelorhood very serious, and that he knew the Party would approve completely of Li-li as a wife for me. I found suddenly that I wanted desperately to see Li-li. I suppose she had always been in the back of my mind, but for years I had not allowed myself to think consciously of her. I had no idea of what I wanted or expected of her now, but I felt that seeing her would help to clarify the muddle of emotions and half-formed thoughts that had reduced me to a state of utter confusion.

The time was about 10 o'clock, but the next day was Sunday and few meetings would be held. On impulse, instead of returning to my own rooms I went out and walked the few blocks to the Chien Mien Hotel. I asked for the number of Li-li's room. I found the room and knocked. The whole incident seemed quite unreal, and I was perfectly calm.

The door opened quietly and Li-li stood in front of me. Now I found that I was speechless. I saw her stiffen and her face grow pale. She said nothing and for a moment she closed her eyes.

"Is it really you?" I finally managed to say.

Li-li came out into the hall and closed the door. "My roommate—I can't ask you in," she said.

She looked older, and her voice was deeper than I remembered, but she was still beautiful. It seemed perfectly natural to take her hands. "You were so close. I had to come here—to find out if you've changed," I said.

279

She turned her head away. "I've changed completely," she said. "Too much has happened—"

"It would be childish to think we could pick up from where we left off five years ago," I said, "but nothing could happen to make us forget each other completely."

She pulled her hands away but looked at me squarely. "Bob, please; I can't stand any more ... emotion. What do you want of me?" she said.

"I just want to talk to you," I said. "Always before we had to hide the fact that we were seeing each other. I have to know what it's like being with you naturally—as a friend—without fear—"

Li-li protested, but I insisted, and finally she agreed to meet me the next morning. In bed, back in my own room, I began to accept as real the fact that I would be with Li-li again. The thought suddenly occurred to me that she could be useful in my escape plan, but immediately I was filled with self-disgust. Survival in the New China forced everyone to be utterly selfish, but if I took advantage of Li-li and endangered her for my own purposes, my life would not be worth living. Nevertheless, I also had the thought that if I did marry her I would never be able to escape. Both ideas were abhorrent, and I put them out of my mind. Oddly enough, however, I had the feeling that everything now would be all right, and I slept better that night than I had for years.

Li-li had never seen the famous Summer Palace in Peking, and I had the delight of showing it to her the next morning. While exploring the beautiful gardens, we told each other stories of the Palace's dramatic history. We were much as we had been during our two weeks together in Hangchow, and in some strange way the years in between seemed to vanish. The illusion was made complete when we rowed on the Palace lake just as we had on the lake in Hangchow.

Li-li acted much as she had then, but slowly I perceived that she was in a dreamlike state. She seemed to be responding to emotions dimly remembered rather than actually felt now. I sensed that for the present at least she was incapable of any real feeling, and the thought saddened me. I understood her better when I pieced together from her fragmentary conversation the story of what had happened to her since I saw her last.

After her husband was sent to labor reform as a counter-revolutionary in 1953, she managed to find work in a sewing cooperative. She earned barely enough to feed herself, and no one dared to speak to her except the authorities, who abused and insulted her and gave her orders. She did not have to describe to me what she had endured; I knew well the stultifying effect of being treated as a hated enemy of society. For her, the treatment must have been infinitely worse because she was regarded as a "degenerate element" as well as a counter-revolutionary's wife. The one slight advantage she had was the fact that she was practically the only literate woman in her cooperative and was of some use in keeping records for her mass organization meetings. Nevertheless, she was harassed constantly and she knew that eventually she would be driven to suicide or disposed of.

But then her husband died. He must have been strong to have endured the hopelessness, privation, overwork and undernourishment for as long as two years; few if any medicines were available to the labor reform prisoners and he, like most of them, sooner or later succumbed to disease, probably dysentery. Shortly after his death, cadres approached Li-li; they asked her to denounce her husband as a really vile counter-revolutionary who had received his just deserts, and to "admit her mistake" in having married him. She was made to understand that if she refused she would be struggled against and might even suffer the same fate as her husband. To survive, therefore, she agreed to sign the statement written by the cadres and containing lies about her own and her husband's past. The statement was given wide publicity.

This, however, was only the beginning. As a reformed counter-revolutionary's wife, she found that she was required to give frequent speeches, also written by cadres, on how she had "seen the light." The months of conscientious labor in the sewing cooperative now helped her. She was also declared a "reformed degenerate element." In this dual capacity she became much in demand as a political lecturer to various women's organizations. Her striking appearance and intelligence were additional assets. Before long, she had learned the Communist terminology and the pattern of behavior and thinking expected of her; she began to write her own speeches and articles. Like me, she found that once she started cooperating with the Communists, a constant effort to push herself upward was necessary; the moment she ceased making the effort to be useful to the regime she would begin the dreaded plunge to oblivion.

Nevertheless, the rewards for the reformed could be great. In Shanghai, for example, an ex-embezzler and safecracker held a number of lofty titles in the municipal government and received much favorable publicity. He existed for the purpose of indicating that in a beneficent Communist society even the most seemingly unregenerate types could be successfully remolded, receive salvation, and earn high position. Potentially, therefore, Li-li's future held much promise and already her status was such that she would be an enviable catch as a marriage partner for someone in my position.

We did not discuss marriage or even the future that day in the Summer Palace. In fact, we talked very little. I think that mostly we were content merely with the wonder of being together without the worry that calamity would strike us if we were seen. In the late afternoon, I took her back in time for her discussion meeting with the other delegates of her group. She would stay in Peking for several more days, but I was leaving the next morning. Nevertheless, she agreed to meet me in Shanghai when she returned.

As soon as I returned to Shanghai, I worked at putting the final touches on my revised lecture for the thought-reform school. The new lecture began with a comparison of the "border of freedom" between China and Russia and the one between Canada and the U.S.A., which, according to my account, bristled with armed guards. Brutal FBI men were on the trail of smugglers and dope peddlers, alert "mounties" were on the lookout for American gangsters.

I explained why many Americans became gangsters. The capitalist system was so heartless, I said, that the poor people could seldom escape antisocial activity. In the slums, both parents had to work so hard for mere survival that their children roved the streets in gangs—unsupervised and committing every type of vile crime.

By way of contrast, I described the Leningrad Pioneer Palace, the U.S.S.R.'s showpiece youth center where young people are provided with the facilities, expert instruction and encouragement for every type of creative activity.

At the same time, I was careful to credit America with the facilities that my audience knew existed. Miami, for example, was known well enough to provide a good comparison with the Soviet Black Sea resort of Sochi. In describing the two places, I made Miami seem the more extravagantly luxurious but Sochi more beautiful. Miami, however, catered only to the debauches of the degenerate rich, while Sochi was meant solely for the common people. In talking about Sochi, I always mentioned the fact that while we were there, a Chinese student was recuperating from an illness in the best hospital. About Miami I said that if I had been ill there, I would have been turned away from any of the hospitals as a worthless "coolie"; in fact, I had often wondered where I would get my next meal, because racial prejudice was an inherent aspect of an imperialist society and the better restaurants discriminated against Chinese.

I ended my lecture with a word of caution about envying the Russian achievements. I pointed out that the Russians had built their paradise with hard work and without outside help. We would have to do much the same; more important than the material aid they were giving us were the inspiration, hope and confidence they could provide.

The value of my lecture was that it put across all the officially prescribed fabrications by distorting existing facts rather than by using completely false information. Moreover, I enlivened the material with stories and personal anecdotes to make it more interesting and thus remove some of the deadly dullness characteristic of most Communist propaganda.

I had informed the Institute officials of my revised lecture, and on the day I first delivered it, two of the officials visited my class. They said nothing afterward, but I received a telephone call that evening from the head of the Institute. He asked me to expand my lecture along the same lines and a week later give it to a special meeting of some top Party members. This was indeed an honor. An ex-national capitalist lecturing Communists was almost unheard of. In spite of myself, I felt a thrill of excitement.

Meanwhile, Li-li had returned to Shanghai, and two days after introducing my new lecture I had dinner with her. I could not help giving her a glowing account of my success. She congratulated me, but she looked so gravely thoughtful that I asked her what was the matter. "Sooner or later, I suppose we'll both become Party members ourselves," she said, "and I was wondering what it would mean."

We both knew what it would mean. The idea that Party membership was the ultimate destination along the road we both were traveling had never before occurred to me. Previously it had been too distant, and I had been thinking mainly of escape, but now I saw it clearly. Once we became sufficiently expert in deceit to be accepted by the Party we would receive the security and material benefits of the privileged class, but we would pay for them by joining the exploiters of the exploited. It was one thing, in order to survive, to deceive the Communists by seeming to cooperate with them, but it was something quite different, merely for our selfish comfort, to join them in suppressing our fellow countrymen. Li-li's words had the sobering effect of making me see my position in its true light.

I remembered that Li-li had always had the effect of bringing out the best in me. When I was with her, I could like myself as well as her. To feel something of self-respect again after years in which my self-esteem had been eroded by lying and cheating was an exhilarating experience. I was aware that night that I was still hopelessly infatuated with her, and I wanted her desperately.

When I saw her again a few days later, I cautiously mentioned marriage, but Li-li stopped me at once. She told me that she had made the irrevocable decision never to marry again or even to encourage a relationship of close friendship with anyone. I did not press the issue, grateful that she still permitted me to see her occasionally. I was aware that I had broken my resolve to make my escape attempt immediately upon returning to Shanghai. I had not necessarily given up the plan; I simply did not think about it during this period.

This period was the busiest of my life, and I reached the zenith of my usefulness to the regime. Because of my new lecture, I found suddenly that I was much in demand. I gave variations of my talk to trade union gatherings, to the various front groups for the "democratic elements," to intellectuals, to women's organizations and even to Party members. Excerpts from my lecture were circulated in the press throughout the country. Also, I was sent to speak in Hangchow, Wusih, and other cities as far away as Nanking. I often delivered my lecture twice—and occasionally three times—a day.

It is important to realize, however, that the anti-Russian pro-American feeling persisted and was evident everywhere. Most of my listeners seemed to find the lecture interesting, but I doubt if even the Communists believed what I said. Nevertheless, I was doing an effective job of proclaiming official policy on the subject of Sino-Soviet relations, and for this I knew that I was coming to the attention of the highest Communist officials.

I began to receive my rewards almost at once. In March 1957, for example, I was given membership in the Shanghai Political Consultative Council. The post entailed no real duties or responsibilities. It represented a rise in status rather than position. My official position was still manager of the three flour mills and I maintained the fiction that I performed duties there by visiting Comrade Yang in our office on rare occasions. I had long since realized, however, that the ex-capitalists were not trusted in the jobs they were fitted to do and were deliberately kept as far away as possible from the enterprises they nominally directed. By now, the enterprises were being managed openly by the State Representatives. Nevertheless, to show outsiders that a Communist society generously rewarded remolded capitalists, we were given impressive-sounding but largely meaningless titles in the government administration. J.P. for example, now was deputy mayor of Shanghai. He received such an important post because he was so well known internationally. People like me, however, were rewarded with higher titles only when they made special efforts to be useful to the regime.

Actually, the real reward for my contribution was less in the new title and more in the fact that I began to be accepted socially, to an increased degree, by high Party officials. Thus I was now invited frequently to the parties at which the head Communists dropped the stern puritanical pose they presented to their subordinates and to the masses, and frankly enjoyed the luxuries of their privileged position. Moreover, the other lecturers at the Institute began to include me in their group, and one of them, Director Win, an official in the Propaganda Department of the Shanghai Party Committee, even treated me as a personal friend.

I was seeing Li-li as often as I could, and the fact became widely known. One day, Comrade Director Win suggested that I bring her with me to a small but exclusive dinner given for the Institute lecturers and a few of their friends. I could see that Win and the others had not expected Li-li to be so attractive. Moreover, her dignity and intelligence obviously impressed them greatly. I was proud of Li-li that night, and I was aware that the others envied me.

The next day, Win invited me to have lunch with him and for a whole hour he talked of nothing but Li-li. He was quite aware, I realized, that I had been devoted to Li-li for many years, but I was caught off guard when he asked me suddenly if I intended to marry her.

I answered truthfully that I wanted to marry her, but that she did not seem interested in having a husband. In order to help her, I added that she seemed sincerely dedicated to the good work she was doing.

Win brushed this aside. "Every woman wants a husband," he

said. "She merely expects you to persuade her." He added that I ought to settle down with a wife, and that Li-li would be ideal for me.

Director Win was only a year older than I, but because his position was much more important than mine, he tended to treat me in a paternal fashion. Accepting this role, therefore, I asked for his advice and help in making Li-li change her mind about marrying me.

"Go after her. Don't take no for an answer," Win said. "Meanwhile, I'll do what I can to put in a good word for you."

I was scheduled to leave for a lecture in Hangchow two days later, and I arranged that Win would take Li-li to dinner while I was gone. When I returned, Li-li told me that Win had been pleasant to her and had spent the entire evening praising me. Thereafter, Li-li and I were always invited together to the official parties and Win usually monopolized her to talk about my virtues. I do not think that Win himself was aware that he had fallen for her. I was not upset by the situation. Li-li certainly could benefit by having such a highly placed admirer. I also had nothing to lose by having Win publicly sing my praises. Moreover he created the impression that Li-li and I were about to announce our engagement, and I am sure this dispelled some of the official suspicion that I might be deliberately avoiding establishing a family in order to escape the country. The truth is that I really did want to marry Li-li. I dreamed that somehow we might escape together, but I knew that this would be impossible. I did not admit it to myself, but I was wavering in my determination to get away.

And then in April 1957 an incident occurred that seriously affected my thinking about escape. One morning, I received a call from the office of the United Front Work Department informing me that I was to attend a secret meeting that afternoon in the auditorium of the Party's Shanghai Committee. Participation in unpublicized activities of the Party was an exceptional honor, and I was both flattered and curious. I thought that perhaps I would see Mao Tse-tung again, and I went to the meeting in a state of suppressed excitement.

About 200 people were gathered in the auditorium. They included thirty nominal leaders of the "democratic elements" and the business community, but the rest were the top Communist officials. The mayor addressed us. He told us that Chairman Mao had made an important speech to the Supreme State Council on February 27, 1957. We who were now assembled were to hear a tape recording of the speech in order to be familiarized with an important development in official policy. Later, the mayor said, the speech would be released to the masses, but meanwhile it was to be kept secret. Thus we were not to take notes on it or talk about it, even among ourselves.

By now, I was really excited. I was sure that only those whom the authorities trusted would be allowed to hear a secret speech by the Chairman. The fact that I was trusted to this extent must mean that I was approaching complete acceptance. Even Party membership was no longer a remote possibility. Nevertheless, I put such thoughts aside, and for the next four hours listened to Chairman Mao's slow calm voice.

His address later carried the title "On the Correct Handling of Contradictions Among the People." Ultimately, the speech would cause much worldwide speculation, partly because subsequently released versions would differ from the secret original and partly because this speech introduced the astonishing "Hundred Flowers" period.

Mao began by discussing the Hungarian "revolt" and the events which had followed it in China. He fully admitted that student agitation, workers' strikes and peasant unrest had occurred. He even described, as a specific example, how a highly placed official had worked hard at night to prepare and distribute anti-Soviet posters. He also mentioned a famous professor who had publicly stated a desire to kill thousands of Communists "for the good of the people." Such incidents, Mao said, were regrettable, but were not necessarily the fault of the people who had instigated them; most of these people were not counter-revolutionaries and thus did not require to be arrested. Instead, the incidents were apt to be the result of "bureaucratism," a fault which had become serious among some of the cadres. Because of this fault, suppression had been used to deal with some of the people's legitimate dissatisfactions, when education and persuasion should have been the proper instruments. The Party cadres themselves, therefore, needed to be shown their mistakes in order to correct them.

I listened to these comments in utter astonishment. They indicated that the Hungarian uprising *had* left an impact on the regime and that the authorities were genuinely disturbed by its implications.

Mao next proceeded to explain patiently his point about "contradictions." There were two types, he said—contradictions among the people themselves and contradictions between the people and the enemy. Contradictions among the people resulted from misunderstandings; they posed no threat to the people's regime and did not require suppression. Contradictions between the people and the enemy, however, were maliciously instigated from evil outside sources; they did pose a threat to the people's regime and thus required a "solution by force." Many cadres, Mao said, failed to differentiate between the two types of contradictions. The result was that force instead of persuasion had been sometimes erroneously used. Several of the campaigns, especially the Elimination of Counter-Revolutionaries, had been car-

290

ried too far and injustices had occurred. Mao promised that these errors committed by overzealous cadres would be corrected and that many people who had been sentenced to labor reform would be released. He even expressed regret that some innocent people had been executed as counter-revolutionaries, but he took the opportunity to deny the "imperialist claims" that the regime had killed a total of 20 million people for this crime. The number "was not much greater than 700,000," he said.

Mao next warned that contradictions among the people, if wrongly handled, could become contradictions between the people and the enemy. In both Poland and Hungary, he explained, the people had had genuine grievances which required a patient hearing and careful consideration. In Poland, Gomulka had handled these contradictions among the people properly and had successfully solved the problem. In Hungary, however, the Communist leadership had been inadequate, enabling the imperialists to distort the situation and to use the legitimate grievances of the people in an attempt to destroy the socialist regime. Thus in Hungary, contradictions among the people had become contradictions between the people and the enemy, thereby making the use of force necessary.

Conversely, this same transformation could come from the opposite direction. Taiwan, for example, existed as a contradiction between the people and the enemy because the American imperialists occupied the island. If the mainland Communists, however, could persuade Chiang Kai-shek to change his ways, throw out the American imperialists and thus bring about the peaceful liberation of Taiwan, then the contradictions would be merely those among the people and force would not be required.

After carefully establishing his theory on "contradictions," Mao returned to the subject of the mistakes made by the cadres. He described more of the mistakes, and he even admitted that high Party officers had been guilty of serious errors. He mentioned specifically that the Tibetan people had been handled so badly that "reforms" had to be postponed for several years. Such mistakes, Mao said, weakened the regime. Correction therefore was necessary. Throughout China, a "rectification campaign" designed to improve the Party cadres' work was to be inaugurated. The campaign, to be successful, required the help of everyone in China. The people were to help the Party by criticizing it. The people were to speak out freely and air their grievances so that social injustices could be remedied. Mao emphasized that no retaliation would be taken against those who spoke out. On the contrary, he said that those who did not voice their criticism "are not our friends."

It was at this point that Mao dramatically called on all of China to "let a hundred flowers bloom, let a hundred schools of thought contend." Party members who took it upon themselves to decide which ideas from the masses were acceptable and which were not indicated that they lacked faith in the people, Mao explained. Moreover, such cadres were guilty of a grievous wrong because they discouraged from the masses the sort of criticism that alone could keep the Party's "working style" at top efficiency. Because, ultimately, only the people could judge what was best for themselves, they needed to learn to differentiate between "fragrant flowers" and "poisonous weeds," which thus must be allowed to bloom side by side.

Mao spoke of other subjects of current interest and ended by discussing his own role in the regime. He compared himself to a leading character in a certain well-known opera, but said that now he was growing too old to play the star's part well; he hinted that he soon might step down to a subordinate role.

At home that evening, I wrote in my diary all that I could remember of the speech. I had two strong impressions about it.

One was that Mao had been utterly sincere. The other was that dramatic changes were in store for us.

Obviously, for example, the coming "rectification campaign" requiring the people to criticize Party officials meant that we were to have a period of free speech. Perhaps other freedoms would be permitted as well. What if we should be allowed to travel freely again to Hong Kong? If this should be so, I might dream that Li-li and I could go together. I knew now that although I still wanted to escape, I could not bear the thought of leaving Li-li just when I had found her again after all these years.

But then the thought occurred to me that the authorities might have really learned their lesson from Hungary. Perhaps we would now enter an era of decency, and human values again would have meaning. If that happened, some of our old dreams might be fulfilled. Moreover, having worked myself into such a secure position, my future here in China could be bright indeed.

I was in a daze. After Mao's speech anything seemed possible. For the first time in many years, I allowed myself to hope.

CHAPTER 12

The lion's roar is a fearless man speaking;
When the beasts hear it, their skulls crack.

—POEM OF BUDDHIST SCHOOL

LATE IN APRIL 1957—two weeks after I had listened to the secret recording—Mao's speech was released on a wider scale. In Shanghai, about 100,000 people heard it. J. P., for example, read a typescript of it to a meeting of the Federation of Industry and Commerce. By such means, the authorities communicated the information in the speech to the people without officially publishing the contents which could have been used by non-Communists abroad to embarrass the regime.

Even so, the version of the speech given to the masses was toned down considerably. For instance, only some of the failures in Tibet were mentioned. The admissions that high Party officials had occasionally blundered and that well-known persons had engaged in anti-Soviet activities were left out, and so was the hint that Mao might step down from his leading role.

Nevertheless, Mao's statement that the Party cadres needed "rectification" remained unchanged. His insistence that the people must begin at once to "bloom and contend"—i.e., to criticize the cadres and air grievances—was as emphatic as before. And his promise that no reprisals would be taken against those who spoke out sounded as sincere as it had in the original version.

The people probably were as astonished by the speech as I had been. For a few days they were too frightened and suspicious to say anything. Only when criticism of the Party by important people began to fill the daily papers did they begin cautiously to unburden themselves. Each mass organization doubled and then trebled its meetings so that every member would have full opportunity to voice his thought. In addition, special "blossom" meetings were held for every segment of society. Within a week the whole country had risen to voice its opinion of the regime.

For eight years, under the Communist regime, every one of us had been controlled by the Party. Through the mass organizations, every brain had been "washed" and every thought "remolded." In the suppression campaigns, we had been taught through terror to act as though we believed the officially prescribed falsehoods. But now, suddenly and inexplicably, we were ordered to reveal what we really felt about the life we led. A kind of frenzy gripped the people, and the campaign gained a frightening momentum.

Anyone who believes that "brainwashing" or "thought reform" were used successfully to make 650 million Chinese *believe* in Communism needs only to read the Chinese newspapers for May 1957. The authorities obviously had been frightened by the fact that in Hungary, the people had risen against a "people's" regime. This indicated that despite the continual use of brute force to suppress the masses, a Communist regime was not secure from a mass uprising. To forestall such an uprising in China, the authorities acted upon the idea that permitting the people a kind of emotional catharsis would release harmlessly any latent impulse to violence. They also apparently believed that after eight years of enforced subservience the people must be docile enough so as not to dare to voice criticism of the regime in any extreme fashion. What the authorities did not realize was that even a slight release of pressure was almost sure to have an explosive effect. Within two weeks, therefore, the "speaking out" developed into a hysterical scream of protest.

Even many Communists became carried away and revealed their true feelings. The Party Secretary in charge of the *China Youth Daily*, for example, wrote that the Communist leaders could be divided into three groups. One included the cynics, who had no political convictions and made no effort except to grasp luxury and privilege for themselves. Another group included the weak, who were so afraid of losing their prestige and authority that they only "yessed" and flattered the other leaders. And the last group included the stupid whose incompetence, conservatism and blindness were mainly responsible for the country's deplorable state.

The most bitter criticism came from non-Party government officials—those who belonged to the "democratic elements" and had been given figurehead positions. The Forestry Minister, for example, stated publicly that tens of thousands of innocent people had been persecuted as counter-revolutionaries, and he demanded that the so-called counter-revolutionary cases be reviewed so that the "obvious wrongs" could be redressed.

Lung Yun, a vice-chairman of the National Defense Council, accused the Russians of stealing industrial equipment from China's northeast provinces, and he questioned Soviet friendliness in allowing the Chinese both to fight and pay for the Korean war. This criticism was especially effective because it refuted

297

"internationalism," in the name of which the Communists justified most of their subversive activities in other countries. The criticism was made even more telling by the fact that Lung Yun had been a member of a recent delegation to the U.S.S.R., where he was meant to acquire love for "our Soviet elder brothers."

Perhaps the most biting criticism came from the intellectuals, who spoke out more boldly and eloquently than any other group. A famous professor from the Chung Nan Institute of Finance and Economy wrote a review of the treatment the group had received from the Communists. Countless intellectuals, he wrote, unable to endure life in the New China, had been driven to suicide. *Even God would be angered by the situation,* the professor wrote. *Are you Communists aware of what the true situation is and are you prepared to face up to it?*

Another intellectual who spoke up emphatically was P.G. Kai from the famous Chinese People's University, which had pioneered the "new education." Kai graphically described the hunger and raggedness of the masses in contrast to the luxuries enjoyed by the Party members. He ended with the comment, "The truth is that the masses want to overthrow the Communist Party and kill all the Communists."

The poet Chan Ko-tza put into words the terrible aloneness that we all had learned was a feature of Communist society. *Everyone feels this lack* [of friendship], he wrote. *Our life is like a flower without dew; it is dry and colorless. . . . We have no friends here.*

As the criticism grew increasingly emotional many people, particularly among the students, workers and peasants, began to combine words and action. The students' "blooming" first became "active" on May 4, 1957, when 8,000 of them held a rally in Peking to commemorate the historic May Fourth Movement, an abortive student uprising 38 years before which the Communists erroneously claimed was "socialist" inspired. At the meeting now, the student leaders charged the Communists with "suppression of freedom and democracy in all the country's educational institutions." They called for nationwide agitation against the regime. Thereafter classes were canceled while students attended stormy meetings and rallies, circulated anti-Communist pamphlets, put up inflammatory posters and held noisy demonstrations. One student leader said that the purpose of the student movement was to "raise an army of a million youths to resist the so-called Communist revolution, to fight Communists and to drive out Communists, the real enemy of the people." "We fight for democracy, freedom and human rights," he declared.

In the countryside, peasant agitation grew increasingly violent. A few of the more brutal cadres were attacked and torn to pieces by angry mobs. Cadres who had been arrogant were driven out with pitchforks. Government granaries were forced open and the hungry peasants ate adequately for the first time in years.

Among the industrial workers a wave of anti-Communist strikes began. Mostly, however, the workers tore down all their previously written "self-criticisms" and the dull "boost production" posters from the factory walls and bulletin boards. Instead they posted daring denunciations of the Party and Youth League. In my mills alone, I saw hundreds of these crude placards; usually they showed the Party cadres as fat and bestial while the workers were emaciated, ragged and beaten down. The workers' meetings were now attended so enthusiastically and the complaints were so long and impassioned that the cadres had difficulty in bringing the meetings to a close. The most common complaints were that "gross favoritism" was shown to Party members, that the cadres were "unjust and undemocratic," and that the State Representatives were "ten times more arrogant than the previous capitalist owners had ever been."

Whenever I appeared at the mills now, the workers cheered me. Comrade Yang was a changed man. He had aged shockingly, and his self-confidence had vanished. At one meeting, when he started to address the workers, he was shouted down with jeers and abuse. I saw Yang's shoulders sag. His humiliation was so complete and in fact the whole situation was so uncomfortable that I avoided the mills as much as possible.

At the thought-reform school, my lecture on the Russian paradise versus the American hell reached the limit of absurdity; Lung Yun's accusations against the Soviet Union were now a favorite subject at blossom meetings throughout the country. Fortunately, because of the frequent meetings, I did not have to give my lecture often. Moreover, because I was not a Communist my listeners did not contradict and argue with me. The other lecturers, however, suffered the outspoken contempt of their students. I heard them accused of "perverting truth and logic to an extent that insults the intelligence of even a simple man." The high Communists seemed unable to believe what they were hearing and attempted desperately to maintain their dignity in the face of the constant abuse. The staff members under them appeared lost and confused, as though they had been abandoned by their superiors. Some were visibly crushed and tried to avoid even being seen by the Institute's "students."

Everywhere, the sight of terrified and cringing Party cadres was common. Considering the insolence and authority which had identified them only a few weeks before, they had fallen far indeed. Several times, in the streets, I saw cadres being reviled, insulted and jeered at by angry mobs. The typical cadre—thin, stoop-shouldered, ferret-faced, humorless and fanatic—suddenly no longer inspired fear, but instead aroused only pity. He cowered before the mob or tried to scurry out of sight.

Even Comrade Ho was forced at last to hear the truth about himself. The three "progressive" members of our tourist delegation to Russia "blossomed" by submitting a scathing denunciation of his behavior during the tour. I would have thought that Ho's arrogance was strong enough to sustain him in any circumstance, but I was told that he actually wept when the complaint was printed in the newspapers.

Some Communist officials attempted to remedy the worst abuses of which the Party was accused. Shanghai's mayor, for example, publicly apologized to a professor who had been unjustly denounced and persecuted by a Party-member rival. Because in reality the intellectuals were the people most hated and despised by the authorities, such an apology dramatized the complete change in attitude. After this apology, other prominent "blossomers" cited cases of other wrongly accused famous people who thereupon were released from prison. One of these was Dr. Henry Ling, who had been President of Shanghai University between 1945 and 1949. I saw him on a Shanghai street a few days afterward. His six years of suffering were plainly visible in his bent and emaciated frame, but he was pathetically happy to be free and to know that China was now following a new course.

The truth was, however, that China was suddenly not following any course at all. The authorities were rapidly losing all control of the situation. I remember, for example, a newspaper story about a hoodlum whom the police had caught trying to attack a woman in a city park. The hoodlum had defied the police. "What do you mean by interfering?" he had asked. "This is a contradiction among the people—it has nothing to do with you—" The police reportedly had scurried off in confusion.

I was confused about the "blossom" campaign from the moment the people began to abandon themselves in criticism of the regime, and I became increasingly uneasy as the emotion and violence mounted. Mao's words, "Any who do not speak out are not our friends," were being used more and more to encourage even further excesses, but instinctively I avoided blossoming. This was easy at first because the meetings of our mass organization were now so well attended, and the other members were so avid to "blossom," that only part of them could get a hearing.

I noticed that J.P. also was trying to avoid a formal statement of criticism, but he was too much in the limelight to escape it entirely. Nevertheless, when he did "blossom," he made no criticisms concerning his own problems. Instead, he came to the rescue of a small businessman who had suffered a grave injustice.

The businessman had owned a pharmacy and his employees originally had been apprentices trained by him. During Five-Anti, the Communists used one of the ex-apprentices as the standard "accuser." The employee was rewarded with Party membership and later, under the Joint State-Private arrangement, was put in charge of the pharmacy as the State Representative. Arrogant in his new status, the ex-employee tried to seduce the ex-owner's widowed daughter-in-law. Her resistance insulted the ex-apprentice, who took out his anger on the old man. This led to a quarrel in which the Communist attacked the old man with a knife, wounding him severely on the arm. The old man reported the incident to the Security Bureau but the police took no action when they learned that the assailant was a Party member. The old man appealed to one authority after another, but could get no one to listen to him, and meanwhile his attacker still ran the pharmacy. Finally, the old man approached J.P. and begged him for help. J.P. reviewed the case carefully and then used it for his "blossoming." He pointed out that if a Party member was permitted to violate a civilized society's basic rules of law and order, then the "new" society was unjust and could not guarantee elementary security to the masses. J.P. spoke eloquently, and his arguments were forceful. Within 24 hours, the ex-apprentice was arrested.

That night, J.P. discussed the case with me and some of his associates. He was happy of course to have been able to redress a small fraction of the immense wrong that had been done within the business community. In addition, however, he accepted the seemingly strange notion that the Party had suddenly become interested in justice, and that therefore he had done the right thing by blossoming. He really believed—and so did the others— that the Communists did want to improve their ways; in fact, he felt that the Communists were forced to improve if they were to continue to hold power.

I did not know what to believe. J.P.'s argument refuted what we had learned thoroughly during the last eight years: the Communists used only brute force to maintain their political power. They used it ruthlessly and effectively, but now apparently they were preparing to adopt other less crude means. If J.P. and his friends were right, then I should begin at once to think out carefully what criticisms to make in my own blossoming. But if J.P. was wrong, we would have to face the fact that the authorities were deliberately perpetrating one of the most vicious acts of treachery in history. Remembering the unmistakable sincerity in Mao's words, I found this as hard to believe as the idea that the Communists were trying to earn the willing cooperation of the masses.

I could not make up my mind, and I stalled, hoping for some clue to the direction that events would finally take. Meanwhile I was obligated to attend a group of special blossom meetings, and the difficulty of avoiding to speak out increased.

The first meeting was called by Liu Chi-pin, a deputy mayor

of the city and an old Party member. He requested a gathering of the former students who had returned to the Shanghai area from Europe or America. About 250 of us met in the Culture Club, which once had been the French Club. We held degrees from some of the most famous universities in the West. Liu, distinguished-looking and poised, greeted us affably, invited us to help ourselves from the ample refreshment table, and then asked us to make freely any comments we might have about the regime.

Obviously, Liu was not prepared for the flood of bitterness that followed. Even I, who knew well how disillusioned the returned students were, was surprised by the vehemence of their attacks.

They all denounced the regime for its lies, deceit and broken promises, and demanded to know why the authorities guilty of these evils deserved respect and support. They also uniformly denounced the arbitrary, unjust and arrogant treatment they had received from the cadres. They were incensed by the uncivilized brutality that had been used during the suppression campaigns, and they demanded the release of imprisoned fellow students.

But most of all, they were bitter about the waste of their talents in the New China. On this subject, dozens clamored to speak at the same time and their voices became shrill with emotion. By now Liu had lost his poise. Sweat was running down his face, his hair was mussed, and his uniform was wrinkled. He sat gripping the arms of his chair and his eyes darted from one shouting member of the audience to another.

The climax came with the complaint of an engineer who had taken his degree in the U.S. He said that in 1951 he had given up a US$800-a-month job in order to return and serve his motherland. Since then the Communists had permitted him to do nothing for the people. Even technical suggestions he made were rejected as being based on "capitalist techniques." During the six years since his return, he had been transferred four times and each time his salary had been "readjusted." He had begun with the equivalent of US$130 a month and now he was given only US$50. The man was becoming visibly angrier and angrier. Suddenly he took off his jacket and rushing up to Liu shook the coat in the deputy mayor's face. "For six years I have not bought a single garment," he shouted. "For six years I have not been allowed to use my ability or my training. Because of what I have endured I've lost thirty pounds. Why? *Why?* How long do you expect us to put up with your stupidity, your indifference? Do you think we will all sit back quietly and let you Communists grow fat and insolent?"

By now everyone was shouting wildly. It was past 8 P.M. and although the meeting had been set for from 2 to 6 P.M., it still showed no signs of letting up. Liu struggled to brush the ragged coat away from his face. He stood up and retreated behind his chair. His features were distorted with fear. "All complaints will be forwarded to the proper authorities," he said in a high-pitched voice. "Another meeting will be called soon so that all can have a full hearing." With that he turned and rushed off the platform, stumbling against a chair in his haste to get away.

At the meeting of the returned students my silence had not been noticed because each of the others had been too preoccupied with his own chance to speak. The next day, however, I was told to attend, a week later, a special meeting for 30 prominent businessmen. At such a small gathering my comments were sure to be requested. I would either have to say something against the Party or confess, in effect, that I did not intend to make any contribution to the blossom campaign. Either course seemed dangerous and I was worried.

Li-li, I learned, was also worried about whether or not to blossom. The night before I was to attend the meeting with the businessmen, she came to my house—apparently on impulse—to ask my advice. This was the first time since our reunion that she had made an effort on her own to see me, and I was delighted. I was unable, however, to give her a straight answer on what she should do. I confessed that I was confused about the situation, but I told her that important men like J.P. Chan were sure that the Communists were sincerely trying to improve. "Mr. Chan believes that the Party *must* improve if it is to stay in power," I said.

Li-li frowned. "Perhaps he is right," she said, "but I am frightened."

I went to the sofa and sat beside her. "What is it you fear?" I asked. "Has anything happened to you?"

She shook her head. "I know something must happen soon, and I feel it will be terrible," she said.

"We both have been intelligent enough to survive so far," I said. I took her hand. "If we keep our wits about us, we'll pull through this crisis as well."

Li-li closed her eyes. "I'm so tired of struggling just to stay alive," she said. "If we live through this crisis, there will be another and then another. You're smarter than I. You might live, but eventually I'll make a mistake—"

"No," I said. I took her in my arms. "We must help each other. If we are together, nothing bad can happen to us."

Li-li's head was on my shoulder, and I was filled with delight, but I could feel that she was still tense. "Do you remember that day in the temple when the priest read our fortunes?" she asked.

"That was only superstition," I said.

Li-li leaned back to look at me directly. "True," she said, "but I know that my future is hopeless. It's not superstition; it's because I'm not strong enough to endure in this new society."

"I can be strong enough for both of us," I said.

Her eyes softened, but she shook her head. "I would only pull you down with me," she said. I started to protest, but she stopped me. "Bob, you should try to leave this country," she went on. "You're clever enough to manage it. Your position is strong enough. I know you must have thought of it. Isn't that why you've never married?"

I held her tighter. "That's past," I said. "I couldn't leave you now. I want us to be married. Even if you're right, and we have only a little time together, it will be worth it."

Li-li sighed as in hopelessness, but she pressed her soft cheek against mine. "Dearest Bob, I knew you would propose to me and I'm thrilled, but I can't—"

"I won't let you refuse," I said, holding her tighter. "We love each other, and that's all that matters."

"Bob, please try to understand," she said. She drew herself gently away. "We do love each other, but to survive we must live by lying and deceiving. Isn't that the opposite of love? If we tried to *practice* love, we would end by destroying our means of surviving—either that, or the life we lead would destroy our love."

I suddenly had a picture of what living with Li-li would be like. The very fact that we would be tied together with strong bonds of emotion would give the authorities a powerful weapon against both of us. If either of us for any reason was found "unacceptable," the other would suffer the same fate unless he or she betrayed and denounced the other. Knowing this, we would instinctively try to protect each other by never revealing our real thoughts or opinions. In the end, we would be living the same lie with each other as we did with everyone else. I remembered Chan Ko-tza's lament, "We have no friends here—" I moaned in anguish, and buried my head in Li-li's shoulder. She was right; love was impossible in the New China, and I knew that rather than destroy my love for her I would give up seeing her. "But what if the Chans are right and the Party will change?" I asked.

"Then you can come back from wherever you are," Li-li said. "But you should try to get away now, while you still have a chance."

I drew back. "Do you believe then that this campaign is only a trick?" I asked.

"I don't know. I don't understand these things," she said. "But they have tricked us before. And now they are losing control over the people. Will they really just sit back and let the people drive them out?"

Suddenly it seemed perfectly clear to me. I am sure that Mao was sincere when he made his original speech, but I think he had deceived himself concerning the extent to which the masses had been made docile by eight years of suppression. I am sure that he and the other top Communists must have been horrified by the intensity of the hatred toward them that the campaign revealed. How would they respond to the hatred? Previously, they had been consistently ruthless; why should they now be expected to show human compassion? Every day, the situation was becoming more tense, and the people were growing bolder. If the authorities were to regain control, they would have to strike soon—and hard. Li-li's feminine instinct was correct. I knew that now, and I knew that our poor country would soon face the worst reign of terror we had endured so far. For a moment, Li-li and I clung to each other, trembling.

But then I drew back. "I have thought of escape, of course—I even worked out a plan," I said. "But I can't do it now. The authorities associate you with me. They think of us as practically engaged. If I got away, you might be in trouble."

"Bob, I beg of you not to think of me," Li-li said. "You can make a life for yourself outside, but I wouldn't know how to do it. I don't care what happens to me, but I would be happy if I knew you were away, and safe."

"It's out of the question," I said angrily. "I will not attempt an escape as long as it might endanger you."

Li-li's face showed affection, exasperation and frustration almost simultaneously. "I wouldn't be in any danger," she said. "Once I knew you were safely away, I could denounce you. I could say that I had felt all along that you were not loyal to the regime."

I brushed this aside. The authorities would not believe her; I knew it, and she knew it. But then I had an idea. "Wait," I said. "If you denounced me *before* I escaped, then you would be safe. It might even help you by making the authorities think you were smarter than they in recognizing my disloyalty."

"But wouldn't that make it impossible for you to escape at all?" she asked.

I insisted that it would not affect my plan, but it was a lie. Her denouncing me might well destroy any chance of escape. I would be gambling on the expectation that my position with the authorities was much stronger than Li-li's and that they would trust their own judgment of my loyalty over hers.

We spent the next two hours drafting a letter which she would send to me a week later. We pretended that I had invited her to my house that night, that I had asked her to marry me, and that when she refused I had tried to make advances to her. In her letter, she said that in gratitude to the Party and Chairman Mao for giving her a chance to live a clean and decent life, she intended to devote the rest of her years to the glorious task of socialist reconstruction. A person like me would hinder, rather than help her. She felt that I was still imbued with bourgeois values, that I lacked sincerity, and that I was opportunistic rather than genuinely devoted to the cause of the New China. Li-li demurred at some of these statements, but I forced her to make the letter cold and unmistakably derogatory.

Until this moment, we realized, both of us had been hoping subconsciously that somehow the obstacles to our marriage eventually would be removed. We understood now, however, that if we were to continue loving each other, we could never be together. I no longer had any reason to delay my escape attempt, but I felt no excitement at the thought that soon I might be leaving this unhappy land. I would be doing what I had to do, and I was quite calm about it.

I even managed to remain calm at the meeting the next night, although the other businessmen became quite emotional in their blossoming. Nevertheless, I felt pride for these men. For the last eight years, every one of them had endured every kind of humiliation and every form of bullying coercion. Many of them, during Five-Anti, had been physically tortured. Yet not one of them now showed fear. In almost every case, the complaint they made against the regime was not that they had been robbed of their property, but that they were not permitted to give the benefit of their superior *efficiency* in the operation of their enterprises. They really asked for little more than that their wealth of experience be acknowledged and that their advice sometimes be accepted.

Charlie Chan was in no position to speak strongly about efficiency and experience, but he blossomed that evening with a complaint about the attitude of his State Representative toward one of the older employees. According to Charlie's story, the old man had accidentally broken a teapot one day and some hot water had been spilled on the State Representative. "I am sure you all know that no worker would purposely harm the all-powerful State Representative," Charlie said. "But our Comrade

Manager screamed abuse at the old man and then fired him. I knew that the old man had a sick wife, and I put in a few polite words in his defense. What a storm broke loose! The Comrade Manager saw fit to call me every vile name I ever heard of." At this point, Charlie's voice grew harsh with bitterness. "Isn't it enough that the State Representative has complete power over our property and our actions?" he asked. "Does he also have to rob us of our last shred of dignity and decency?"

Poor Charlie, how different he was from the happy-go-lucky character I knew once. Listening to his excited criticism I felt now, with no doubt whatever, that the authorities were not going to accept such talk and that eventually Charlie would have to pay horribly for the luxury of his emotional outburst.

My turn to blossom followed his. I already had planned what I was going to say, but I dreaded to say it because I knew the reaction it would have on my companions. "I also have something to criticize in our Comrade Manager at the mills," I began. "Comrade Yang, our State Representative, has not given me proper guidance in my efforts to eradicate my past shortcomings and to remold myself for a place in the socialist society. I come from a capitalist family and I was educated in the United States. Because of this background, I am badly tainted with bourgeois individualism. When I attend the mills I am frequently late in arriving, although this is in violation of the company rules. Comrade Yang, however, rarely takes notice of my faults and thus does not help me. Although I realize the seriousness of my undisciplined individualism, I find difficulty in making sufficient effort to correct my attitude. I earnestly hope that the State Representative will be more strict with me from now on and help me overcome my deficiencies—"

In the brief silence that followed my talk, I could feel the loathing of every businessman in the room. In a quick glance,

I caught the look of surprise and disgust in Charlie's face, and then I could look at him no longer.

Nevertheless, the Communist Director who had sponsored this meeting approached me smiling. "Mr. Loh," he said, shaking my hand, "we are glad to have your kind of constructive criticism. I will inform Comrade Yang at once so that he can help you. I hope you will feel entirely free always to bring forward this sort of helpful suggestion that can enable our State Representatives to do a better job."

There was no doubt about it. The Communists might *say*, "Let a hundred flowers bloom," but they would accept only sweet bouquets of flattery thinly disguised as "criticism." I had learned from the beginning that the Party could not accept real criticism. How could I have allowed myself to forget it, even for a moment?

None of the others had been thanked by the Comrade Director, and I left the hall alone, acutely conscious of the black looks from my friends and associates. Nevertheless, on the way home my mind was working feverishly on the letter I would write to my escaped friend Pao in Hong Kong.

Later that night, my hand shook as I penned the characters for the secret message: *My cousin is feeling well these days.*

CHAPTER 13

*The east wind blows through the north garden
Where flowers of all kinds blossom.
Knowing they will fall in a little while,
I come to gaze on them many times a day.*

—PO CHU-I

I WROTE MY letter to Pao on May 18, 1957, and thereafter I lived under extreme tension. My escape plan now seemed flimsy and transparent. I became supersensitive to the attitude of others and tended to read hidden meanings into the words of anyone who spoke to me.

I had my first fright with this the next day when I went to the office at the mills. I had expected Comrade Yang to be pleased with my blossoming the evening before; for weeks he had endured the insults and humiliation from the mills' workers, and my request for his guidance and correction should have made him feel that his authority was not entirely lost.

Nevertheless, he greeted me coldly and with an unmistakable

look of suspicion. I immediately felt a chill of apprehension. "I have been informed of your complaints against me, but I do not understand them," he said bluntly.

I could not speak. I thought that he was preparing to denounce me, and I waited in dread for his next words.

"Why is it," he continued, "that the comrade workers to whom our Party is dedicated speak out so unjustly, while you, a person from the bourgeoisie, find so little to complain about?"

His question was so naïve that I could not believe he meant it literally; I was sure that it contained an accusation, and in my mind I searched the words desperately for a clue to the crime for which I was being charged.

Finally, however, I saw that comrade Yang really was perplexed. I had been associating with the higher Communists long enough to forget that many of the lower Party cadres actually believed the official fantasies. Thus, to Yang, the workers, having been designated the new ruling class, were expected to show fawning gratitude. When instead they showed bitter resentment at being treated like slaves, Yang was dumfounded; he thought that the workers were being "unjust." I could not expect to break open such a fanatically closed mind, but I hoped to overcome his suspicion of me, and I launched into a dramatic description of my position.

I explained that, except for the Party and Chairman Mao's leadership, I would still be an unimportant university instructor; I would be earning a bare living and would have little hope for the future. Now, however, my hopes were limitless. My salary was higher than I had ever hoped to earn. In addition, the regime accorded me honor and status and gave me the privilege of extensive travel. Most of all, the Party freed me from the burden of my past errors, and taught me the true happiness of working for the people's welfare. My voice trembled, and my words stumbled over each other in my effort to be convincing. I ended by saying, "The simple laborers may not always understand and appreciate what the Party does for them, but how could I do other than show gratitude?"

Comrade Yang's face relaxed. He considered my words for a moment. Then he actually smiled at me. "To be honest, Mr. Loh," he said, "I had never believed that an ex-bourgeois could ever resolve the contradictions in his background. I see now that I was wrong. I confess to the error of having lacked sufficient faith in the Party's judgment." He stood up and offered me his hand.

I was shaking with relief, but I realized that I had become capable of endangering myself through my own fears. I had deceived Yang into thinking that my nervous apprehension stemmed from sincerity, zeal and awe of his authority. In a similar situation with one of the more astute higher officials, however, something of the true nature of my anxiety might be guessed at. If that happened, the arrival of my brother's letter would confirm the suspicion about me, and I would be finished. I determined to hide my fears at all cost.

Nevertheless, my fears were increased even further the next morning. For the previous month, the newspapers had been printing harsh criticisms of the regime, but occasionally an item or two criticizing the criticizers would appear. On this day, however, the number of those who blossomed against the other blossomers suddenly increased. Supposedly, these news items came from individual workers and peasants who viewed with alarm some of the "unfair" comments about "the great Communist Party which was engaged in the splendid task of leading the mother country into socialism." In reality, of course, they were written by the cadres whose special language was unmistakable. These news items, therefore, suggested that the Party was pre-

315

paring to slam down the lid on the freedom of speech which had been permitted during the blossom campaign.

In the papers the following morning the number of blossomers who criticized those who criticized the regime was much greater, and the tone was sharper. I no longer doubted that an ominous reversal of policy was being introduced. This could mean only that a new suppression campaign—perhaps the most brutal one we had endured so far—was being planned. I could hope to obtain an exit permit only during a period of exceptional leniency when the authorities were interested in maintaining the pretense that such liberties as free travel were permitted under their regime. In the hysteria of a suppression campaign, however, everyone would be suspected; leniency would disappear and even to request an exit permit could invite suspicion that might prove catastrophic. Thus I felt now that I was in a race against time.

Nevertheless, my first reaction to the changed tone in the press was fear for Li-li. I found, however, that she was equally aware of the change and even more fearful than I; her worry was chiefly for me. I waited for her that afternoon outside the entrance to her sewing cooperative, and I walked with her to a meeting which she had to attend. Her intuition told her that events would move quickly, and she pleaded with me to leave the country before it was too late. I told her that my plan was already in motion, and I instructed her to send me, that very night, the letter in which she refused my marriage proposal and denounced me as an "opportunist." She demurred, feeling that such an accusation now would be sure to jeopardize me; only when I insisted that I would not make my escape attempt at all without first having her letter did she agree.

I also made her agree to blossom at her meeting that evening. She had managed to avoid it so far, but the line now was clear and she should put herself on record, as quickly as possible, as disapproving of criticism against the Party. "I suppose you're right," she said. She looked older than I had ever seen her. "How much longer can I go on making such compromises merely to stay alive?" she added.

The following morning, May 31, 1957, the press comments against those who blossomed against the Party were even more numerous. The atmosphere everywhere was changing. The emotionalism of the past weeks was giving way once more to fear. Oddly enough, the immediate effect was to increase the intensity of the blossoming against the Party. Those who had permitted themselves to speak out their true thoughts about the regime now subconsciously began to suspect that they had been treacherously trapped. The implications of this were almost too terrifying to face. Instinctively they tended to reject the suspicion by speaking out even more vehemently and by seeking safety in numbers. All those who had voiced severe criticism now pressed everyone else to do the same; evidently they felt that if the whole country expressed equal dissatisfaction with the regime, the authorities would be unable to take revenge on any particular group.

In any case, the notes on the Institute's bulletin board that day contained the most bitter anti-Communist statements I had seen so far. As I was reading them, Director Win approached me. He asked me what I thought of them.

This time I made a great effort to hide my fears, and I managed to shrug with seeming indifference. "I suppose Chairman Mao must be right when he said that some of the Party cadres need rectification," I replied, "but these criticisms seem unnecessary. Would you chop down a whole cherry tree just because one or two cherries have worms in them?"

Win raised his eyebrows. "Nevertheless, the background of

317

the people who wrote these notes is the same as yours. It seems odd to me that you do not make similar criticisms."

"But why?" I said, trying to put indignation in my voice. "I personally can find nothing to criticize. Am I expected to lie and fabricate some false accusations?" Win was smiling but he was watching me through narrowed eyes. I felt myself beginning to perspire. "You know me thoroughly," I went on. "Comrade, can you think of one reason why I should be dissatisfied?"

"Still, something is obviously bothering you," Win said smoothly. "You look like you've not slept for a week, and I've never seen you so nervous."

I let my shoulders droop, pretending to abandon any further attempt to hide my secrets from him. "It's Li-li," I said. "I'm getting no place with her."

"Ah, so?"

"I asked her to my house a few days ago," I continued. "I tried to remember your advice, but she would not listen to me. She would not even let me touch her."

I caught a gleam of satisfaction in Win's eyes before his face expressed polite sympathy. "Really, old Loh," he said, "you cannot continue to let such a small matter upset you. Your work will begin to suffer."

I nodded, seemingly in mute misery. Win's words were stern but his voice was friendly and now he laughed at me. "We must talk further about your problem," he said, and he invited me to dine with him two evenings later, on June 2, 1957, which was a Sunday.

In bed that night I went over every detail of my conversation with Win. Unquestionably he was far more shrewdly observant —and therefore more dangerous—than Comrade Yang, but finally I decided that I had handled the situation to the best of my ability. At least nothing in Win's attitude suggested that I had made a serious mistake.

What surprised me most about our conversation was that he had called me "old Loh." In effect, this confirmed that he was trying to establish a relationship of personal friendship with me. Such a relationship between a high Party official and an ex-national bourgeois, however, was extremely difficult simply because the difference in social status was too great. Until now he had always addressed me with the coldly formal title of "Mister," although his voice had been friendly.

It now occurred to me that he had been *ordered* to become friends with me. This explanation of his attitude was much more likely. It suggested that I was being considered seriously for Party membership. The fact that Win had been chosen to prepare me for it indicated that I would be assigned a function within the Propaganda Department. This made sense because, from the time I had written J.P.'s voluminous "confession" during Five-Anti, my major successes in cooperating with the regime had been in the speeches, lectures, articles and reports I had prepared.

I began to wonder, however, why the offer of Party membership was being delayed. If I were trusted enough to be considered for it, why did not the authorities speak to me openly about it? Did they still have some doubts about me? Were further tests of my loyalty deemed necessary? At this point, I remembered that underground Party members still existed. Considering my usefulness from the viewpoint of the authorities, I realized that they would regard me more valuable without open Party membership. At the Institute the cadres thought that my lectures were more effective when I spoke as a businessman to businessmen. Moreover, as a secret Party member I could still belong to the Federation of Industry and Commerce; I could continue to work at deceiving foreigners about the regime's policy toward the "democratic elements," and in addition I would be able to act as an informer against my companions. All of this would explain why Win was approaching me so cautiously.

I was sure now that I had correctly deduced what the authorities were planning for me. I considered how these plans might affect my chances of being granted an exit permit. If I were to be offered secret Party membership soon and assigned at once to an important project, I might find that the time for a trip to Hong Kong would be denied me, even though I might be trusted adequately. Conversely, I knew that my "emotionalism" concerning Li-li would be regarded as a bourgeois weakness that would tend to make the authorities hesitate in offering me the security and privilege of Party membership. Between these two possibilities, I decided I would be safer to win the confidence of the authorities as much as possible. My "weakness" for Li-li would be considered unimportant as long as my work at the Institute was not adversely affected. I determined therefore to improve my lecture and because I could not sleep anyway, I spent the rest of the night working on it.

The next day I received Li-li's letter. Reading it now, knowing that I must show it to the authorities, the letter sounded much more harshly condemning than I remembered. The implications that I was politically unreliable and an opportunist were extremely serious even if they were only suggested rather than stated openly. Li-li would make such comments about me only if she were militantly loyal to the regime and had been grossly provoked by me. If I did manage to escape, however, her accusations would sound then like a brilliantly astute analysis of my character, and she would be commended.

Meanwhile, surprisingly, I found that I was worried less about the implication that I was "politically" deficient than I was about another comment the letter contained. I had made Li-li hint that when she was at my house, I had tried to force myself physically upon her. This was intended to explain her extreme indignation. I realized now that while the authorities might accept their own evaluation of my political loyalty rather than the emotional outburst of a female and a reformed "degenerate element," they would be forced to accept her accusation that I had behaved boorishly with her. The puritanism of the Communists would be rasped; worse, because of the Communists' pretense that they championed the laboring classes, they would not be able to dismiss lightly the fact that an ex-bourgeois had molested a member of the proletariat. Of course, the Communists also would modify their attitude to any extreme for someone whom they regarded as useful, but I would be putting my own usefulness to a severe test in showing Li-li's letter. I spent another sleepless night planning carefully my act for Director Win.

When I met him the following evening I looked so haggard that he commented on it at once. "You must advise me," I said, and if hysteria edged my voice it probably was genuine. "Look at this letter she wrote me."

Win laughed and put a hand on my shoulder. "It can't be as bad as all that," he said as we sat down. But his smile faded as he read the letter and by the end of it he was frowning. He handed it back to me and lit a cigarette before speaking. "You made a bad mistake when you lost control of yourself and tried to take her by physical force," he said.

"I swear I didn't intend what she implied in that letter," I said. "I meant only to be affectionate—"

"Perhaps," Win replied. "But you need to be more subtle. Try to put yourself in her position." He handed me a cigarette and reached over to light it for me. "Here is a girl who once suffered every kind of degradation from people of your class. Now she is leading a clean life. She has discovered what it means to be useful and respected. Naturally she remembers her old life with horror, and she still associates people like you with it. Understandably, therefore, she is oversuspicious of you; she is prejudiced against you simply because of your background. She feels more at ease with the comrades. Eventually, of course, she will overcome her suspicions and prejudice, but meanwhile you must be patient."

The smug hypocrisy of his words sickened me, and I wondered if he really believed them. Nevertheless, I pretended he was imparting great wisdom to me. "Yes, you're right," I said. "What you've said explains her attitude exactly." But then I added tensely, "I beg of you to talk to her for me. Explain to her. Tell her I am aware of my bourgeois faults, but that with her help I can overcome them."

Win sat frowning for a moment. "Very well," he said finally. "I'll do what I can."

He spoke thoughtfully, but the eager expression in his eyes indicated that he was deliberately controlling his voice. I realized suddenly that Win was now fully aware of wanting Li-li for himself. I found that jealousy was like hot acid inside of me, and I hated him murderously.

In the days that followed, however, I managed to suppress these dangerous emotions. I told myself constantly that if I were successful in making my escape, I would be leaving Li-li safeguarded by a powerful protector. Toward me, Win was more friendly than ever. This proved that the accusations in Li-li's letter had not damned me, even though Win may have been tempted to use them as a means of removing me so that he could have Li-li to himself. Li-li perceived that I might be endangered if he became jealous of me. To forestall this possibility, she pretended to be flattered by his attentions, and cold if not hostile toward me. My own part in this intrigue was to continue showing that I suffered badly from unrequited love. At the same time, I pretended to have high hopes for the success of Win's intervention with Li-li in my behalf. Finally, I concentrated on making my lecture at the Institute as effective as possible; this was to prevent the authorities from thinking that my feelings for Li-li had a bad effect on my work.

During this period, however, my relationship with Li-li was not as much of a threat to my escape plan as the now rapidly changing political climate. By the first of June 1957, the hostility in the press toward criticism of the Party was plain and daily became more intense. The effect of this was to create mounting waves of fear and confusion. After eight years of suppression and rigid control, the blossom campaign had provided relief from the pressure and, what is more, it gave hope that at least limited freedom might eventually be possible in the New China. Now, however, the fact that the Communists were still morbidly preoccupied with opposition was becoming apparent. The suspicion that the blossom campaign had been only a trick to identify for suppression all those who harbored anti-Communist thoughts gradually spread. In its wake, those who had revealed their true thoughts and now were doomed either surrendered to fear or made desperate attempts to avoid facing the situation. The rest, having experienced again the delight of free speech only to have it snatched quickly away, sank even deeper than before in hopelessness and despair. We all understood that the blossom campaign had revealed the people's violent hatred of the regime and for that very reason the authorities would use even greater violence to suppress it. We knew that the usual methodical preparations for another campaign were being made, and we now expected it to begin any day. Once the new wave of violence was started, I would have no hope of escape.

After June 7th, therefore, I began to expect the letter from my brother, and I waited for it with increasing anxiety. I had sent the code message to Pao, rather than to my brother, in order to have nothing on record which would suggest that the letter had been planned by me. The arrangement was that when Pao received my message he would immediately inform my brother, who would then write to me the words I had originally dictated. As a means of further discouraging the suspicion of collusion, I had cut down drastically on the correspondence with my brother; in fact, my last letter to him had been sent when I was in Moscow, nearly six months before. Thus I had little news of him. I began to fear that he might be on some long trip away from Hong Kong or that he had lost the copy of the letter which I had dictated to Pao.

Just when I was beginning to despair, the letter arrived. It was on Tuesday, June 11, 1957. My hands shook so badly that I could barely read the words. The letter was written precisely as I had dictated it, but my brother had cleverly added a few touches that brought it up to date. Here is what it said:

MY DEAR YOUNGER BROTHER,

We have not heard from you directly for a long time, but our relatives tell us that you are well. We understand also that under the guidance of the Communist Party and the People's Government your character has improved greatly. This makes us proud indeed. We can well understand your enthusiasm for the New China; even we overseas Chinese here in Hong Kong find that our situation is much improved because of the impressive changes taking place in the mother country.

In your last letter written to us from Moscow, you invited us to return to Shanghai to visit you. So far, our business has kept us from making the trip but we are looking forward to it, and we hope to see you there sometime within the next year.

Meanwhile there is a matter which disturbs me greatly and, I fear, will disturb you even more. The bank trustees have informed us that we must settle our father's estate without further delay. For the past month, I have been negotiating with the trustees in the effort to get the money released so that the division can be made and your share sent to you. The British laws on these matters, however, are extremely rigid. Despite the help of expert lawyers we cannot work out a way of releasing the funds without your presence. We are told that the three sons sharing the estate must sign in the presence of the court officials.

We know that you must be extremely busy. We also have serious problems, and in fact it is imperative that I go to Singapore within two months. We have committed ourselves to a good-sized manufacturing venture there and have plans for establishing a large branch plant. Thus, I need rather badly the funds from my share of our father's estate, and that is why I am trying hard to get it settled quickly.

I hate to ask you to take time away from your own affairs in order to help us, but I have no choice. Actually, the matter could be taken care of quickly with your presence; you should not need to be here more than a week or so. Also you would be able to take your share of the money with you in any way you choose. The estate is well over HK$200,000 and your share therefore will amount to at least HK$70,000. We understand that you are in no need of money; nevertheless, the division carries out our father's wish and I hope you use your share to buy government bonds.

Our share of the estate will be most helpful in the Singapore undertaking and thus we hope you will let us know by cable when we can expect you.

This letter made several points which I was sure would impress the authorities. The first was that my brothers in Hong Kong were "patriotic businessmen" who were sympathetic to the

325

People's Government and had no objection to my working for the Communists.

The letter also showed that my family had influence and interests outside of Hong Kong. The Communists, I had learned, were much interested in influencing the overseas Chinese, but did not include the Hong Kong Chinese in that category.

Next the letter indicated that my previous correspondence with my relatives had been pro-Communist. The invitation for my brothers to visit me in Shanghai was an example.

I had had to give much thought to the amount of money I supposedly was inheriting. If the sum were made too large, the authorities might become suspicious enough to investigate the matter. If the amount was too low, they might not think it worth the risk of letting me go to pick it up.

I also had carefully set a time limit. If I had not made the matter seem urgent, the authorities might advise me to postpone the trip and in the end I might not be able to make it at all. In fact I had told Pao originally that if no word was received from me within two months of sending the letter, he and my brothers could know that my escape attempt had failed.

Finally, the letter was carefully worded to give the impression that I would not want to go to Hong Kong; at the same time, however, my brother gave no hint of suspecting that I would have any difficulty in making the trip, if I were merely *willing* to do it as a favor.

I reread the letter time and again, trying to imagine how the Communist authorities would react to it. I spent almost the entire night rehearsing in my mind how I would present it.

At the Institute the next morning, I went at once to Win's office. Another sleepless night had made me look haggard again and Win greeted me with a comment on how bad I looked. "More troubles," I said, handing him the letter. "I need advice."

Win scanned the letter once and then, frowning, read it again more carefully. He shrugged, however, when he handed it back. "That shouldn't cause any trouble," he said. "Go to Hong Kong and get the money."

"But it may take two weeks," I protested. "If I'm away that long now, I'll lose Li-li for sure."

"Nonsense," Win said, and then I saw that the prospect of having Li-li to himself for two weeks occurred to him. "The thing to do is to go as quickly as possible and get it over with," he said brightly. I pretended to be glumly doubtful, and he came over to put a hand on my shoulder. "Don't worry about it, old Loh. I'll look after Li-li while you're gone, and I'll see that she doesn't forget you."

I now permitted myself to look happier, and I thanked him effusively. Obviously Win felt that I would be doing him a favor by letting him look after Li-li during my absence, and he had the decency to brush my thanks aside. "Take that letter to the Director of the United Front Work Department," he said to me at the door. "That will expedite the matter."

Back in my own office, I collapsed into a chair, my knees shaking, but I felt that I had somehow crossed the first hurdle.

An hour later I called the office of the United Front Director and made an appointment for that afternoon. The fact that I was given an appointment the same day suggested that he had already been told about me. Nevertheless he greeted me in his office with impersonal formality. "What is your problem?" he asked when I was seated by his desk.

"This letter," I replied. "I don't know what I should do about it."

The Director took my letter and read it slowly. Then he read it again and then a third time. "I gather you want to go to Hong Kong for this money," he said finally.

I frowned. "Frankly," I replied, "I would rather not go. The time is so inconvenient for me. My course at the Institute is ending, but I am very busy with preparations for the next session. Moreover, I have accepted a number of lecture engagements. I feel that my work is extremely important, and I do not believe it should be interrupted for such a trivial matter." The Director made no comment, but he was studying me intently. To cover the awkward silence, I stumbled on. I confessed to being somewhat fearful of going to Hong Kong. "I have heard that it is so full of KMT and imperialist agents that one cannot be safe there," I said.

"I am not familiar with the current situation in Hong Kong," the Director said, "but I do realize the importance of your work at the Institute. If you will leave your letter with me, I shall consider the matter of whether or not you ought to make the trip at this time. Meanwhile, you shouldn't let the problem worry you. I shall be in touch with you."

At home that evening I slept well for the first time in weeks. I felt now that I had done everything I could do and whether or nor I received the exit permit would depend largely on luck. I did not allow myself to hope for the permit or to think what receiving it would mean. Nevertheless, I was fully prepared for refusal. If that happened, I did not think I would be in trouble; after all, I had insisted to everyone that I did not want to leave.

Two days later, on June 13th, I received a call from the Director's office and was asked to see him at two that afternoon. He was busy with some files and while I waited for his attention I felt like a man on trial waiting for the jury's verdict.

"I'm afraid I have bad news for you," the Director said finally. "I must ask you to make the trip to Hong Kong." For a moment, I think my heart had stopped beating, but now it pounded furiously. "The policy that applies in this instance concerns foreign exchange," he went on. "Remember Chairman Mao's words, 'One cent of foreign exchange is equal to one drop of human blood.' "

I frowned and made myself look disappointed. This inspired the Director to explain more reasons why the trip would be beneficial. I would be refuting the imperialist slander that the People's Government denied the people the right to travel freely abroad. Also I would have the chance to describe to influential relatives and their friends the progress being made by the People's Government, and perhaps I could persuade some of them to visit the motherland to see for themselves the great strides that were being taken. As for my personal problems, the Director was sure that the Party Secretary at the Institute would help me fit the time for my trip into my teaching schedule. As for my "duties" at the flour mills, the Director believed that the State Representative, by working extra hard, could manage to get by without me for a fortnight.

The Director stood up, and it was my turn to show the proper response. "I know that what you say is right," I said, glumly but dutifully. "I shall of course accept the Party's instructions."

The Director shook my hand. At the door he told me to send in at once my application for an exit permit, suggesting that I make it apply for a month, rather than for only two weeks, "just in case there might be unexpected delays." As an afterthought, he added that I ought to notify the Bank of China in Shanghai that a remittance of about HK$70,000 could be expected. I understood that the bank in Shanghai would thereupon notify the branch in Hong Kong; without such notification the Hong Kong branch officials might suspect that such a large unexplained sum was intended for paying secret enemy agents on the mainland and the remittance would be delayed.

Outside, I went immediately to the police station in the district where I lived. As I handed in my application for an exit permit,

I said casually to the police officer, "Please inform the United Front Work Department of this." The remark indicated that my trip was authorized from high quarters, and this in turn would obtain prompt handling for my application.

I put off going to the bank until the next day. After telling the manager that the remittance of funds from my father's estate could be expected, I felt that I was finally committed irrevocably to the escape and from this moment on was dangerously exposed. The truth was, of course, that the British law was not as strict as my brother's letter had suggested and my physical presence for the settling of an estate would not have been absolutely necessary. Moreover, my father's estate had consisted entirely of his business enterprises which were left in charge of my brother, and I assumed that the real details of my father's will could be checked without much difficulty.

Thus, if the Shanghai bank official, in notifying the Hong Kong branch about my supposed remittance, should happen to ask to have the matter checked, I was sure that I would be found out immediately. The same would happen if any of the government officials who knew about my proposed trip were even slightly suspicious of me and requested a check through the bank. Even though I had surmounted the most difficult obstacles, therefore, I was still by no means safe. In fact, I was now more fearful than before. This was partly because of the danger that the true details of my father's will might be discovered but partly also because the political situation was now quickly approaching a climax. The whole country seemed on the verge of hysteria, and I felt that at any moment something could happen that would destroy my chance for getting away.

When my exit permit was received on Monday, June 17, 1957, however, I felt finally a great sense of relief and when, that same day, I obtained reservations for a week hence on the train to

Canton, I allowed myself for the first time to think that my escape was possible. My exhilaration was almost uncontrollable, but it lasted less than 24 hours and then my fears returned intensified.

On the morning of June 18, 1957, the *People's Daily* carried the purported full text of the "contradictions" speech that Mao had made secretly on February 27th. The formally published speech differed radically from the previous two versions. Some of the criticism of the cadres was deleted as well as the examples of blunders made by Party officials. The whole tone of the speech was altered so that little of the dramatic call to speak out freely remained. Even more significant than the deletions were some additions that now were made to the speech, and by far the worst of the additions were the so-called "six criteria" for correct blossoming.

A person was judged to have blossomed correctly if his words and actions of criticism 1) helped unite rather than divide the various Chinese nationalities; 2) benefited rather than harmed socialist transformation and construction; 3) consolidated rather than weakened the people's democratic dictatorship, and 4) democratic centralism; 5) strengthened instead of weakened Communist Party leadership; and 6) increased rather than decreased "international socialist solidarity and the solidarity of the peace-loving peoples of the world."

In short, anyone who had said anything even remotely critical of Communism, Communists or the various Communist countries had not "blossomed correctly" and could be accused of harboring "reactionary thoughts" at best or of engaging in treasonable "counter-revolutionary activity" at the worst. It goes without saying that after eight years of suppression under the Communists, no one would have blossomed if the criteria had been announced in the beginning. In fact, no one would have dared to speak out if Mao had not said that those who fail to do so "are not our friends" and if the promise had not been made repeatedly that no retaliation would be taken against those who did. From the moment Mao's speech was printed, anyone who even mentioned aloud the previous official promises would expose himself to physical danger. No one could doubt any longer that the people would suffer more frightful brutality as soon as the authorities could complete the logistics necessary for "people's courts," the labor reform gangs and execution grounds.

The next six days were the longest of my life.

CHAPTER 14

Of the thirty-six ways, escape is the best way.
—CHINESE PROVERB

DURING THE six days I had to wait until my train would leave for Canton, I saw Li-li briefly every day. I would wait for her in the evening outside her sewing cooperative and then either take her to her home or to one of her group meetings. She pretended to others that my attentions were unwelcome, but usually we found a moment or two during which we could drop the complicated pretenses. She was terrified that the blow we expected momentarily to fall would prevent me from getting away. I was equally terrified that she would be caught in the coming suppression campaign, and I made her check with me every statement she intended to make in her meetings. Actually, she had been prudent, and she had made no blunders that I could see. Nevertheless, under the cover of the violence and hysteria of a suppression campaign, the authorities also disposed of people whom they simply no longer found useful, and someone in Li-li's position could never be sure when the authorities would again turn on her.

For this reason, I was no longer jealous of Win's attentions to her. I felt now that he represented the best hope for her safety. He took her to dinner once during this period, and Li-li told me that he obviously was looking forward to seeing her frequently while I was gone. I gathered she herself was indifferent to his attentions—neither pleased nor displeased—but I begged her to be pleasant with him and to encourage his friendship.

During the day, my lecture schedule had been stepped up so that I could finish the course before leaving. Thus I had as many as three lectures to make in one day, and each was at the Institute's branch headquarters for a different one of the city's 18 districts. I welcomed, however, being kept so busy; it kept my mind off my worries, and prevented me from allowing my hopes to build up too high.

On the night before I was to leave, J.P. gave a party for me. The guests included relatives and friends of mine as well as some of my Communist associates at the Institute. Even the head of the Institute was pleased to attend one of J.P.'s pleasant dinners. Surprisingly, Li-li also was invited. J.P. had never met her before, and I had the delight of seeing him succumb to the spell of her beauty and charm. "I understand now your feelings about her," he said to me. "You're a lucky man."

I had not wanted J.P. to have this party for me—I was afraid that it would look like too elaborate a celebration when supposedly I would be gone for only a fortnight. Nevertheless, J.P. had insisted, but to my relief he used the fact that I was inheriting some money—rather than the fact that I was leaving on a trip—as the reason to celebrate. Before the party was over, however, I learned that he had his own reasons for giving it.

During a lull in the conversation near the end of the evening,

334

he suddenly turned to me and said in a loud voice, "Bob, I want you to promise me one thing—"

"What is it?" I asked.

Everyone in the room heard his next words clearly. "I want you to promise me solemnly that you'll come back here from Hong Kong."

I was so startled that I almost gave myself away. J.P. *knew* what I was planning to do. I realized now that because J.P. had blossomed, even though mildly, his position was sure to be weakened in the coming suppression campaign. The fact of my defection could make matters worse for him. Thus he was preparing now for the time when all my friends and relatives would have to denounce me. He was publicly establishing that he had "doubts" about me and that he had tried his best to ensure my return.

"What do you think I am?" I said, pretending indignation. "Of course I promise to return." My broken promise would give the authorities more excuse to blacken my character, but it would help to clear J.P. of any connection with me.

Only a few minutes later, one of my uncles drew me aside and to my chagrin I learned that he also knew what I had planned to do. He was a man in his forties with a twelve-year-old son. He said that although nothing remained in life for an old man like him, he hoped I would remember his son. He added that perhaps sometime in the future the boy would need me and I might be able to help him. This was his way of saying that I would be in the free world where I would have the priceless gift of hope. Some day, conditions in the mother country might change and then perhaps I would be able to give the same gift to the boy. The fact that a man of his age must look upon his life as finished seemed unbearably sad.

As the guests were saying good night to the hosts, Charlie

335

gripped my hand in both of his, and I saw him struggle to twist his ugly face into a grin. I wondered if we would ever meet again. "Can I get anything—do anything—for you in Hong Kong?" I asked.

He nodded. "Have a binge—a real superduper binge," he said softly in English, "—for me."

Li-li and Win came back with me to my house. This had been planned before, and it had been Win's suggestion. Ostensibly the idea was to help me pack, but Win had also suggested that after a polite interval he would leave Li-li alone with me so that I could have another chance to plead my case with her.

When the three of us were alone together, however, the atmosphere was strained and our conversation was awkward. I had very little packing to do because supposedly my trip was to be short. Thus I dared not take more than two summer suits and a few changes of linen. A minute was required to put these in a bag. I added a picture of Li-li, explaining that I wanted to show her off to my family as the girl I hoped to marry. I also added the pictures taken on my tour of Russia, saying that my brothers would be interested in them.

At this point, Win suddenly drained his drink and stood up. "Come," he said to Li-li, "we must leave ol' Loh to get some rest." I looked at him questioningly, but he avoided my glance. He took her arm and propelled her toward the door.

I still wonder what made Win change his mind about leaving Li-li alone with me. I am inclined to believe now that he also knew I was planning to defect. The other authorities, of course, could not have suspected it, but Win may have guessed it from the moment I had given him my brother's letter. In fact, my permission to make this trip may have been granted *only* because he thought I would not return, thereby allowing him to have Li-li to himself. What a sharp piece of irony *that* would be!

In any case, while the three of us were alone together in my house on the evening of June 23, 1957, he must have sensed that the relationship between Li-li and me was quite different than outward appearances suggested. Jealousy would prevent him from wanting Li-li and me to be alone together if he thought now that we were secretly fond of each other.

Fortunately, I had not had the chance to tell Li-li about Win's plan, and thus she did not have to hide surprise when it was suddenly changed. She said good-bye calmly, but her eyes were warm with affection. I think we both knew that we would never see each other again.

The next morning, I discovered that even the old servants knew I would not be coming back. They had not been tearful when I had left on a two-month tour of Russia, but now when ostensibly I was to go to Hong Kong for only two weeks, they wept copiously. We had a tender farewell, although none of us mentioned a word to suggest that I would not see them again soon.

Win and the Party Secretary of the Institute picked me up at my house. They drove me to the station and saw me settled on the train. This send-off, simple as it was, could not have been more "official" if I had been a Party member myself; it helped to relieve the almost unbearable tension I was feeling now that the prospect of escape was beginning to seem real.

The only other passengers in the two "soft seat" cars of the train were foreigners except for one old man. He and I shared adjoining berths. I learned that he was the president of Chusan University in Canton, and an old Party member. He had seen me in the company of two obviously important Communist officials and he treated me with humility and respect despite the fact that I was much younger than he. Later, I happened to say that I had been educated in an American university; his attitude toward me immediately became coldly superior and contemptuous. But when I casually mentioned that I had been to the Soviet Union and now was headed for Hong Kong, he apparently concluded that I held high position and his attitude promptly switched back to cringing servility. Arrogant or subservient, bully or coward—how sick I was of Communists with their built-in robotlike responses and their stilted language which perverted the meaning of words.

Nevertheless, I was grateful to learn that going to Hong Kong gave me high status; I was able to use the knowledge effectively the next day. We arrived in Canton late in the afternoon, and I went at once to the Shung Fung Travel Bureau with which I was registered. I found the office crowded with angry shouting people. To my dismay, I learned that a wait of about a week was necessary before a passenger could get accommodations on either the boat or the bus to Macao. One man—an Indonesian student —was in a particularly bad temper and was hysterically shouting that he had been waiting now for ten days.

I haughtily asked the clerk to take me to the manager. I then treated the manager with contempt, and he responded with cringing servility. The moment I identified myself as one of the arrogant bullies, he became one of the craven cowards. I told him that I had to get to Hong Kong immediatey. I did not say that I was on government business, but I gave the impression that I was. I worked in a mention of the fact that I had returned recently from Moscow, and I implied that anyone who delayed my travel would be holding up the nation's affairs. The result was that he promised somehow to get me on the bus that left early the next morning. He also obtained for me a reservation for that night in the Ai Chun, the showpiece hotel reserved for foreign visitors.

An extraordinary aspect of the trip I was making was that it was "illegal." To go to Hong Kong legally would have meant applying through the British Consulate for a visa; the process would have required months and in the end the visa might be refused. Thus an elaborate system for smuggling people into Hong Kong had been established and was used by almost everyone who went there from the mainland. In fact, several "travel bureaus" advertised openly in the mainland papers, offering safe and immediate "passage" to Hong Kong. I had merely registered with one of these bureaus in Shanghai and had stated that I would go by first class. The Canton branch of this travel bureau then would arrange to get me to Hong Kong and the "fare" would be collected only after I had landed there safely.

The catch to the system was that the fare had to be paid in Hong Kong dollars. The rates fluctuated, but at the time I made the trip, they were HK$500 for first class, HK$250 for second class and HK$150 for third class. These amounts covered all expenses from Canton to Hong Kong; they included food and lodging, but the cost of clothes needed for disguises was charged to the "passenger." The whole system, of course, was sponsored by the Communists; it was the means whereby they sent their agents abroad. Its most important use, however, was as a source of foreign exchange. Hong Kong was now the only practical means of egress to the free world; when it is remembered that more than two million refugees from the mainland are residing in Hong Kong alone, it is obvious that people escaping from Communism make a highly profitable business for Communists.

This would suggest that the authorities would encourage—or at least would allow—practically anyone to go to Hong Kong who could pay the fare in foreign exchange; the truth was, however, that exit permits were granted with extreme caution. The authorities knew that the vast majority of the 650 million Chinese on the mainland would escape if they could. Also the Communists had plenty of evidence that almost every mainland Chinese

339

who managed to get to Hong Kong refused to return. Thus the question was whom the authorities would *allow* to escape.

By far the largest percentage of escapees were simple, uneducated people. The truth is that the Communists looked upon the proletariat with contempt and could not believe that people outside would take seriously anything said by a mere worker or peasant. Many of these escapees were too ignorant to understand clearly or describe accurately what the conditions were on the mainland. Thus the authorities had little to fear from them and at the same time earned valuable foreign exchange while getting rid of many mouths that otherwise they would have to feed. Even so, these escapees were almost always required to leave close family members behind as hostages to guarantee their behavior outside.

Practically everyone else, even high Party officials, was required to leave such hostages when going to Hong Kong. The only important exceptions were people with close relatives among the influential overseas Chinese whose goodwill the authorities were especially anxious to earn. Nevertheless, a member of this group was permitted to leave only when holding him would result in more unfavorable publicity than he himself was likely to spread once he was away from Communist control. My friend Pao was typical of this type. During the years he had been held in Shanghai, he had actually seen little of how the regime worked. The authorities knew that outside he would speak unflatteringly about the New China, but the effect of continuing to hold him would have been worse.

The rarest group of escapees were people in positions similar to mine. They were capable of seeing through the Communists' pretenses, perceiving the truth about the Communists' motives, assessing the facts about the regime's achievements, and worst of all, they could effectively communicate such information to outsiders. The authorities always assumed that these people would escape if given the chance. Thus they were never granted exit permits without providing numerous close family members as hostages and without some exceptional reason for the trip—a reason that promised much benefit to the regime. A number of these people did refuse to return. This meant that, in order to protect their families left behind, they would have to remain mute about conditions on the mainland. It meant that they could never see their families again, and would have to live the rest of their lives in strange lands as barely tolerated foreigners. It also meant, therefore, that they found the atmosphere of freedom irresistible.

Under all these circumstances, the fact that I obtained an exit permit without providing even one hostage was exceptional indeed. In fact, as far as I know, the case is unique. It can be explained only by the fact that I applied for the permit during one of the rare periods of leniency, that the authorities were greedy for the foreign exchange of my supposed inheritance, and that I had convinced them finally, after eight years of constant effort, of my apparent loyalty. This explanation sounds cogent enough, but quite possibly the only real reason I received the permit was Comrade Win's desire to get rid of me—as humiliating as it is for me to admit it.

On the morning of June 26, 1957, however, I cared nothing about the reasons why my permit had been granted. I still could hardly believe that the plan I had thought about for so long was actually working and that I was really on my way to escape. The papers were announcing the opening that day of a forum of the National People's Congress. Premier Chou-En-lai would make an important speech. Because Mao's famous speech on contradictions had been formally published eight days before, the forum obviously would concern the policy changes which would clamp down on the free speech of the blossom campaign. I realized that I was getting away barely in time, and even during the four-hour bus ride from Canton to Macao I actually sweated with the fear that we might be stopped and sent back.

The other passengers who crowded the bus obviously felt the same. The atmosphere was tense almost to the point of hysteria. We rode in silence, but whenever the bus stopped because of some traffic obstruction, we would become restless and some of the passengers would burst into high-pitched querulous complaints or violent cursing.

At noon the bus reached its destination, Kun Pei. This was a small village containing a large customshouse. A hundred yards or so beyond the building was the border to the Portuguese colony of Macao. The border was protected by barbed wire and was well patrolled and guarded. The border itself was marked by a small stream. No bridge crossed the stream; the road went from the customshouse, through the yellow mud of the stream and then on up to the gates in the wall of Macao city. The distance from the customshouse in China to the wall in Macao was about 100 yards, and seeing the road I had a nearly irresistible impulse to make a dash for it.

Nevertheless, I forced myself to endure the two hours of customs formalities. We were lined up and our exit permits were taken from us. This was frightening; without the permits we felt helpless and vulnerable. If a mistake occurred, if one's permit should be mislaid, the consequences could be so terrible. The officials were cold and curt and unsympathetic.

Next, our money was taken from us. We were allowed to buy HK$8, but the remaining currency could not be taken out. I sent the rest of my money by postal order to the servants at my house in Shanghai.

Finally our permits were returned to us, much to our relief, and we were lined up for the inspection of our luggage. The inspection was thorough and the wait was long.

Two of the travelers, six or seven people ahead of me in the line, were not allowed through. I could not hear what was said, but I could see that the travelers were arguing and pleading with the tight-lipped inspectors. After about 20 minutes, police were called and the two men were dragged away. One of the prisoners whimpered pathetically as he was propelled along. The memory of these sounds and the expression on the faces of the two prisoners haunt me to this day.

Thus, by the time I reached the inspectors, I could scarcely control my trembling. If my escape attempt failed now, when I was so close to freedom, I knew I would collapse. But I had nothing to fear. I had put the pictures of my Russian tour on the top of my clothes in the bag. The inspector took one look at the pictures, quickly closed my bag and respectfully motioned me on.

Outside the building we faced the dirt road which dipped down through the muddy stream and then climbed to the wall of Macao. Yet none of us moved toward the road. There were no officials to give us orders, and we therefore waited dumbly like animals until someone would tell us what to do. Our group grew larger as we were joined by other travelers who had passed through the customs inspection.

One of the new arrivals was a big fellow who looked like a tough workman. I noticed that his face was twisted into an ugly grimace. As soon as he was outside, he turned and looked back into the building. He stood with his feet apart and his fists over his head. Suddenly he began shouting. In the most vile language, he cursed the Communists, the Party and the regime. From his comments, I gathered that he had gone from Hong Kong a year before to work in Canton and had been trying for eight months

343

to get away. He was working himself into a violent rage describing his experiences, and I drew away from him terrified, expecting violence at any moment.

Other travelers, however, converged on him; they told him that he was not in Macao yet. The man immediately grew silent. His face turned into a sickly gray mask of terror. Then he pulled away from the group and sprinted along the road. In his haste, he fell twice and by the time he reached the Macao gate he was covered with mud.

Nevertheless, the noise he had made brought two of the guards out of the customshouse. They looked at us contemptuously and motioned toward the road. "Go on," one of them said.

Our group now contained about 100 people. We began to move slowly, even reluctantly, along the road. It seemed almost too good to be true that we had only to walk a hundred yards to freedom. Gradually, however, our pace quickened, and suddenly a kind of panic gripped us. We broke into a run which became a wild, sobbing, clawing scramble.

Through the gate we found ourselves in a street guarded by Negro troops who tried to herd us into line. They and the Portuguese officials treated us like cattle. Paradoxically we had rushed from the "progressive" society of Communist China into the arms of eighteenth-century colonialism, but we travelers were too jubilant to care. Cursing us in crude Chinese, the Portuguese officials managed to "process" us quickly. Our exit permits were merely gathered up, taken into an office and then returned to us ten minutes later. The troops now prodded us to move along.

We paid little attention to them. By this time our group had become hysterical with joy. Some were weeping, others screaming, and others shouting, singing, laughing or trying to do all three at the same time. I found myself pounding the back of an old workman and shouting, "We made it! We made it!" He seemed to find this extremely funny; he doubled over with laughter and finally sat down in the street. He rocked back and forth, laughing uncontrollably. Near by, a young man and two elderly ladies had joined hands. They were jumping up and down and shouting nonsense. It was so ludicrous that I also began to laugh and finally I too had to sit in the street beside the old man.

We became aware at last that Chinese representatives from our travel bureau were trying to round us up and make us climb into two waiting trucks. Our hysteria evaporated, and a few minutes later I found myself standing in the back of a crowded truck which bounced along through rough city streets. Ten minutes later we pulled up in front of a three-story house. The ground floor, we found, was the office and lounge of our travel bureau. The two upper floors were dormitories. We were to wait in the lounge until our names were called, but I was called almost immediately.

At the desk a polite young man described to me, for the first time, the three classes of travel for being smuggled into Hong Kong. First class meant that one went across on the regular ferry. Before leaving, the "passenger" was given a uniform and he went aboard as a member of the ferryboat crew; in Hong Kong he disembarked also as one of the crewmen.

I was told, however, that this class was temporarily discontinued. Only four to six people per trip could be smuggled in this manner, and occasionally the Hong Kong police tightened up their inspection so that even this small number were temporarily unable to get through. I was told that I would have to wait a week or two if I insisted upon going first class.

Second class was by motor fishing boat. The passengers were hidden in the cargo hold which normally was used for fish. Third class was in a fishing boat without a motor. The young man said frankly that risk was unavoidable in both these classes but that the third class could be really dangerous. The sailboats moved slowly and were helpless in bad weather or if suspected by the Hong Kong harbor police. Subsequently, I learned that hundreds had died in the third-class gamble for escape from the mainland.

Nevertheless, I was told that if I would accept second-class travel, I might get out that same night. I signed up for the journey without hesitation; the matter of the fare was handled like a loan; the paper I signed was a promissory note payable in Hong Kong dollars. I understood that the note was payable after I had been safely delivered in Hong Kong.

The young man said nothing, but he obviously thought I would be wiser to wait for a first-class journey. I found, however, that my impatience was uncontrollable. I did not realize it yet, but months would be necessary to get over the fears with which I had lived constantly for eight years. I wanted to get as far and as quickly away as possible from the China mainland, and I think I would have taken any risk even to save a few hours of waiting.

Having settled the travel business, I went into the lounge. The place was furnished with only a few rough chairs and benches, but to me—and to my fellow travelers—it was the most beautiful room we had ever seen. It contained large stacks of newspapers and magazines from the free world. We pounced on these, and we now had the indescribable delight of reading calm rational news again instead of grimly emotional propaganda. Oddly enough, we were all intrigued the most by the "yellow" journals. We had forgotten that anything was ever published for the sole purpose of entertainment. We looked with utter astonishment at the pictures of attractive women and we studied the jokes, too bewildered to find any humor in them.

And then we made the most wonderful discovery of all: conversation. It began when one of us would read some news item which he felt irresistibly moved to share with the rest of us. "Listen," he might say suddenly, "*they* [he meant the Communists] never told us about *this*." Slowly we realized that we were no longer under compulsion to watch every word we uttered, and we began to talk. We did not launch into diatribes against the regime—politics of any kind seemed abhorrent—we merely used our voices to experience the exquisite delight of speaking without fear. The old workman, for example, described some dishes his mother used to cook for him. A young student quoted verses from a poet whom the Communists considered "frivolous" and yet listening to the boy we were deeply touched.

Our group was strangely drawn together. Most of the people were peasants or laborers; there were a few overseas Chinese students returning to Asian countries. Nevertheless, we felt that we understood and sympathized with each other. Although, in reality, these people were strangers, I trusted every one of them. I wanted to help them. They were my friends. In the lounge, we were served plain but tasty food, and to our special delight, American and British cigarettes were passed around. Nevertheless, I can remember nothing that equaled the pleasure of simply chatting with my new friends.

Later, I went to the floor above to find the cot which had been assigned to me in case the journey for that night should be called off. The dormitory was starkly furnished, but I doubt if any traveler here ever complained about it. On the cot next to mine, however, a man was sitting with his shoulders bent, apparently in despair. He was not from our group, but in my newfound love for humanity I spoke sympathetically to him. He told me that the bureau had delivered him twice to Hong Kong but both times he had been arrested by the Hong Kong police who had

347

deported him back to Macao. He was now waiting to make his third attempt. The bureau at least was honest and efficient. If the attempt to smuggle a "passenger" failed and he was picked up, the attempt was repeated as many times as necessary. Meanwhile, the passenger was provided free food and lodging and when he finally had been successfully smuggled in, he paid only the originally stipulated amount. The worst danger, I learned, was being arrested in Hong Kong itself. The illegal immigrants were put temporarily into concentration camps where they were fingerprinted. Once a person's fingerprints were on record, his chances of ever becoming a legal resident of the colony were slim.

I therefore began to feel apprehensive when, late in the afternoon, 15 of our group were called into a separate room and told that we would make an attempt that night to get through. We were warned that from now on we must follow to the letter the instructions given to us. The bureau official said that different people would be in charge of us at different times, but that we would always know the leader and that our lives depended upon doing immediately and exactly what he ordered.

We now changed into the type of clothes worn by the people in Hong Kong. This would enable us to lose ourselves at once in the crowds on the British island. We turned over to the travel bureau everything except these clothes we were wearing. Our possessions would be delivered to us later in Hong Kong. At eight in the evening we began the actual journey. Leaving the bureau headquarters, we were told to walk casually and to straggle along so that we would not seem a group. After several blocks we came to a small hotel on the riverbank. We entered one at a time and made our way to a room which previously had been pointed out to us. The room was furnished as an office. The shades were pulled down and the lights were turned off. We were told in whispers that we must be absolutely quiet. Our names were checked off and then we waited for a half hour. Finally, the members of our group began to be led out one at a time. Soon I found myself on a darkened pier. We were put into a small sampan. The boat was rowed quietly, keeping in the shadows of deserted fishing vessels.

After another half hour, we pulled up alongside the dark hulk of a larger boat. We scrambled aboard and were told to drop down through the hatch to the bottom of the hull. The hatch was replaced. We had to sit crowded together, our knees drawn up, on the rough planking. It was pitch-dark, hot, airless, and it stank of rotten fish.

We were upset the most, however, by one of our companions, a middle-aged man with a repulsive skin disease; huge scabs covered his head and face. The danger of catching his unpleasant disease did not bother us—such things were meaningless in the life-and-death business of our escape. The disease, however, made him extremely conspicuous. Thus if the police spotted us, he would be easily traced, and the rest of us would be caught with him. We worried about him as the minutes dragged on in that stifling hold.

After two endless hours, the boat began to move and now sea-sickness added to our misery. Several of my companions began to vomit uncontrollably and two others fainted from the heat. Just when we thought we could not stand the hold another minute, the hatch was removed and we were permitted to come out. I remember sucking in great gulps of air, and then I found a corner where I could sit leaning against a coil of rope. I managed to doze a little.

At 2 A.M. we could see mountains on the horizon and soon after, the lights on Hong Kong's peaks. A breeze came up, warm and damp, and the sea roughened; the boat rolled and pitched badly so that further sleep was impossible.

349

At 4 A.M., when we were nearing Hong Kong, we were made to go down into the hold again. If possible, the place seemed even worse than before, and all of us soon became violently sick. The motor stopped. We could hear the sailors putting up the sail and getting out fishing nets. The boat now wallowed in the waves. I was dimly aware that it was being idled along while the sailors pretended to fish, but the motion was sheer torture. To make it worse, the heat was increasing rapidly. I was half faint, and all of us were moaning. Suddenly, one of the group could stand it no longer. He pushed open the hatch and stood up. A sailor immediately hit him on the head with a wooden pole. Thereafter we were quiet while the hours dragged on. I think we were all half dead.

When the hatch was finally opened again, we needed to be helped out. When my eyes adjusted to the light, I saw that the time was 9 A.M. We were indescribably filthy and we reeked so badly that even the sailors wrinkled their noses at us. We had had nothing to eat or drink for 15 hours, but the sailors now were frantically impatient to get rid of us.

We found that we were in the harbor of a tiny uninhabited island northeast of Hong Kong. A sampan had pulled alongside. We were taken quickly to the land. We were told to lie flat in some thick bushes and were warned that we might be shot if we moved or made a noise. For two more hours we endured the blazing sun, myriads of insects, and worst of all the torture of thirst.

Three small fishing sampans then entered the harbor. We were divided into three groups of five each. I was fortunate not to be included with the man who had the skin disease, but I was past caring about anything except water.

Again I found myself cramped in the dark hold of a boat's hull, but now the sun was high and the heat was unbearable. I think I did faint this time. My lips and tongue were so swollen I could not speak. Time had lost all meaning, but we must have been on the sampan for at least an hour. At about noon we were put ashore again, this time at the foot of a steep mountain. We were permitted the time to clean ourselves a bit in the sea water. Then we began the climb.

There was no path and the undergrowth was thick. Somehow we managed to reach the top, which was about 500 feet above the shore. At the summit we were made to hide in a clump of woods, and our guide left us alone.

I think this was the worst part of the journey. We were covered with scratches. Our clothes were torn from the thorny brush of the mountain. We were exhausted. We had not had a bite to eat nor a drop to drink since early in the previous evening. But worst of all we now waited so long that we feared we had been abandoned.

Just after 6 P.M., two well-dressed men suddenly appeared in the woods. Our relief was indescribable, but we could make only incoherent grunts to express our gratitude. We now were led down the far side of the mountain. I think we stumbled and fell more than we climbed.

We came out at last on a highway. Two motorcars were parked near by. One was a Ford and the other a Plymouth and both were 1956 models. They looked incredibly luxurious but I was in a dreamlike state and nothing could surprise me. Three of us went in one car and two in the other. I sank back into the cushions and felt myself being wafted down the hill road.

Before long we reached Kowloon. This would indicate that our mountain had been on the coast of New Territory. We were driven to Kaitak Airport and let out at a bus stop. Another guide was waiting for us, and we three travelers got on a bus with him. I looked like a coolie who had had a hard day's work, and no one paid any attention to me. The bus took us to the Kowloon Ferry. The guide took us into the third-class section and we were not in the least conspicuous. Ten minutes later we were in Hong Kong.

Because of impatience—or thirst—I could stand no more of the bus routine. I had HK$5 left; I gave it to the guide and indicated that he should get a taxi for us. The guide nodded and a minute later we were riding through familiar streets.

I realized now that we travelers had been divided according to the addresses of our destinations. One of my companions was dropped off first. Our guide went with him and returned after about five minutes. My turn was next. Moments later the guide accompanied me to the door of my brothers' apartment.

I rang the bell. Almost immediately a woman's face appeared at the peephole in the door. I had never seen her before, and she looked at us coldly. She gestured at us to go away. The guide immediately became angry. He called me a liar and a cheat and he made vague threats. My mouth was too swollen with thirst to speak, but I understood dimly that he thought I had given the travel bureau a fictitious address and did not have the money to pay for my passage. Almost beside myself with frustration and despair, I began to pound on the door with my fists.

A moment later my brother's face appeared at the peephole, and then the door flew open. For a long moment, we stared at each other in silence. I saw his eyes widen in horror and pity. "My God, what have they done to you?" he said finally.

At this point, I felt myself sinking. The guide and my brother caught me, and I was half carried inside. The guide demanded to know if I was expected here. When he learned that I was, he wanted confirmation that my passage "loan" would be paid. My brother offered to give him the money at once, but the guide refused it, saying that someone else would come for the money.

In spite of myself, I began to laugh with weak hysteria. The whole arrangement of my passage had been so typically Communist. Each separate function had been assigned to a separate person in such a way that each was a check on the other. Would I never get away from it?

But the guide left finally. I was alone with my brothers and the contrite servant woman who had turned me away at first. My brothers embraced me, pounded me on the back and deluged me with words I only dimly understood. I made them understand that I was thirsty and a glass of carbonated cola drink was pushed into my hands; I drank three bottles of it without stopping and found then that I could talk a little.

Nevertheless, I was completely dazed. Other faces appeared. I recognized my friend Pao. His arm was around my shoulder and he was shouting at me, "You did it! You did it! You *really* did it!" Everyone laughed so often and so easily. I had forgotten about how people laughed—

Next, I found myself soaking in a soothing hot bath. Soon after, I was stretched out between clean sheets in a soft bed. Slowly my nerves slackened and I began to relax luxuriously.

But then I remembered my father. I remembered being here with him eight years before. I thought of the eight long years I had lost because I had not listened to him, and I wept bitter tears into my pillow.

CHAPTER 15

When will the sorrows
of the Emperor's subjects
come to an end?

—YO FEI

I SPENT JUNE 28, 1957, my first full day of freedom, resting from the physical exertion of the escape. Whenever I dozed off, nightmares wakened me almost at once. I suffered periodic spasms of trembling. I was in a daze and only half realized where I was.

Pao and my brothers were sympathetic, but their idea of therapy was a party that night in the Repulse Bay Hotel. I borrowed some clothes and dutifully allowed myself to be taken to the celebration, but I cannot say that I enjoyed it. The bright lights which I had not seen for so long created an atmosphere of wild gaiety, and the merriment of my relatives and friends seemed wrong in some vaguely immoral way. I felt better when I was alone again in the peace and safety of my own room.

355

The next morning, my brothers took me to the Aberdeen Cemetery and discreetly withdrew as I knelt by our father's tomb. I closed my eyes and seemed to feel his presence. I wanted to believe that he was aware of my escape, because I knew that it would make him happy. This thought had the effect of releasing much of my tension, and from that moment I began the long process of learning to live again as a free man.

Nevertheless, I still faced the danger of being arrested as an illegal immigrant in Hong Kong. That afternoon, therefore, we made the preliminary arrangements for obtaining my residence permit.

I was taken through a maze of back streets and up some rickety stairs to a small crowded room. A woman instructed me to write down my name, my birth date, and the date of my arrival in Hong Kong, which I was to say had been April, 1953. My brother gave the woman HK$50. She then pointed to a man who, she said, would meet me outside the immigration office three days later.

As I approached the office building at the appointed time, the man greeted me and then drew me into a doorway for a whispered consultation. He warned me to say nothing to the immigration officer. When I reached the desk, I was to give the officer the paper on which I had written out my vital statistics. Just before handing him the paper, I was to make a tiny fold in the lower right-hand corner. If the officer should ask me why I had not registered before, since supposedly I had come to Hong Kong in 1953, I was to mumble that I could not read or write and had known nothing about the regulation.

At the entrance to the building, I found that at least 500 people were waiting to register. The man placed me between him and the line, and we walked toward the head of it. Suddenly the man gave me a slight shove, and I stumbled into the line about 30 places from the front. I expected the people behind to object, but instead the man in back of me caught my shoulders to steady me and gave me a reassuring pat. I realized that my "immigration agents" had some of their own people planted in the line. Moreover, many of the people there must have been in circumstances similar to mine and thus were in no position to complain. If another person were put in front of me, for example, I would not have dared to say anything about it.

The registration proved more simple than I would have believed. The immigration officer even filled out the form for me, and no questions were asked. The only trouble was that he gave me a slightly different name. The Chinese character for my name is read as "Loh" in Shanghai but as "Luk" in the Cantonese dialect. The residence permit was written in English, and the officer transliterated my name character according to the Cantonese; thus, legally, I now became "Luk" instead of "Loh."

I considered this a small sacrifice to make for the privilege of living again in a free country. I found, however, that my Hong Kong residence permit did not automatically banish the fears I had had for so long. The reason for them, in Communist China, had been real enough, but now my fears were "nameless." I was constantly apprehensive, but I could not tell why. At night, my dreams were so frightening that I dreaded sleep. If a stranger merely stared at me, I would begin to tremble uncontrollably.

Even worse was the difficulty I had in talking naturally to my relatives and friends. On the mainland, conversation between two people was apt to be primarily for the purpose of proving political reliability. Conversing under these circumstances had become an ingrained habit, and now if anyone revealed personal thoughts or opinions to me, I reacted with painful embarrassment or even panic.

I was not bothered by this discomfort with other refugees.

We could share the delight of free speech, but we instinctively avoided the subjects that still could awaken anxieties. I was happy to be with my brothers and old friends again, but I found that I was more at ease with others who also had escaped recently from the mainland. Without exception, the refugees regarded Hong Kong as a paradise. The vast majority of the two million escapees lived on steep mountainsides in shacks made of flattened-out tins and used burlap bags that often were washed away by heavy rains; they walked miles for water which they had to carry in jars; they had no jobs, no change of clothing, and so little food that they were never without hunger. And yet they used the word "paradise" to describe Hong Kong.

I soon learned that the refugees had a grapevine system which could furnish up-to-the-minute news of events on the mainland. We who were literate, of course, had learned how to read fact from the fiction printed in the Communist publications. Many who corresponded with relatives and friends back home had worked out simple codes with which they evaded the censors and exchanged much real information. And a wealth of fresh detail was brought out by the daily new arrivals.

Within only a day after my arrival, however, the stream of refugees dwindled to a trickle. The suppression campaign which we had been dreading began with the speech with which Premier Chou En-lai opened the People's Congress forum on June 26, 1957. The main part of his speech attacked "certain right-wing elements who have made a number of utterances of a destructive nature, using the pretense of helping the Party with the rectification campaign." He said that the views of many of these "rightists" were "aimed directly against the basic state system of our government." He added that the rightists were trying "to get our State power away from the vanguard of the working class—from the leadership of the Communist Party."

These comments were the cue for the lesser Communist officials to speak out with increasing violence against the "rightists"; i.e., against those who by word or deed had shown anything but utter subservience to the Party. The pretense was maintained that the rectification campaign was still going on, but now the "rectification" was extended mainly to those who had criticized the regime. Instead of blossom reports, the papers were suddenly filled with the speeches of high officials. The titles of a few of the more famous speeches illustrated the new policy: "Right Careerists, Where Is Your Conscience?" "Rightists Are Guilty." "The People Rise to Meet the Noxious Challenge of the Rightists." "Warn the Rightists to Repent." "Attack the Rightist Traitors." "Break the Bones of Those Who Oppose Socialism." "Crush the Right Careerists."

At the same time, the familiar system of enforced "confession" was begun. The "confessions" revealed that a vast and fiendishly clever plot had been put into operation by the imperialists whose agents, apparently, had penetrated into every corner of the country. The imperialist agents had worked upon a few mild dissatisfactions which did exist among certain elements of the people and had succeeded in transforming well-meant and constructive criticism of the regime into an attack on the very existence of the People's Government. Thus, just as Mao had so brilliantly "foreseen," contradictions among the people had been turned by imperialists into contradictions between the people and the enemy. Fortunately, the Communist Party, always alert to the people's welfare, had uncovered the plot in time. Moreover, the Party, always patient, wise and tolerant, understood that some of the "rightists," still secretly unregenerate in their reactionary thinking, had cooperated knowingly with the enemy. Others, however, had been duped through their ignorance to aid the enemy. Having exposed the imperialist plot, the Com-

359

munists beseeched those who had participated in it to confess fully; thereupon the Party, always democratically subservient to the people's will, submitted the confessions for the people's judgment.

The first confessions began to appear in the mainland papers by the middle of July 1957. They came from well-known figures, and their statements, cringing and abject, set the pattern for the thousands that would follow. Here again the titles of a few of the more famous "confessions" illustrate the trend: "Why Did I Become a Traitor?" "I Surrender to the People and Beg for Forgiveness." "I Hate Myself for Having Been a Rightist." "To the People I Am a Traitorous Criminal." "I Bow to the People and Confess My Crimes." "I Failed to Live Up to the Confidence and Honor Bestowed Upon Me by the People." "I Plead for the Chance to Start My Life Anew."

Along with the confessions came the penalties. The number of people executed did not compare with that in the earlier campaigns, but a new punishment called "learning through labor" was introduced. It was similar to "labor reform," and the prisoners succumbed just as quickly, but they were paid a nominal wage for their forced labor.

High non-Party officials with international reputations, however, usually fared better. Generally, they were stripped of their nominal titles and honors and put under house arrest for certain periods. This happened, for example, to Lung Yun, the National Defense Council vice-chairman who had blossomed by denouncing the Russians. It also happened to Minister of Forestry Lo Lung-chi, who had demanded a review of the "so-called counter-revolutionary cases."

The intellectuals, as usual, fared the worst. Hundreds were sent to labor reform, or to "labor learning." Usually they were publicly humiliated and degraded first. This happened to Ting

Ling. She was the country's most famous woman writer, and she had been a Party member for 30 years. When she was declared a rightist she was stripped of all her titles, even those with the China Writers' Association. She was made to scrub the floors in the Association's building for a year or two and then was sent to "learn through labor" in the wastelands of the Siberian border.

The businessmen were similarly treated although as a whole they had not spoken out so scathingly against the regime as had the intellectuals. At the minimum, those who had blossomed even mildly were made now to serve as office boys, sweepers or janitors in the establishments they once had directed.

In Hong Kong, the people who had never lived under the Communist regime viewed the "anti-Rightist" campaign with disapproval and sometimes were embarrassed by the maudlin tone of the confessions. None of them, however, really understood what their compatriots on the mainland were suffering, and occasionally they would even joke about the situation.

We refugees, on the other hand, watched the events with mounting horror. I was especially affected, because I now realized how close my escape had been. The campaign had begun with Chou En-lai's speech on June 26, 1957, the day I had left Canton for Macao. If my journey had been delayed by even one more day, I probably would never have escaped. It is certain that I would not have been able to get out if the journey had been put off for as long as a week. I can still lose a night's sleep if I allow my mind to dwell on this thought. At the time, however, our worst apprehensions concerned the fate of those we had left behind.

The first person I knew who was caught by the campaign was the young engineer who, at the blossom meeting for returned students, had shaken his ragged coat in the deputy mayor's face.

He confessed to some fantastic activities in behalf of the "enemy" and was sentenced as a counter-revolutionary.

The next group included the three pro-Communist delegates on our trip to Russia. These were the ones who believed that they would help the regime by telling the truth about Comrade Ho. All three of them "confessed" and were declared rightists. They were sentenced to "labor learning."

Dr. Henry Ling, the ex-president of Shanghai University who, during the early phase of the blossom campaign, had been released from prison as a wrongly accused counter-revolutionary, was suddenly put back in prison, and his death was reported not long after.

But I was upset the most by what happened to Dr. Stewart Yui, the old teacher whom I loved and who had persuaded me to return to Shanghai in 1949. Since the early Thought Reform Campaign he had held a menial post at Fu Tan University, and for the past year he had been bedridden. Nevertheless, he was one of those chosen now to be struggled against. His cot was dragged into the court of the university. The students, under the direction of the cadres, were made to crowd around him and to abuse and vilify him. After four hours of being shrieked at, spat upon and threatened in order to make him confess, the old man lost consciousness. His cot was then moved back into the building, but he was informed that the struggle would begin again in the morning and would continue until a confession had been wrung out of him. During the night, Dr. Yui managed to get out of bed, find a razor and slash his wrists. Dr. Yui had been a brilliant teacher; he also had been one of the kindest and most gentle people I had known. Although old, infirm, degraded and helpless, he had never once compromised his honesty, honor or dignity. He had dramatized the qualities that the authorities feared most in the people and took the most pains to exterminate.

As long as Dr. Yui had lived I had been able to hope that ultimately in the New China the spirit of man must triumph over the tyranny. Now, however, I accepted that the spirit of an entire people could be stultified; with enough suppression the people could be reduced to unthinking, unfeeling cattle who functioned only as they were directed.

My immediate concern, however, was to ensure that my defection would not increase the difficulties for my closest friends on the mainland. I had time to give the matter much thought because until my exit permit expired, the authorities would not know that I did not intend to return. About a week before the exit permit would expire, I sent three carefully worded letters to Shanghai; one was to Li-li, one to J.P. and one to Comrade Yang at the flour mills. In all of the letters I said that I was found to have a serious case of ulcers and that the doctors had ordered eight months of complete rest for me. I added that my brothers were giving me the care I needed and that when I recovered I had decided to join them in the family's business enterprises, which needed my help badly. To Comrade Yang, therefore, I formally submitted my resignation as manager of the mills. To J.P., I apologized for breaking the promise I had made to him about returning. And to Li-li, I professed to the realization, at long last, that she did not care for me or even think very well of me, and that henceforth I would bother her no more with my attentions.

The purpose of these letters was to establish the idea that my decision to remain in Hong Kong was spontaneous and stemmed primarily from circumstances beyond my control. As long as I was not thought to have planned in advance to defect, no one on the mainland could be accused of having aided or abetted me.

To establish this idea adequately, however, I had to make my letters sound casual and completely innocent of any thought that I was doing something wrong. It was as though in a Communist society—as in any democratic society—the individual had perfect freedom to make the choices which affected his future. The pretense that such freedom existed was always verbally maintained by the authorities, especially in front of foreigners, but no one living under the regime could be so stupid as not to realize that his every action was rigidly controlled. In effect, therefore, I was taking advantage of the pretense. The Communists could not deny my letters without admitting that the freedom I so casually assumed was not permitted in their society. Nothing ever infuriates the Communists so much as to have their pretenses exploited and used against them. They were forced to act upon the idea that none of my associates in Shanghai could have been in collusion with me, but they turned on me savagely. Subsequently I learned that I was accused of many serious crimes; for example, a small fire that in 1954 had been caused by a short circuit and had damaged one of the motors in the flour mills was now credited to me as an act of sabotage. Also, I was described as one of the diabolical secret agents which the imperialists had used to transform "contradictions among the people" into "contradictions between the people and the enemy."

Unpleasant as these accusations were, I was relieved that none of my friends suffered because of having known me. Nevertheless, they had to face the consequences of their own acts during the blossom campaign. J.P., for example, was accused of having "aroused the businessmen against the Party" when he had blossomed by asking for justice in the case of the ex-pharmacy owner who had been attacked with a knife by the firm's State Representative. J.P. unquestionably would have been convicted as a rightist for this crime except that he was in an unusual position. For years he had put on an act for hundreds of foreigners from every part of the world suggesting that businessmen could work happily with the Communists. If now he was accused of having been secretly antagonistic to the regime all this time, a good many important people throughout the world would know that he had been forced to do his act and that the Communists therefore were guilty of fraud. Thus, in J.P.'s case, the authorities did not convict him of being a rightist and they settled for a mere "public confession." He was made to humble himself before 30,000 people gathered at a rally in the Shanghai Culture Square. He said that although he was not guilty of any "rightist actions," he had had "rightist *thoughts*." Because of these thoughts, the rightists had been able to use him, without his realizing it, in their attacks on the Party. J.P. pointed out that the case of the ex-pharmacy owner had been not only trivial but exceptional. By publicizing it, he had increased its importance disproportionately. The intention of the rightists had been to undermine thereby "the noble quality of the cadres" and to mislead the public about the "noble aims of our Party." J.P. concluded in the usual manner. With the Party's help he now realized what harm he had done to the Party and the people. He promised henceforth to increase his vigilance against rightist thoughts and to seek every opportunity to make himself into a new and better man. And finally, he was infinitely grateful for the "magnanimity" shown him by the Party.

The Communist State Representative who had tried to kill the ex-owner of the pharmacy was released from detention and reinstated in the pharmacy. The ex-owner was declared a rightist and sent to "learn through labor." Thus J.P., who had made such an effort to see justice done in this one instance and had thought that his success was proof of the Party's desire to change, now saw all of his work undone.

Charlie's effort to protect the old workman who had been dismissed by the State Representative for spilling hot tea water was also undone. Poor Charlie did not have the protection of an international reputation. For casting aspersions on the "noble qualities of the cadres," he was sentenced to two years of "labor learning." Subsequently, I heard that he lived through it, but that his health had been broken.

I received news of Li-li two months after arriving in Hong Kong. She and Director Win were married. The fact that a Communist official as important as Win married an "ex-degenerate element" caused gossip among the Hong Kong refugees. In trying to find out as much as I could on the subject, I discovered that Li-li had an aunt living in Hong Kong, married to a bank clerk. The aunt corresponded with Shanghai relatives and on rare occasions exchanged letters with Li-li herself. I met the aunt, who thereafter would tell me at once whatever news she had about Li-li. I did not dare send Li-li any messages no matter how well disguised; now that I had been declared an enemy, I would endanger anyone whom I contacted on the mainland. Nevertheless, knowing that I was not completely out of touch with Li-li helped my mental outlook immeasurably. I gathered that she was well, that she was popular with the top officials, and that she was busy with important work. I did suffer occasional pangs of jealousy, but the knowledge that she was safe was a great relief to me, and from now on I had less trouble in readjusting to the free world.

My brothers did not really need me in the family enterprise, but Pao's father was short of help, and he hired me as his secretary. The job had no future and the pay was insignificant, but I now wished for little, and it provided all I wanted. I had the leisure to catch up on reading the truth of what had been happening in the world during the past eight years, talk frequently with the other refugees, and follow the now rapidly unfolding events on the mainland.

The anti-Rightist campaign reached the height of its frenzy during the late summer of 1957, but it lasted into early 1958. By this time, of course, the rhythm of the regime's suppression tactics was clear to everyone who had lived under the Communist rule. One segment of the population at a time endured the authorities' malevolence. When these people had been reduced through terror to complete subservience, the attention was turned to another segment, and then to another and another until everyone had felt the awful weight of the regime's power. The whole process, then, was repeated. The anti-Rightist campaign represented, in effect, the "third round" for the intellectuals and ex-bourgeois and the "second round" for the civil servants. Even before the campaign finished, therefore, everyone knew that the workers and peasants would now have their turn for further suppression. The next victims began to show signs of panic even before the first propaganda guns were fired. Among the workers, for example, a new wave of maudlin praise for the Party became apparent and replaced the complaints and criticisms they had voiced during the "rectification." Individual workers, obviously, were struggling to put themselves on record as politically pure in hopes that their own punishment would be less harsh. In Hong Kong, the prices of eggs, chickens and vegetables suddenly began to soar. These commodities were imported from the mainland, and the peasants began desperately to consume their own produce, knowing that when the regime attacked them they would lose everything.

The attack against the workers and peasants was opened in the spring of 1958 with a campaign that became known as the "Great Leap Forward." In this particular campaign, however, the workers suffered the most. The "Great Leap" was intended to be a monumental "voluntary" effort to increase the national productivity. Everyone was to participate by "contributing" extra hours of daily labor. Difficult goals were set in every aspect of national activity, but the increases demanded from agriculture and especially from industry were fantastic.

In industry, the emphasis was placed on the "backyard" production of steel. Thus, homemade furnaces sprang up everywhere. The workers, having labored a full day at their regular jobs, worked after-hours in these smelters. For months at a time, fifteen to eighteen hours a day, seven days a week of the most grueling labor possible was normal for the average workers. The aged, the women and children also were forced to "volunteer" for this endless toil. To feed the homemade furnaces, hysterical campaigns were waged for the collection of scrap metal. The campaigns intensified, and the people donated many of the few metal utensils they owned. In the end, they often were made to *buy* metal to be melted down in the furnaces.

At first, the authorities made astronomical claims about the increases achieved through the "Great Leap." Later, when any outside economist could prove—using the Communists' own figures—that the regime's statistics were fabricated and that the campaign cost more than it earned, the authorities "readjusted" their claims. Although the propagandists continued to use the term "Great Leap," its failure was evident.

The failure resulted from a mistake that occurs frequently in Communist societies. Because decisions in every phase of the national activity are made by the politically pure rather than by the expertly trained, the regime lacks full advantage of expert advice. Also, the Communists invariably are so suspicious of anyone with the intellectual capacity to be an expert that they deny themselves much of the help he could give them. For example, anyone in China who knew anything about making steel could

368

have advised that even the very best of the homemade smelters was incapable of producing a usable product. Moreover, the transportation system was barely adequate for coping with normal production; a system several times as large and efficient would have been required to handle the distribution problem of keeping tens of thousands of tiny additional smelters operating. The result was waste on a tremendous scale. Millions of hours of manpower and astronomical amounts of fuel were spent on melting down useful items into useless blobs of metal which could not even be moved away. The extra strain on the transportation system reduced its capacity even further and before long, not even the normal distribution could be maintained, and the whole economy suffered a setback.

Nevertheless, the campaign's political profit, particularly in the neutralist countries, was large. The concentrated propaganda about the Great Leap and the fantastic production claims for it left the impression that Communist China was indeed suddenly acquiring enormous material strength and that the Chinese people, solidly united, were happily making astonishing, voluntary contributions to the State out of love for the Communist Party and the "socialist" way of life. Despite the proven failure of the campaign, many of the more naïve neutralists still believe that it was an impressive achievement.

Any worker who lived through the Great Leap, however, knows that the campaign also had the effect of suppression. The people were made to work constantly to the very limit of human endurance—and in many cases beyond. They were not merely too tired to harbor any thought of opposing the regime. They were broken. It was as though the authorities, in a vicious fury at the antagonism shown them by the people during the blossom period, had sentenced the whole population to the slave gangs of labor reform. Proof of the punitive nature of the campaign was

369

in the fact that people from the other classes and strata who incurred the Party's disfavor were sent as *punishment* to "learn from the masses" by giving their labor along with the workers and peasants.

When the peasants were sufficiently broken down by the hard labor of the Great Leap, the ultimate in dispossession was forced upon them. In the spring of 1958, the mainland press carried hints that some of the farm cooperatives had "merged." In July, one group of cooperatives was said to have "taken on characteristics of the commune." In August, Mao toured the countryside and described the "communes"—plural—he had visited. This was the cue. In September 1958 one of the most intense propaganda campaigns of the previous nine years was begun. The farmers who once had "demanded" that the regime put their land and implements into collective ownership now suddenly "demanded" that all the property and all their possessions should be taken by "the people." By the end of September, the authorities claimed that 98.2 percent of the peasant households of the entire nation had been taken into the communes.

The result was that the peasants now were completely regimented. They owned nothing. Each person was put into a production team which was assigned specific tasks within the large area that his commune incorporated. He was given a place in a communal mess hall and assigned shelter either in a room of a village house or, later, in a large dormitory. He worked as the authorities directed. For the still continuing Great Leap, he "donated" more labor during what was theoretically his spare time. During the off-season, his "team" was sent to labor on roads, canals and water conservancy projects. He was not permitted to resign from his team nor was he allowed to choose the team with which he labored. If he had a wife, he cohabited with her only when the separate work assigned to his team and hers allowed it. Their children were raised in nurseries and educated to be "red and expert"; i.e., they were given concentrated political indoctrination along with technical training in the jobs to which the authorities would assign them. Finally, each commune member could get nothing to eat except in the one mess hall to which he was assigned and was therefore tied to his commune as effectively as a serf was held to a fiefdom. In short, the difference in status between a slave and a member of a Chinese Communist commune was indiscernible.

Outside China, there has been much speculation about the success or failure of the commune "experiment." Economists pointed to the shocking decline in agricultural production following the establishment of the communes, and concluded that the system was a failure. It is true that within two years the mainland was facing famine on a nationwide scale. A large percentage of the foreign exchange had to be spent on enough Canadian and Australian grain merely to keep the army and security forces fed. Moreover, nothing in the situation indicates that it can improve within probably a decade, and because agriculture is the basis of the economy, the entire industrial program has had to be sharply modified. By 1961, deaths due to starvation were increasing rapidly and diseases of malnutrition were widespread throughout the country.

Nevertheless, despite these seeming evil results, the commune system from the regime's viewpoint is a success. Anyone who has lived under Chinese Communism learns one lesson quickly and thoroughly: the authorities give priority first and always to the problem of eliminating any kind of opposition to their control. The blossom campaign revealed the extent, nature and location of opposition. The anti-Rightist campaign reduced the educated classes to voiceless subservience. The Great Leap made the workers into robots that would work uncomplainingly to death if the authorities commanded. And now the communes brought each of the more than 500 million peasants under a control so complete that every bite of food he received depended upon whether the authorities found him useful and acceptable. Tens of millions of people may well starve to death to consolidate further the Party's power, but the possibility now of any uprising to dislodge the despots is almost nil.

The work of consolidating power kept the Communists extremely busy during 1958 and 1959. In early 1959, Mao turned over his chairmanship of the People's Republic to Liu Shao-chi, but he retained his chairmanship of the Party; henceforth Mao gave his full attention to ensuring that the Party maintained its discipline under the stress and strain of assuming complete control over the masses. From the beginning of this final effort, however, the Communists obviously were confident of their success, and a new arrogance in their relations with other countries became apparent at once. In late 1958, for example, the authorities ordered the shelling of Quemoy and Matsu islands, apparently in preparation for an invasion. This warlike act of the "peace-loving Chinese People's Republic" "disturbed" the Asian neutralists. The Communists responded, with more insolence than logic, by labeling any who criticized their act as "warmongers controlled by the imperialists." They desisted from the shelling only when the Americans indicated that an invasion would be resisted.

The Communists then turned their attention to the weaker countries to the west. The exploitation of Tibet had already been stepped up; the resulting revolt of the Tibetans led to the escape of the Dalai Lama, but the Red Army proceeded to suppress the uprising with a methodical brutality rarely equaled in history. Again the Asian neutralists expressed "disappointment" and even disapproval, but now the officials in Peking seemed indifferent to outside opinion. They increased their subversive activities throughout South Asia, and they began to claim and occupy pieces of Indian and Burmese territory. When the people in these countries objected, the replies from Peking alternated insults and threats with offers to "negotiate." Generally, the Communists permitted the neutralists to devise their own soothing explanations for the behavior of the People's Republic.

To those of us who were familiar with the Chinese Communist methods, the reason for the regime's new truculence was plain. It indicated that the authorities at last felt secure in their complete control of the people and that they were almost desperately anxious to hide the material weakness of the country. With famine becoming worse each year and with industrial production stagnating if not retrogressing, the leaders began to bluff and bluster in the attempt to frighten outsiders into believing that the country is strong.

During the three years of these developments, my quiet life in Hong Kong had a dreamlike quality; reality for me was the grim events taking place on the mainland. In March of 1960, however, the ARCI (Aid to Refugee Chinese Intellectuals) helped me to return to the United States. This seemed a miraculous stroke of good fortune. Hong Kong was a pleasant place to live for someone in my position, but I always felt an impermanence about the place, as though it had been precariously caught on a snag in the stream of time, and must soon be swept up and lost again in the rushing flood of events. Oddly enough, I felt less at home there than I did in the United States.

Thus I returned to the United States with reawakened enthusiasm. I hoped to find there something that would give me hope for the future of my countrymen still imprisoned on the China mainland. America, I saw at once, had changed considerably. The cities were bigger, the lights brighter, the traffic noisier, the cars fancier, the prices higher, the people friendlier and the pace faster than before. In short, the more the country changed, the more it was the same thing; it gave me the wonderful feeling of permanence and stability.

To my dismay, however, the attitude in America toward Communist China had *not* changed. I often felt that in returning to the U.S., I was stepping back eleven years in time. I heard now the same arguments based on the same wishful thinking that I had listened to before; the same fallacies were being used to explain the same misconceptions.

This was especially true, I felt, of my fellow Chinese Americans. I met again many of the Chinese students I had known before, those who had remained here instead of returning when the Communists won control of the mainland. Almost without exception, I found that while they disapproved of some of the regime's policies, they were proud of the strength which they credit the Communists with giving to the motherland.

I have tried desperately to explain that the motherland no longer exists. What we think of as the motherland consisted of a tradition, a culture and a particular pattern of social values that were unique to the geographical area called China. The tradition, the culture and the values have been stamped out; the area has been made into a huge concentration camp.

I have also argued endlessly that the seeming strength of Communist China is based only on lies and fraud. Materially as well as spiritually the country is humiliatingly weak. The unity of a chain gang and the bluster and threats of a cutthroat do not comprise strength worthy of admiration.

It is natural, I suppose, that such comments are resented. Even close friends make such replies as, "Naturally you're anti-Communist; you came from the bourgeoisie"; or "Admit it—you left the Communists because you figured you could do better for yourself here."

The injustice of these reactions fills me with despair. The truth is that despite my background, I went to Communist China ready to dedicate my life to the Communist cause. The fact of my bourgeois background *in itself* was no obstacle there. Many of the Communists came from the bourgeoisie. Moreover, in Communist China I received many material benefits, even luxuries. I achieved high status, and if I had remained I unquestionably would have become an important official. I cannot claim that I personally suffered physically in any way under the Communists. In America, conversely, I have far fewer comforts, and I have no hope whatever of earning a position here comparable to the one I had there. Thus when I still say that living in Communist China was hell, one would think that my argument would carry some weight.

On the whole, I found that non-Chinese Americans tend to have an open mind about Communist China, but generally the subject is too complicated to be explained easily to them. Perhaps the most difficulty comes from some of the "old China hands"— Westerners who spent many years in the China of the previous regime and remain sentimental about it. These people often cling stubbornly to the illusion that the old civilization still exists, under the surface, and that the Communists have done nothing more, really, than to introduce much-needed "reforms." They sometimes naïvely suggest that the Chinese people will change Communism more than Communism can change them. We refugees from the new regime find this attitude infinitely sad.

Conversely, we are apt to be impatient sometimes with the comments on Communist China made by scholars and journalists whose knowledge of the subject is only academic. The perfectly natural tendency of these people is to base their opinions and conclusions upon what the Communists *say*. Because what the Communists in China say and what they *do* have nothing in common, the scholarly approach can produce some strange fantasies. For example, much material has been written on the subject of the blossom period and the anti-Rightist campaign. Researchers are apt to have only the final version of Mao's speech on "contradictions," because this was the only one published. Thus many scholars have taken the attitude that the Chinese people were rather stupid to have spoken out so vehemently when Mao had established the "six criteria" for correct blossoming. It is incomprehensible to the average scholar that an important statesman can make a pronouncement one day, and then the next day calmly announce that what he really said the day before was something quite different.

Finally, we refugees tend to be disturbed the most by the bickering on the subject of Communist China between Westerners of different shades of political opinion. In the world today a true understanding of the Chinese Communist process, and an accurate evaluation of China's strengths and weaknesses are too important to be lost in mere partisan politics.

The Chinese Communists, like the comrades everywhere, have only one strength. They have succeeded in identifying themselves with and in exploiting for their benefit the almost irresistible demand for reform and social improvement that is being made by the hitherto quiescent and voiceless mass of the world's population. The relative political, social and economic merits of capitalism and Communism are quite beside the point. Equally invalid are the facts that under the Marxist-Leninist-Maoist system the promises made to the masses are not kept and that people are made to live under a despotism of the most primitive type. The essential point is that, until someone else can inspire more hope in the world's masses than the Communists are able to do, the trend certainly will continue to favor them.

The conservatives among the Westerners, however, still attempt to deny the desire for change that is shaking the world. They tend to identify any social reform with the Communist enemy and therefore to resist it. This, of course, plays into the hands of the Communists who, in fact, count on the conservatives to set the stage for revolution.

Many of the Western liberals, however, are equally as dangerous. While recognizing the need for reforms, they often mistakenly associate the Communists with reformers. If the Communists did what they say they do—if they provided even a fraction of what they promise—the world probably would have been Communist some decades ago. The liberals who do not recognize Communists as enemies of reform are also contributing to Communist strength.

In short, the only advantage the Communists have in the world ideological struggle comes from weaknesses among the Westerners. If selfishness, disunity, blindness, ignorance, prejudice and indifference are dominant factors in the democratic societies, then the Communists will be strong indeed.

Until recently I had thought that the weaknesses in the West gave the Communists predominant strength. To my mind, however, the most noteworthy news now coming out of Communist China concerns increasing graft and nepotism among the cadres. If absolute power corrupts absolutely, then a degeneration among the new despots can be anticipated. The Chinese Communists proved the hitherto incredible fact that a small group can achieve complete control over 650 million unwilling people. Maintaining the control, however, depends entirely on the discipline that the Party can continue to exact from the members.

The East-West struggle is probably a race between the length

377

of time that the Communist bloc can maintain Party discipline and the time required for the Westerners to seize the ideological initiative by beginning to put into full practice the democratic ideals in which they believe.

I believed even more in the potential strength of the West after having lived for eight years in Communist China. I had no difficulty in adjusting to a frugal life in the U.S., but I still cannot enjoy the safety and security I have been fortunate enough to find without feeling corresponding sorrow for the misery and hopelessness of my compatriots in China. As the weeks passed, my life here became more real, and my own years under the Communists seemed increasingly like a bad dream, but I am haunted constantly by the terrible suffering of the millions of human beings in what was once our motherland.

In early 1961 I received news that Li-li was dead. She had drowned and her body was found in the river. Her aunt wrote that the death was ruled accidental. I have no way of disputing this, but I am inclined to believe that Li-li reached the limit of her endurance and ended her life. I found that I was not surprised by the news, and in fact I had subconsciously expected and prepared for it.

Strangely, she became more real to me now that I did not have to think of her as an "ex-degenerate element, ex-counter-revolutionary's widow married to a Shanghai Director of Propaganda."

Often I seem to sense her presence. On summer nights, sometimes, when the city streets are wet with recent rain, I half expect her to appear suddenly out of the crowd of strangers walking toward me. If that should happen, here in New York, no more pretenses would be necessary. I would simply take her arm and we would go on together.

The thought comforts me, for the moment, and I am at peace.

378